BASKETBALL DRILLS, PLAYS, AND STRATEGIES

A Comprehensive Resource for Coaches

B
BETTERWAY BOOKS
Cincinnati, Ohio

Clinton M. Adkins • **Steven R. Bain** • **Edward A. Dreyer** • **Robert A. Starkey**

Foreword by Sean Miller, Head Coach of Men's Basketball at Xavier University

For more fine titles from Betterway Books, visit our Web site at www.fwbookstore.com.

16 15 14 13   10 9 8 7

Distributed in Canada by Fraser Direct, 100 Armstrong Avenue, Georgetown, ON, Canada L7G 5S4, Tel: (905) 877-4411; Distributed in the U.K. and Europe by David & Charles, Brunel House, Newton Abbot, Devon, TQ12 4PU, England, Tel: (+44) 1626 323200, Fax: (+44) 1626 323319, E-mail: postmaster@davidandcharles.co.uk; Distributed in Australia by Capricorn Link, P.O. Box 704, Windsor, NSW 2756 Australia, Tel: (02) 4577-3555

Library of Congress Cataloging-in-Publication Data
Basketball drills, plays, and strategies : a comprehensive resource for coaches / by Clinton M. Adkins ... [et al.].
    p. cm.
  Includes index.
  ISBN-13: 978-1-55870-810-5 (pbk. : alk. paper)
  1. Basketball--Training. 2. Basketball--Coaching. I. Adkins, Clinton M.
  GV885.35.B38 2007
  796.323'2--dc22

                    2007015617

Edited by Michelle Ehrhard
Designed by Claudean Wheeler
Illustrations by Michelle Ehrhard, Kelly Piller, Grace Ring,
    Josh Roflow, Eric West, and Claudean Wheeler
Production coordinated by Mark Griffin

F+W PUBLICATIONS, INC.

DEDICATION

To the families and friends of the authors.

ACKNOWLEDGMENTS

Special thanks to Sarah Luers for her time. And thanks to Michelle Ehrhard for making this whole thing possible.

ABOUT THE AUTHORS

CLINTON M. ADKINS has played basketball for more than twenty years, including at the NCAA college level. He is an assistant varsity coach at Lakota East High School in Liberty Township, Ohio. He runs a shooting camp for grade-school and high-school players in the summer and is also involved in the Greater Cincinnati Basketball Camp. He lives with his wife and two sons in Cincinnati, Ohio.

STEVEN R. BAIN has been involved with basketball for more than twenty years, including playing at the NCAA college level. He currently coaches at Elder High School in Cincinnati, Ohio, and has been part of the team's back-to-back Elite Eight appearances in the high school tournament. Steve resides with his wife in Cheviot, Ohio.

EDWARD A. DREYER has more than twenty years of coaching and playing experience, including playing and coaching at the NCAA college level. Most recently, he was the head coach at Hughes Center High School in Cincinnati, Ohio. He also coached at the College of Mount St. Joseph and Defiance College. He lives near Defiance, Ohio.

ROBERT A. STARKEY is currently the head boys' basketball coach at Villa Madonna Academy in northern Kentucky. He also runs Villa's boys' basketball summer camps and is one of the school's assistant athletic directors. He previously coached basketball at Roger Bacon High School. He has more than twenty years experience with basketball and played at the NCAA college level. He lives with his wife in Cincinnati, Ohio.

CONTENTS

FOREWORD

BY SEAN MILLER, HEAD COACH OF MEN'S BASKETBALL AT XAVIER UNIVERSITY

I n today's world of sports, basketball is being played at a level that has never existed before. More kids are participating at a younger age, more adults are coaching at all levels, and this great game is now being played throughout the world twelve months a year.

As coaches in the game of basketball, we are the teachers. We all want our game to become better. In order to accomplish this, as coaches, we must first improve our ability to lead, to coach, and to teach today's young athletes. Fundamental development, game strategy, special situations, etc., all need to be taught with a philosophy and purpose behind them.

In this book, *Basketball Drills, Plays, and Strategies,* you will find the tools necessary to coach the game of basketball more efficiently, and with better results—at all levels. Whether you coach a fourth grade AAU team or a varsity team at the high school level, this book becomes your great resource—a road map to greater success.

There are drills, set plays, and special situations inside this book that are detailed and explained with great clarity by some of the best high-school coaches in the Greater Cincinnati area. I highly recommend *Basketball Drills, Plays, and Strategies* to any parents or coaches that want to become better teachers of the game of basketball regardless of the age or level of the player or team that they coach.

INTRODUCTION

We hope this book has something for every coach and that it is helpful no matter what level of play you are coaching or what stage of the season you are in. We've tried to combine our knowledge of the game to create a quick and easy reference to help all coaches. We know from experience that, as coaches, we can always use fresh drills, new plays, and better ways to explain concepts to our players. We hope this book can help you with all of that.

Before you get started, there are some things you should know about how this book works. In part one, you will find drills for practices along with diagrams that show how the drills work. Part two contains plays and strategies you'll use during games, again, including diagrams to help illustrate the concepts. The key on the next page will help you decipher the diagrams so you can understand exactly what is happening in them.

Throughout the book, we also use the standard terminology for basketball positions, and although the word "man" often accompanies these positions, basketball is certainly a sport for boys and girls, men and women. So throughout the book, please be aware of what the following terms mean.

> **1-man:** point guard position
> **2-man:** wing/shooting guard position
> **3-man:** wing/shooting guard position
> **4-man:** post player
> **5-man:** post player (oftentimes the tallest post player or center)

There is also some other standard terminology we use to describe spots on the court. These terms are used throughout the book:

> **Elbow:** The area on the court that is three feet to the right or left of the center of the free throw line. This area may also be referred to as the high post.
> **Free-throw line extended:** The area on the court outside of the 3-point line, fifteen feet above the baseline.
> **Top of the key:** The 3-point area on the court that is directly in the center of the court.

Two other common terms that are used in several chapters are:

Jump-stop: Landing simultaneously on both feet so that either foot can be used as a pivot foot. When a player lands, her feet should be a little wider than shoulder-width apart, with the knees bent. This position sets her up to be in a triple-threat position.

Triple-threat position: An athletic stance used when a player has the ball; feet are shoulder-width apart, knees are bent, and the ball is held in a way that the player can either shoot, pass, or dribble without tipping off the defender as to which of the three he will do.

(Any other terms you'll need to know will be described in the chapters that use them.)

KEY OF DIAGRAM SYMBOLS

⟶	Player movement
∿⟶	Dribble
·······▹	Pass
⊢	Screen (a close out when indicated)
O	Player (neutral or offensive)
✕	Player (neutral or offensive)
◉	Player with ball
✖	Player with ball
▲	Player from third team in specific drills
C	Coach
Ⓒ	Coach with ball
1 1	Numbers indicate specific players
❶ ➀	Numbers indicate specific players with ball

Fundamentals
and Practice
Drills

Dribbling

The fundamentals of dribbling the basketball should be the first area of the game taught. Handling the ball is the foundation of the game. Teaching proper technique at beginner levels is vital to the development of the youth basketball player. Beginning at these young stages, coaches should focus on players dribbling the ball on the pads and fingertips of their hands, seeing the floor as they dribble, utilizing both hands, keeping the dribble around waist level, and pushing the ball out in front of their bodies. Even as players grow and mature, a major emphasis on these fundamentals should remain.

How many times do you see players pound the basketball continuously with no apparent reason? Or dribble the basketball once and then pick up their dribble, leading to a trap, double dribble, or bad pass decision? Or pound the basketball while the other players stand around and watch? There are three reasons why players should dribble the basketball. The first reason is to attack the rim using dribble penetration. Dribble penetration is what makes defenses break down and leads to high-quality shots. The second reason that players should dribble is to create better passing lanes for themselves. That is why it is so important that players do not waste their dribble. The last reason that the dribble should be utilized is to relieve full-court pressure, which ties in with reason number two. In a press situation, a player is attacking pressure to create better passing angles for herself, which will lead to open opportunities at the basket.

Like all basketball skills, dribbling is something that comes with hours of prac-

COACHING KEYS

- Make sure your players are outstanding dribblers. Dribble penetration is the toughest thing to guard in the game. Penetration breaks down defenses and leads to open looks on the offensive end. That is why it is so important to stress the repetitive use of ball-handling drills throughout the season, as well as during the off season.
- Make sure every player on your team, from point guard to center, is able to handle the ball. The more players you have that are deft at dribbling, the more dangerous your team will be. Use that as a selling point to your players.
- Stress to your players the importance of pushing themselves outside their comfort level when doing ball-handling drills. If they don't, they will not see a major increase in their skill level.

tice that should start at the first stages of a player's career. This chapter contains various ball-handling drills (which can be adapted for any skill level) that can help your players become successful ball-handlers and utilize various game moves. When using these drills, practice them at game speed so that players can adapt to game situations.

KEY TERMS

Between-the-legs crossover: A game move where a player quickly changes direction by exchanging the basketball between his legs (front to back), from one hand to another via a bounce.

Crossover: A game move where a player quickly changes direction by exchanging the ball from one hand to another via a bounce.

Dribble penetration: A game move in which a player beats his defender by using the dribble in order to get to the basket, create space for a shot, or increase a passing angle (which many times leads to an open shot).

Hesitation: A game move where a player slows down his dribble, trying to get the defender to come out of his stance, and then quickly blows by to the basket. The effectiveness of this move is all predicated on quickly changing speeds in an attempt to get a defender off balance, allowing for the blow by.

Game moves: A movement made with the basketball in hand in order to penetrate to the basket, get a defender off balance, relieve pressure (create space from a defender), or create space for a shot.

Inside-out: A game move where a player fakes the exchange of the basketball from one hand to the other by pushing the ball "in and out" while using a head-and-shoulders fake in order to blow by the defender. It is very important that players keep their dribbling hand on the top, inside portion of the ball when utilizing this move in order to keep from bringing their hand underneath the ball, which is a violation.

Pull-back crossover: A game move where a player quickly dribbles backward two dribbles with her body at a side angle in order to protect the basketball from the defender, then quickly changes direction by exchanging the ball from one hand to another via a bounce. This is a great move to relieve pressure.

STATIONARY BALL HANDLING

INSTRUCTIONS

1. Players set up in a circle, making sure they have adequate space. Each player needs one basketball.
2. Players start in a game-like position (similar to a triple-threat position on page 7) with their knees bent and feet shoulder-width apart (or slightly more than shoulder-width).
3. Players begin to smack the ball back and forth from the left hand to right hand for thirty seconds.
4. Players then toss the ball back and forth between both hands using their fingertips while keeping the ball in front of their body for thirty seconds. (Note: More advanced players can take the ball above their heads, down to their toes, and back up.)
5. Players then move the basketball from hand to hand, circling it around their heads for fifteen seconds in one direction, then fifteen seconds in the opposite direction.

Difficulty Level: Beginner

Skills Practiced: Dribbling

Number of Players: At least 1

Number of Basketballs Needed: Each player needs 1

Ideal Practice Time: Beginning

6. Players then do the same maneuver, but around their waists, switching direction after fifteen seconds.
7. Players repeat the maneuver again, but around their knees, for fifteen seconds in one direction, and then switch to the opposite direction for another fifteen seconds.
8. Players then interchange the basketball between both hands, circling from their heads to waists to knees and back up. After fifteen seconds,

TIPS

You need to push the players to go hard. If players never mess up, that usually means one of two things: they have mastered these ball-handling skills and need to be challenged, or they are not pushing themselves. Losing the basketball is okay! That means players are pushing themselves out of their comfort zones.

Beginner: Use this drill at the beginning of every practice help to improve the players' feel for the basketball.

Advanced: It is very important that players keep their heads up when doing stationary ball handling, so hold up your hand displaying a different number of fingers and have your players constantly verbalize the number of fingers you hold up.

the players switch and go the opposite way for fifteen more seconds.

9. Players then continuously pass the basketball between their legs, interchanging the ball between both hands. After fifteen seconds, they switch and go the opposite direction.

STATIONARY TWO-BALL DRIBBLING

Difficulty Level: Advanced

Skills Practiced: Dribbling

Number of Players Needed:
At least 1 (can be done individually)

Number of Basketballs Needed:
2 for each player

Ideal Practice Time: Beginning

INSTRUCTIONS

1. Players set up in a circle, making sure they have adequate space. Each player needs two basketballs.

2. Players start in a game-like position with their knees bent and feet shoulder-width apart (or slightly more than shoulder-width). (Teach your players to play in a low position because they are more athletic—balanced and mobile.)

3. Once players are in this position, they begin dribbling both basketballs. Each ball should hit the floor simultaneously and come up to the players' chests/armpits.

4. After players have done this for thirty seconds, they repeat step three, but the ball now only bounces up to the players' waists (optimal spot).

5. After players have done this for thirty seconds, they repeat step four, but the ball is dribbled at knee level.

6. Once players have finished with step five, they will repeat steps three through five. However, instead of a simultaneous dribble, players use an alternating dribble, where one ball is hitting the floor while the opposite ball is in their hands.

TIPS

Both players and coaches must be patient when first utilizing two-ball dribbling because it can be challenging. However, if you utilize the drill on a daily basis, you will see progress in the ball-handling skills of your players.

Beginner: Use one basketball instead of two as this can be very difficult, even for skilled players.

Advanced: Challenge your players with more options as they become more advanced. For example, add crossing over the basketballs or rocking both basketballs back and forth at the players' sides. Be creative.

TWO-BALL DRIBBLING ON THE MOVE

Difficulty Level: Advanced

Skills Practiced: Dribbling

Number of Players Needed:
At least 1 (can be done individually)

Number of Basketballs Needed:
2 for each group

Ideal Practice Time: Beginning

INSTRUCTIONS

1. Players form groups of two on the baseline.
2. One player from each group steps up to the baseline. Each player who has stepped up has two basketballs.
3. On your signal, players begin to dribble both basketballs toward the opposite baseline.
4. As the players are dribbling, each ball should hit the floor simultaneously and come up to the players' waists (See page 15 for an illustration).
5. Once each player reaches the baseline, he stops, turns around, and completes steps three and four until he reaches the baseline where his partner is waiting. The next player takes both balls and repeats the same steps.

TIPS

Teach players to keep their heads up and push the ball out in front of their bodies as they dribble. When dribbling with two basketballs, players have a tendency to look at the ball instead of up the floor.

Beginner: Have players walk, instead of run, while dribbling with two basketballs.

Advanced: Mix up the different ways the players dribble the basketballs. Use an alternating (pitter-patter) dribble, where one ball hits the floor while the opposite ball is in the player's hand. (See page 15 for an illustration.) Have the players dribble the balls unusually high or low. For exceptional ball handlers, challenge them to cross over both balls or alternate taking the balls behind their backs. Be creative.

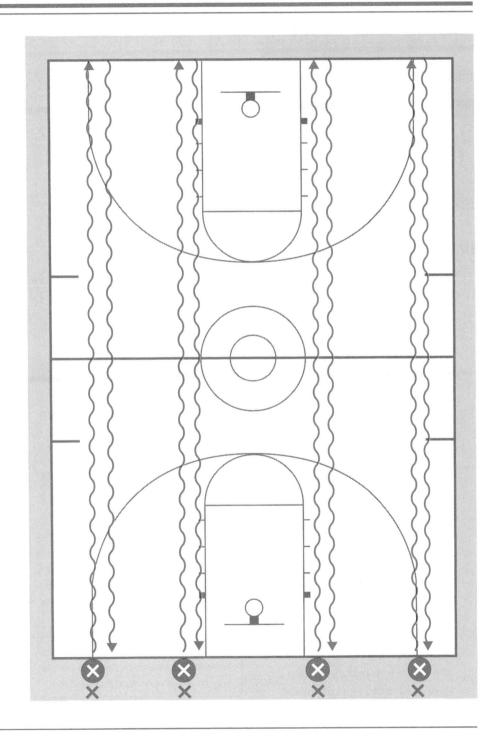

DRIBBLE SERIES

Difficulty Level: Intermediate

Skills Practiced: Dribbling, game moves, lay-ups, jump shots

Number of Players Needed: At least 4

Number of Basketballs Needed: At least 2

Ideal Practice Time: Beginning

INSTRUCTIONS

1. Players form one line at the free-throw line extended, opposite of the basket they are dribbling toward.
2. The first two or three players in line have balls.
3. The first player in line dribbles hard to the wing at the opposite end of the floor using his outside hand (the hand closest to the sideline).
4. Once the player reaches the 3-point line, he makes a game move (see page 10), simulating beating his imaginary defender to the basket. (Once the player reaches the 3-point line, the next player in line goes).
5. After making the move, the player goes hard to the basket and shoots a lay-up.
6. The player rebounds and starts dribbling toward the middle of the floor.
7. Once the player passes the 3-point line on his way back, he makes the same game move he made before.

8. The player continues to dribble until he passes the half-court circle. He then jump stops and makes a solid chest pass to the next player in line.

TIPS

Have players mix up the game moves they are making. For example, have the players do the same move four times and then switch to another move. Also, have players mix up their finishes. For example, one rep they may shoot a lay-up and the next time they may shoot a pull-up jumper.

Beginner: Players should work on the fundamentals of dribbling, keep their heads up and the balls at waist level, and finish with proper form when making lay-ups. Teach players to use the weak hand to develop skill.

Advanced: The more advanced a player becomes, the more he incorporates different game moves, as well as the way he finishes around the basket.

BASKETBALL DRILLS, PLAYS, AND STRATEGIES

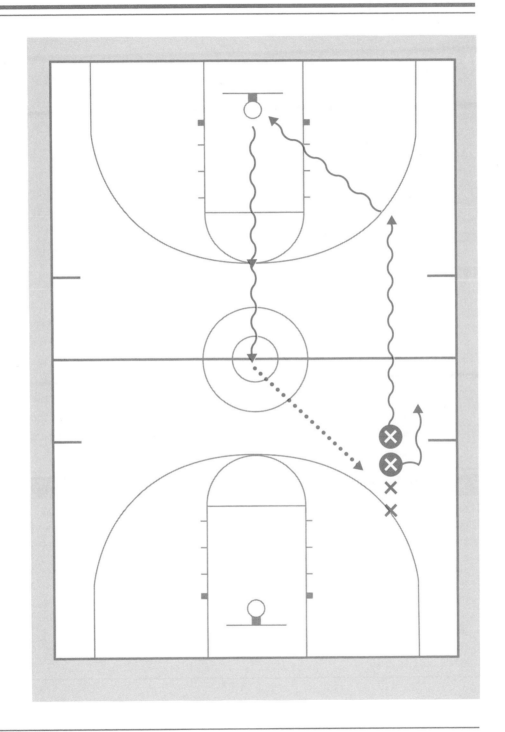

HURRICANE GAME MOVES

Difficulty Level: Intermediate

Skills Practiced: Dribbling, game moves

Number of Players Needed: At least 6

Number of Basketballs Needed: 1 for each line

Ideal Practice Time: Beginning

INSTRUCTIONS

1. Players form groups of two on the baseline.
2. One player from each group steps up to the baseline. Each player who has stepped up has a basketball.
3. Inform your players what game move you will be practicing. On your signal, the players begin dribbling toward the opposite baseline.
4. When the player comes to the free-throw line, half court, and the opposite free-throw line, he makes a game move and continues dribbling toward the opposite baseline.
5. Once the player reaches the opposite baseline, he jump stops and then pivots so that he is facing his partner.
6. The player then dribbles back to the baseline where he started, doing the same things he did in step four.
7. Once the player reaches the baseline, he jump stops and hands the ball to his partner, who will repeat the steps.

TIPS

In order for players to get the most out of this drill, they need to push themselves at game speed. Make sure that when players make game moves, their movements are in straight lines, not lateral (lateral movement allows defenders to get back in front of a player more easily).

Beginner: Players utilize a basic dribble and make a jump stop instead of a game move at each line. After the jump stop, players then begin to dribble to the next line where they will once again make a jump stop. This teaches players how to go from a triple-threat position to dribbling without traveling.

Advanced: Players utilize various moves at each line at game speeds to become more skilled ball handlers.

BASKETBALL DRILLS, PLAYS, AND STRATEGIES

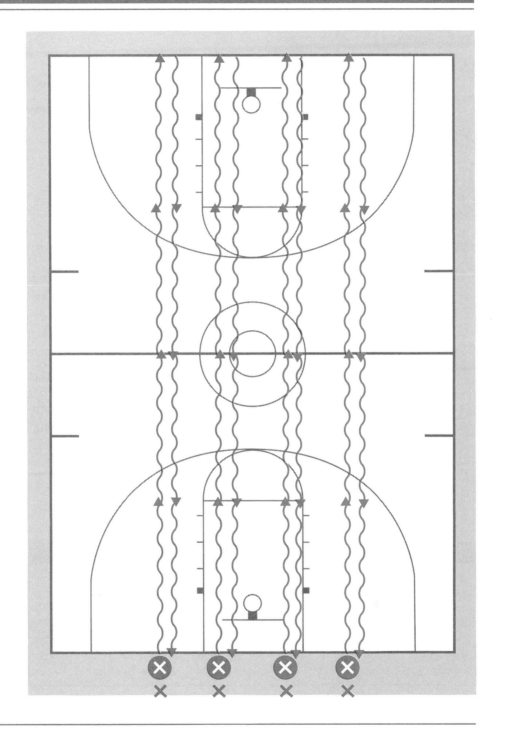

POISON

Difficulty Level: Intermediate

Skills Practiced: Dribbling while protecting the basketball

Number of Players Needed: At least 5

Number of Basketballs Needed: 1 for each player

Ideal Practice Time: End

INSTRUCTIONS

1. Every player has one basketball and, all players are located on one side of half court.
2. On your whistle, the players begin dribbling.
3. Players then attempt to slap away the basketballs of the other players while continuing to dribble their own balls.
4. A player is eliminated from the contest once he loses control of the ball, whether it is deflected away by another player or it is an unforced error. A player can also be eliminated if he steps out of the given zone.

(Note: A player may not kick away the ball of another player; the ball must be deflected away by hand.)

5. As the number of players knocked out increases, the space you are using on the court should get smaller. (Example: Once the number of players is decreased to three, move the dribbling zone to one side of the lane.)
6. The winner is determined when there is only one player left.

TIPS

In order to get players to compete at their highest level, offer incentives to the winners (for example, one less sprint at the end of practice).

Beginner: The space that the players have to compete in the drill should be larger with less-skilled players.

Advanced: Utilize a rule that players can only dribble using their weak hand when competing in the drill; using their strong hand results in removal from the drill.

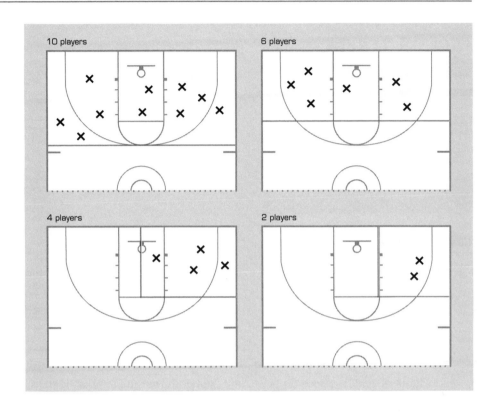

FULL-COURT MOVES SERIES

Difficulty Level: Beginner

Skills Practiced: Dribbling

Number of Players Needed: At least 1

Number of Basketballs Needed: 2

Ideal Practice Time: Any time

INSTRUCTIONS

1. Set up three cones on each side of the floor. The first cone is placed just below the free-throw line extended, centered between the lane and the sideline. The next cone is placed at half court on the outside of the circle. The third cone is placed on the wing (3-point line) on the opposite end of the first cone.

2. Divide players in half, sending one group under one basket and the other group to the opposite basket. The first player in each line has a basketball.

3. Simultaneously, the players begin dribbling toward the first cone. When the player arrives at the cone, she makes a game move to the inside of the cone.

4. The player continues to dribble to the next cone, where she makes a game move to the outside of the cone.

5. The player then attacks the last cone, making a game move either inside or outside the cone, and then makes a lay-up.

6. The next player in line, standing underneath the hoop, takes the ball out of the net and repeats the steps.

TIPS

Have players mix up the moves they make at each cone, as well as their finish at the hoop.

Beginner: Remove the cones and have players work on a full-court basic dribble while finishing with a lay-up. It is important that you switch sides of the floor so that players use both hands. (Players should use the hand closest to the sideline.)

Advanced: Have a coach at each end with a blocking pad to make contact with the players as they are finishing at the hoop to simulate game contact.

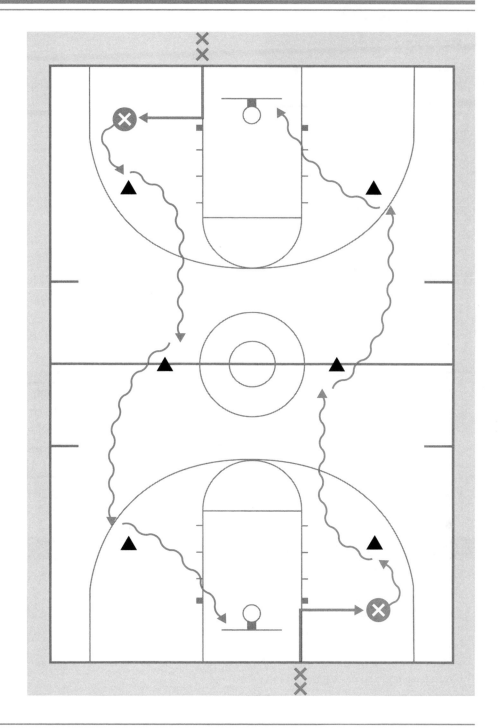

DRIBBLING LINE DRILLS

Difficulty Level: Intermediate

Skills Practiced: Dribbling at fast speeds

Number of Players Needed: At least 1

Number of Basketballs Needed:
1 for each line

Ideal Practice Time: Middle or end

INSTRUCTIONS

1. Divide players into two groups.
2. The first person in each group steps up along the baseline; each player has a ball.
3. On the coach's whistle, the players dribble the ball with their right hand to the free-throw line, quickly change direction, crossing the ball over to their left hand, and dribble back to the baseline.
4. After touching the baseline, players quickly change direction, crossing the ball over to their right hand, dribble to half court, and then return to the baseline with their left hand.
5. After touching the baseline, players dribble to the opposite free-throw line with their right hand and back to the baseline with their left hand.
6. After touching the baseline, players dribble to the opposite baseline with their right hand and back through the baseline with their left hand.

(In the illustration, each line shows just one progression of the drill.)

TIPS

Teach players to push the ball out in front of them instead of dribbling with the ball at their side.

Beginner: Push players to dribble at faster speeds than normal (expect balls to go flying). If players never push themselves to faster speeds, they will not see progress in game situations.

Advanced: Give players a set time in which they must complete the drill as an incentive to push them to go at game speed.

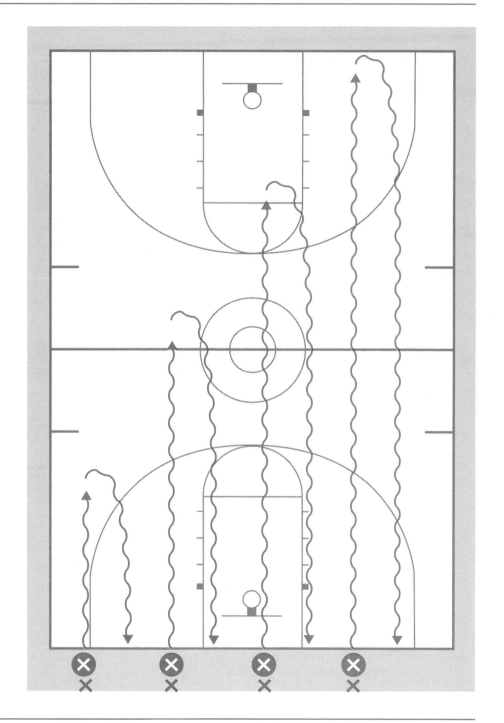

CONE DRIBBLING

Difficulty Level: Beginner

Skills Practiced:
Dribbling while making sharp cuts

Number of Players Needed:
At least 1 (can be done individually)

Number of Basketballs Needed:
1 for each player

Ideal Practice Time: Beginning

INSTRUCTIONS

1. Set up eight cones in a straight line, evenly spread out down the middle of the floor, utilizing the entire court.
2. Players form one line underneath the basket with the first player starting on the baseline. Every player in line has a basketball.
3. The first player dribbles to the first cone with his right hand. Once he reaches the cone, he crosses the ball over from his right hand to his left hand and continues on to the next cone while dribbling the ball with the left hand.
4. Once the player reaches the second cone he crosses the ball over from his left hand to his right hand and continues on to the next cone while dribbling the ball with the right hand.
5. The player continues to interchange steps three and four until he gets to the opposite baseline, where he stops. After finishing the drill, the player dribbles down the sideline (around the drill) to the opposite end of the floor and gets back in line.
6. The next player in line starts the drill when the previous player reaches the second cone.

TIPS

1. Players should cross over the basketball below their knees and before they reach the cone. In a game situation, this translates into protecting the ball from a defender.

2. Players must keep their shoulders square to the baseline while dribbling in as straight a path as possible. Players must make sharp cuts around the cone.

Beginner: Use fewer cones.
Advanced: Use more cones and have players mix up the moves they make when they reach the cones.

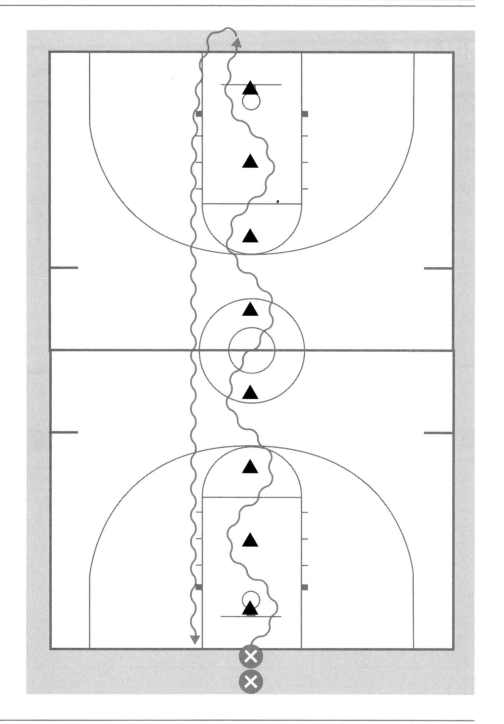

1-ON-2 DRIBBLING

Difficulty Level: Intermediate

Skills Practiced: Dribbling under pressure

Number of Players Needed: 3

Number of Basketballs Needed: 1

Ideal Practice Time: Any time

INSTRUCTIONS

1. A coach takes a basketball out on the baseline.
2. Two defenders line up on opposite elbows with a dribbler in the middle of the lane.
3. The coach inbounds the ball to the dribbler, who then tries to proceed to the other end of the court.
4. Once the dribbler has the basketball the defenders attempt to steal it by trapping and fouling.
5. The dribbler has the entire floor to work with and tries to beat the defenders down the court using his game moves.
6. If the ball is stolen, the defenders put the ball in the hoop and the drill starts over with the coach inbounding the ball to the same dribbler.
7. The dribbler completes the drill once he gets past the defenders and reaches half court.
8. Once the first group has finished the drill, a new group of three players will step on to the court and do the same drill. When a group repeats the drill, make sure the players rotate spots.

TIPS

1. This drill will give you a good idea of who can handle the basketball in pressure situations (that is, who will be good at breaking a press).

2. A key for the dribbler is to try to keep the ball in the middle of the floor. Sidelines are trapping areas for teams that prefer to press.

3. Teach players to attack the outside shoulder of one of the defenders versus trying to split them with the dribble.

Beginner: Put only one defender on the court instead of two, and focus on players trying to blow by their opponent in a full-court situation.

Advanced: Condense the amount of space the offensive player has to work with in order to simulate a game situation, where a player won't be able to use the entire floor because of other defenders.

BASKETBALL DRILLS, PLAYS, AND STRATEGIES

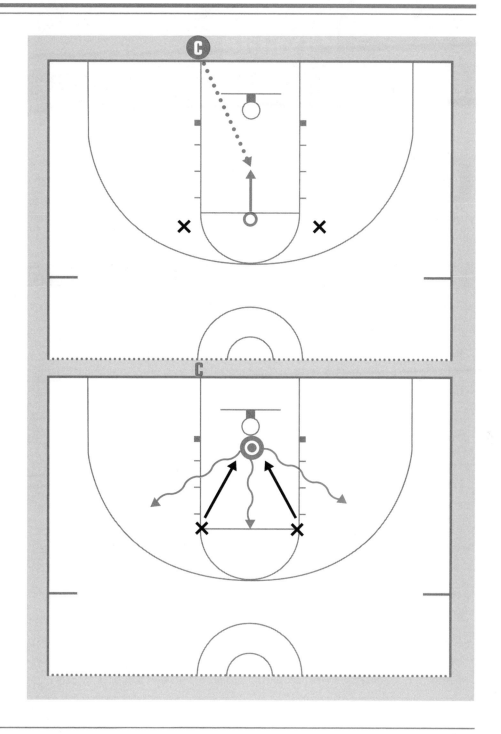

Passing

One of the most overlooked skills in basketball is passing. Many coaches place most of their emphasis on shooting drills, but how do you get good shots if you can't make good passes? Every team needs good passing to get the ball into a scoring position. As a coach, it is important to stress the fundamentals of passing to increase your team's chances of success.

KEY TERMS

Backdoor cut: A player fakes a cut away from the basket and once his defender is moving that way, he cuts to the basket looking for a pass for a lay-up.

Bounce pass: A pass in which the ball is bounced off of the ground about halfway between the passer and the receiver. The bounce pass uses misdirection and can be thrown below the defensive player's hands.

Chest pass: A pass mainly from the chest to a teammate's chest or target hand. It is considered the quickest and most reliable pass.

Entry pass: Usually considered any pass into the post player from a perimeter player. Perimeter players employ good passing angles and pass fakes while looking to make entry passes.

High-low feed: A pass from the high post into the low post. It is used when defenders are playing in front of a post player while the ball is on the wing. The ball is passed from the wing to the high post and then into the low post behind the defensive post player.

Lob pass: A pass in which the ball is thrown over an opponent to a teammate. It is usually used when entering the ball into the post either from the wing or the high post.

Outlet pass: An overhead pass made by a player who just rebounded the ball, usually to a guard to move the ball quickly up the court. By incorporating strong, successful outlet passing, a team can sometimes beat the defense down the court and score quickly.

This chapter includes drills that incorporate chest passes, bounce passes, and outlet passes. The chest pass is one of the quickest and most reliable passes because it goes in a straight line to the player receiving the ball. The bounce pass is a great alternative because it uses misdirection and can be thrown below the defensive player's hands. A player who gets a rebound can make an outlet pass to a guard moving quickly up the court to beat the defense to the basket.

Have players practice the proper way to pass. The passer should always step toward her target to ensure a strong pass, and her thumbs should be pointing down with her fingers pointed out when she is finished passing the ball. Just like following through on a jump shot, this helps ensure a strong pass.

Remind passers that misdirection and deception are effective ways to ensure successful passing. By faking a pass low and passing high, or faking high and passing low, a passer can increase her chances on making a complete pass to her teammate.

COACHING KEYS

- Players should always step to their target and remember to "follow through." Their thumbs should be pointing down and their fingertips should be pointing at their target.
- Players who are receiving a pass should always have their hands up, giving the passer a target, and they should always meet the ball.
- Players should always use pass fakes wisely.

PARTNER PASSING

Level: Beginner

Skills Practiced: Passing, ball control, pass fakes, shot fakes

Number of Players Needed:
An even number

Number of Basketballs Needed:
1 per pair of players

Ideal Practice Time: Beginning

INSTRUCTIONS

1. Players line up down the middle of the court about ten feet across from a partner. Each player on the left starts with a ball.
2. The player with the ball makes a pass fake or shot fake and then makes a strong pass to her partner.
3. The receiving player steps to the ball and catches it in a triple-threat position (see page 7).
4. The player who catches the ball then makes a pass fake and passes back to her partner.
5. Players practice chest, bounce, and outlet passes.

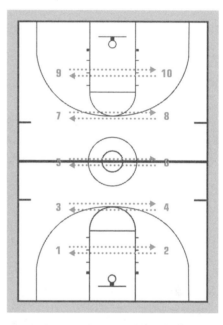

TIPS

Make sure players don't travel when they work on pass fakes and shot fakes.

Beginner: Shorten the distance between partners.

Advanced: Add a third partner to try to steal each pass, or allow a dribble move for each passer.

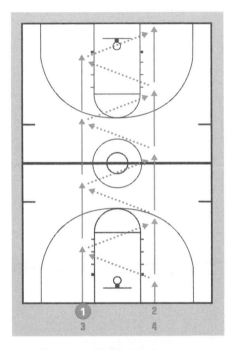

DOWN-AND-BACK PASSING

Difficulty Level: Beginner

Skills Practiced:
Passing, ball control, conditioning

Number of Players Needed: At least 2

Number of Basketballs Needed: 1

Ideal Practice Time: Beginning for a warm-up or end for conditioning

INSTRUCTIONS

1. Players line up on the baseline one on each side of the free-throw lane.
2. The player on the left starts with the ball and makes a strong pass to the player in the opposite line.
3. The player who receives the ball makes a strong pass back to his partner.
4. Both players move from baseline to baseline passing the ball back and forth to each other.
5. When finished, players pass the balls to the next players in line.

TIPS

Have players alternate from bounce passes to chest passes.

Beginner: Have players move slowly up and down the court, using a defensive slide, facing their partner the entire time.

Advanced: Have players run up and down the court while passing to each other. Use two balls and have one player use chest passes while his partner uses bounce passes.

POST PASSING

Difficulty Level: Beginner

Skills Practiced: Passing to a post player

Number of Players Needed: At least 2

Number of Basketballs Needed: 1

Ideal Practice Time: Middle

INSTRUCTIONS

1. Place one player on the wing and another on the opposite block.
2. The player on the wing starts dribbling the ball, while the player on the opposite block flashes to ball-side.
3. The player with the ball takes a dribble toward the baseline and makes a pass to the post player.
4. The post player makes a post move and takes a shot.

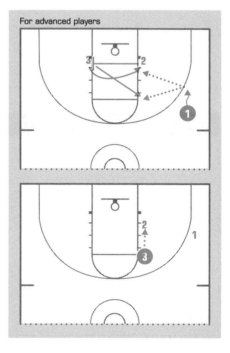

For advanced players

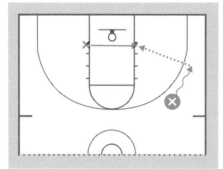

RAPID-FIRE PASSING

Difficulty Level: Intermediate

Skills Practiced: Passing, ball control

Number of Players Needed: At least 5

Number of Basketballs Needed: 1

Ideal Practice Time: Beginning

TIPS

1. The passer may stand in one spot or shuffle from one end of the line to the other.

2. The ball should move quickly and crisply.

3. Players should keep their eyes on the ball and always pay attention.

Beginner: Pass the ball slowly from player to player.

Advanced: Use two balls, moving the ball quickly to every other player.

INSTRUCTIONS

1. Players line up on the sideline about arm's-length apart. One player with a ball stands on the court, facing this line.

2. The player with the ball gives a strong chest pass to the first player in the line.

3. The player who receives the ball quickly passes back to the passer.

4. The passer then gives a strong pass to the second player in line.

5. The passer continues passing back and forth until every one has caught and passed the ball twice.

6. The passer then moves to the end of the line and the player at the beginning of the line becomes the passer.

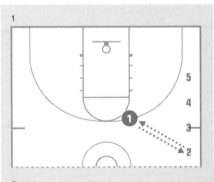

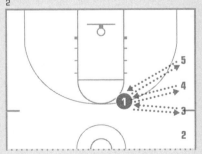

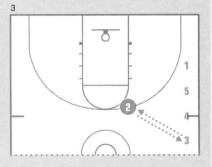

FOUR CORNERS

Difficulty Level: Intermediate

Skills Practiced:
Passing, ball control, teamwork

Number of Players Needed: At least 8

Number of Basketballs Needed: 4

Ideal Practice Time:
Beginning, as a warm-up

INSTRUCTIONS

1. Using the half court, players form even lines in each corner.
2. The first player in each line starts with a ball and passes it to the second player in the line to her right using a strong chest pass. The player then follows her pass and gets in the back of the line to her right.
3. The player who receives the pass then turns and passes to the next person in the line to her right.
4. Players will pass continuously until given further instructions.

TIPS

1. Have players pass to the left after a certain amount of passes or time limit.

2. Have players switch from chest passes to bounce passes, or add pass fakes.

3. Passers should always step to their target and call out the name of the player they are passing to.

4. Players receiving the pass, should always have a target up and be ready to catch the pass.

5. When players receive a pass they should always step to the ball.

Beginner: Shorten the distance of each pass, and use two balls instead of four.

Advanced: Alter the distance of each pass. Allow players to make a cut before receiving a pass, and allow players to pass off of a dribble move.

Challenge your team with a certain amount of time to do the drill without any bad passes or missed assignments. If a mistake happens, hold your team accountable until they do it right for the appropriate amount of time.

BASKETBALL DRILLS, PLAYS, AND STRATEGIES

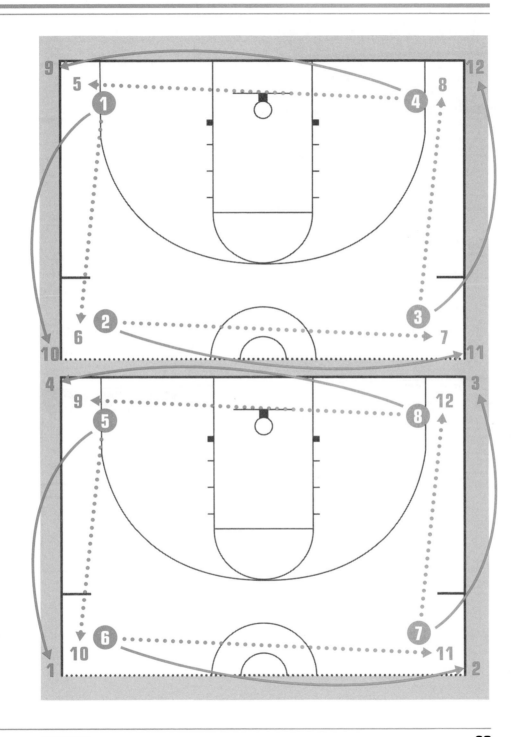

FOUR CORNERS II

Difficulty Level: Intermediate

Skills Practiced:
Passing quickly and accurately

Number of Players Needed: At least 8

Number of Basketballs Needed: 2

Ideal Practice Time: Beginning

INSTRUCTIONS

1. Using the half court, players form even lines in each corner.
2. Players 2 and 4 start in opposite corners with balls.
3. Players 1 and 3 sprint into the middle of the court and receive passes from players 2 and 4.
4. Once players 1 and 3 catch the pass, they quickly pass to the opposite corner from which they came (player 1 passes to player 7, and player 3 passes to player 5) and then follow their passes and fill in those lines.
5. Once players 5 and 7 have received their passes, players 2 and 4 cut to midcourt and receive passes from them.
6. Then the players repeat steps three through five, rotating through all players.

TIPS

1. It is important that players communicate and move quickly.

2. Players need to hit their targets to avoid dropped passes.

Beginner: Have players move slowly and jump stop when they catch a pass.
Advanced: Quickly change between chest passes and bounce passes.

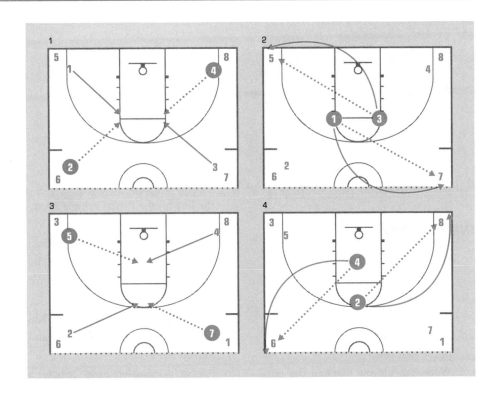

LIGHTNING PASSING

Difficulty Level: Intermediate

Skills Practiced:
Passing, ball control, dribbling

Number of Players Needed: 12

Number of Basketballs Needed: 4

Ideal Practice Time: Beginning

INSTRUCTIONS

1. Using the half court, players form even lines in each corner.
2. The player at the beginning of each line starts with a ball and dribbles with his right hand into the center of the half court.
3. When the players meet in the center court, all four players simultaneously jump stop, make an outside pivot on their right foot, and pass to the line on their right using a strong chest pass.
4. Once the player has passed the ball from the middle of the floor, he runs to the end of the line he just passed to.
5. The player who receives the ball begins dribbling into the center and repeats the drilla.
6. Repeat using a left-hand dribble, a pivot on the left foot, and a pass to the line on the player's left.
7. Repeat using bounce passes.

TIPS

1. Make sure passers step to the player they are passing to and call out that player's name.

2. Be sure players from each line jump stop and pass at the same time.

3. Insist that players hustle to the next line after they pass to keep the drill going.

Beginner: Have passers point to the player they will pass to before they begin dribbling. Keep a coach in the middle to make sure players come in at the same time and keep players at a slower pace. Shorten the distance of each pass.
Advanced: Have all players move more quickly. Have a coach in the middle try to slap the ball out of players' hands when they jump stop to make sure the players are strong with the ball. Quickly change from chest pass to bounce pass.

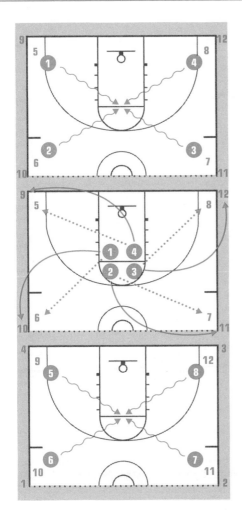

THREE-MAN WEAVE

Difficulty Level: Intermediate

Skills Practiced: Passing, ball control, lay-ups, conditioning

Number of Players Needed: At least 9

Number of Basketballs Needed: 1

Ideal Practice Time: Beginning

INSTRUCTIONS

1. Players form three lines on the base-line. One line is under the basket while the other two lines are about three feet from each sideline.

2. The player in the center line starts by throwing the ball against the backboard, then grabs the rebound and makes an outlet pass to either sideline.

3. The passer runs to replace the player he passed to, while the player who received the ball passes to the player in the third line across the court.

4. All three players run down the court, passing the ball back and forth. The passer always replaces the player he passed to.

5. When the player with the ball reaches the free-throw line on the opposite end of the court, he makes a strong jump stop and passes to the next player, who shoots a lay-up.

6. The last passer gets the rebound or the ball out of the net, and the drill is repeated back to the other basket.

TIPS

1. Players must release the ball quickly and crisply after receiving a pass.

2. Players must always step at their target without traveling.

Beginner: Players may skip the weaving and just pass down the court. Players may be allowed to make two dribbles before passing.

Advanced: After weaving down the court, the players run back to the other end playing 2-on-1. The player who makes the lay-up should be the defensive player, with the two other players are on offense.

For a different challenge, add two more lines under the basket and make the drill a five-man eeave.

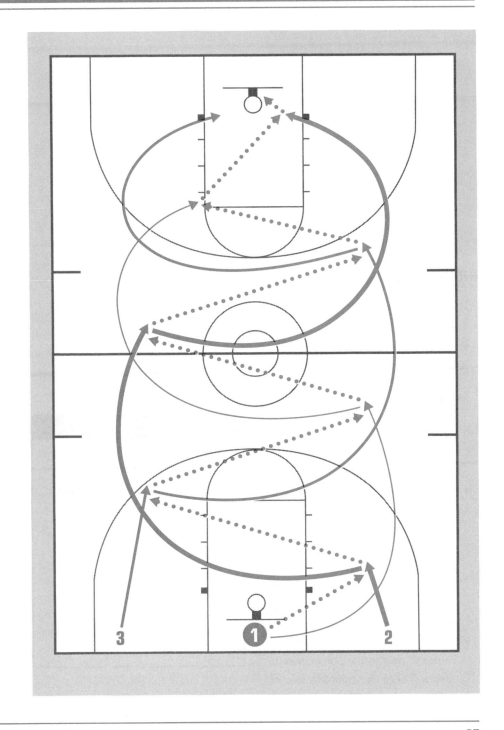

TRANSITION PASSING

Difficulty Level: Intermediate to advanced

Skills Developed:
Passing in transition, ball control

Number of Players Needed: At least 5

Number of Basketballs Needed: 1

Ideal Practice Time: Middle

INSTRUCTIONS

1. Start with five players inside the free-throw lane.
2. A player puts the ball through the net, and the 4-man takes the ball out of bounds, simulating the opposing team just scoring.
3. The 1-man cuts from wherever he is standing when the shot goes through the net to receive the ball at the free-throw line extended.
4. The 3-man runs down the left side of the court while the 2-man runs down the right side. The 5-man runs down the center of the court to the right block. The 1-man squares to the open floor, takes one dribble, and passes the ball quickly to the 2-man running down the court.
5. The 2-man cannot dribble, but has a choice to pass to the 3-man, who is running down the opposite side of the court to the basket, or to the 5-man who is posting up. The 4-man trails the play and sprints to the left elbow, then looks to rebound.
6. Whichever player receives the ball makes a move and shoots the ball. Once a shot is made, the ball is taken out of bounds and the drill repeats the same way to the other basket.

TIPS

1. Players need to make strong passes to their moving teammates.

2. Players need to work on leading their receivers and not traveling.

Beginner: Allow dribbles to shorten passes.

Advanced: Add defenders. Allow the wing player (2-man) to reverse the ball to the trailing 4-man who looks for a high-low lob pass to the 5-man or a backdoor cut (see page 32) from the opposite wing (3-man).

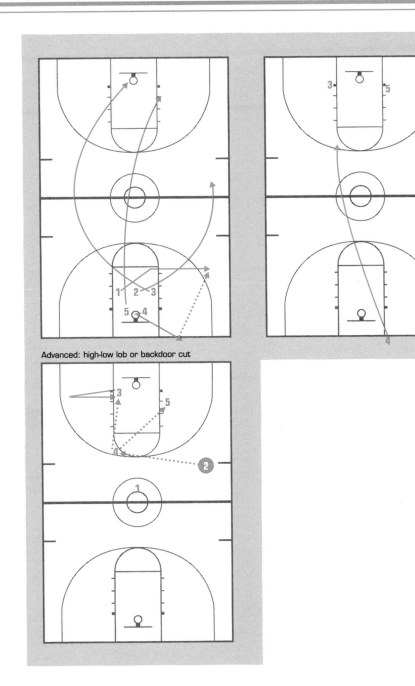

Advanced: high-low lob or backdoor cut

THE GAUNTLET

Difficulty Level: Intermediate

Skills Practiced: Passing on the run, passing against defense

Number of Players Needed: At least 5

Number of Basketballs Needed: 1

Ideal Practice Time: End

INSTRUCTIONS

1. Players 1 and 2 start on the baseline on each side of the lane.
2. One defensive player is positioned in the middle of the court at the closest free-throw line, one at the half-court line, and one at the opposite free-throw line.
3. Player 1 dribbles toward the first defender, while player 2 begins running down the court. When the defensive player moves to guard player 1, player 1 passes the ball to player 2 using a chest pass or a bounce pass.
4. Once player 2 receives the ball, he dribbles toward the defensive player at half court. When that defensive player jumps to guard him, player 2 passes back to player 1, who is running up the court.
5. Once player 1 receives the ball, he attacks the defensive player at the far free-throw line.
6. When the defender jumps out to stop player 1, player 1 makes a pass to player 2, leading player 2 to the basket for a lay-up.

TIPS

1. Make sure offensive players use either a bounce pass or a chest pass depending on how the defense is playing them.

2. Make sure players use strong jump stops when applicable.

Beginner: Have the players move slowly from defender to defender. Add an extra offensive player on the other side of the passer.

Advanced: Add an extra defender at each defensive spot to guard the passer and the cutter.

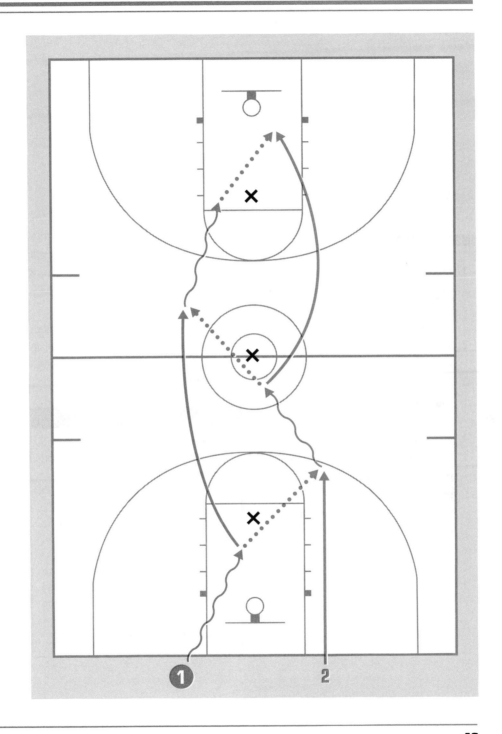

FLASH PASSING

Difficulty Level: Intermediate

Skills Developed: Passing to a cutter, receiving passes after cutting

Number of Players Needed: At least 6

Number of Basketballs Needed: 1

Ideal Practice Time: Beginning

INSTRUCTIONS

1. Place players in three lines, one line on each wing and another underneath the basket. Players rotate to the line that they pass to.
2. The first player in the line underneath the basket starts with a ball.
3. Player 2, in the line to the left, steps away and then flashes towards the left elbow.
4. The player with the ball passes the ball to player 2, who receives the pass in a triple-threat position and passes to player 3 on the right, who has just stepped away and is flashing to the right elbow.
5. Player 4, the second player in the line underneath the basket, steps away and flashes toward the right block. Player 3, at the right elbow, passes to player 4 on the block, who makes a post move and scores.
6. Player 4 grabs the ball as it goes through the net and passes it to player 5, to his right, to start the drill over.

TIPS

1. Players are stepping away to simulate cutting to the ball or running off a screen.

2. Emphasize good cuts.

Beginner: Keep short distances between players to shorten the length of passes.

Advanced: Move lines farther away to increase distance of passes. You may add players as screeners for cutters to run off of or add defensive players to include token defense.

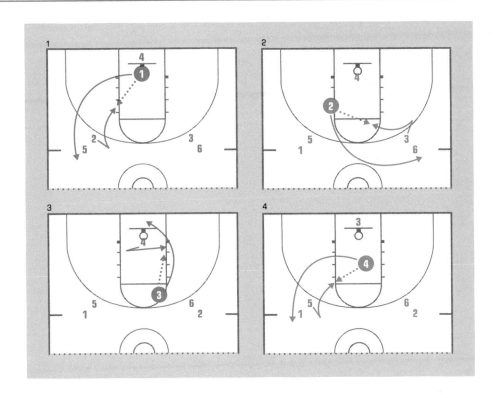

OUTLET PASSING

Difficulty Level: Intermediate

Skills Practiced: Passing (outlet passes and fast break passes), dribbling, shooting, conditioning

Number of Players Needed: At least 2

Number of Basketballs Needed: 1

Ideal Practice Time: Beginning or during individual workouts

INSTRUCTIONS

1. One player starts inside the lane, while another player starts at the free-throw line extended.
2. The player in the lane tosses the ball off the backboard and catches it at its highest point. This player keeps the ball above his head and makes an outlet pass to the player at the free-throw line extended.
3. The player who receives the outlet pass quickly dribbles the ball down the sideline to the other end of the court.
4. The player who made the outlet pass runs down the middle of the floor to the ball-side post.
5. The player with the ball makes a pass to the player on the post, who catches the ball and makes a lay-up.

TIPS

The rebounder must run the floor as fast as possible to try and beat the player with the ball down the court.

Beginner: Have lines of players on each end to give players a break from running up and down the court too often.

Advanced: For increased conditioning, have players run the drill down the court and back.

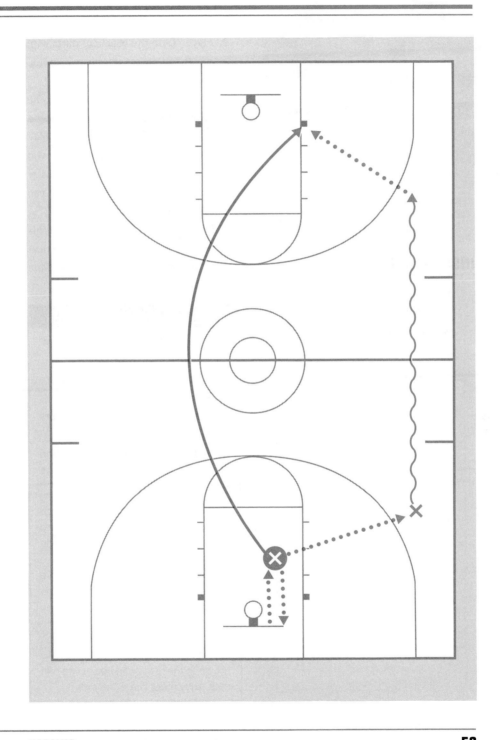

THREE-LINE PASSING

Difficulty Level: Intermediate

Skills Practiced:
Passing, shooting, dribbling

Number of Players Needed: At least 6

Number of Basketballs Needed: At least 2

Ideal Practice Time: Beginning

INSTRUCTIONS

1. Place players in three lines: one on the left-side baseline, another on the right wing, and another on the left wing.

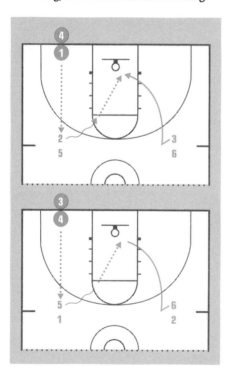

2. Player 1, on the baseline, starts with a ball and passes to player 2, in line on the left wing.

3. After player 2 receives the pass, he dribbles to the left elbow and makes a strong jump stop, then passes to player 3, in the line on the right wing, who is cutting to the basket. The passer must hit player 3 in stride so he can easily make a lay-up.

4. Player 3 makes the lay-up and gets his own rebound, then passes to the next player on the baseline and goes to the end of the line on the baseline.

TIPS

1. Instruct players to go to the end of the line that they just passed to.

2. Emphasize strong and accurate passes.

3. Have the line on the baseline work on outlet passes.

4. Switch sides to work on shooting from both left and right sides of the basket.

Beginner: Place the shooting line on the block so players will not have to catch a pass on the run. This will help eliminate dropped balls.

Advanced: Have the players move back and shoot jump shots as well as lay-ups. Time your players and see how many shots they can make in two minutes. Set a goal and set consequences if it isn't reached. (For example, if players don't make sixty lay-ups in two minutes, they must run a line drill.)

BACKDOOR PASSING

Difficulty Level: Intermediate

Skills Practiced:
Passing, moving without the ball

Number of Players Needed: At least 2

Number of Basketballs Needed: 1

Ideal Practice Time: Beginning

INSTRUCTIONS

1. Players stand in two lines, one line at the top of the key, the other line on the wing. The players at the top of the key are the passers, while the players on the wing are the shooters.
2. The player at the wing makes a strong V-cut by getting one foot in the lane and returning to his wing spot with his outside fist up. (This tells the passer he's making a backdoor cut [see page 32].)
3. While the cutter is returning to the wing, the passer takes two dribbles toward the wing.
4. The cutter then cuts back toward the basket as the passer makes a strong bounce pass to him, setting him up for a lay-up.
5. The cutter makes a lay-up, rebounds the ball, and passes it to the next passer in line.

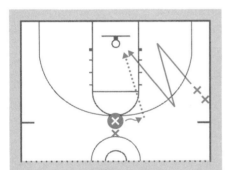

TIPS

The passer should always step toward the cutter when making the backdoor pass. After they complete the drill once, have the cutter go to the passer line and the passer to the end of the cutter line.

Beginner: Have players move slowly, and teach cuts before doing this drill.
Advanced: Add defenders to guard the cutter and passer.

5

Shooting

A team's goal going in to each game is to win. If the goal is to win, then each team is trying to score more points than the other team. The only way to score more points than the other team is to shoot and make more shots in the game. Every coach is different: Some encourage their team to shoot more 3-pointers, while others try to shoot and make more free throws than the other team attempts. As a coach, no matter what your philosophy, you have to include shooting drills that simulate the shots your players are going to take during games.

The following drills should be described and demonstrated correctly to players before they actually practice them. Through the explanation, the players will come to understand that each shooting drill must be practiced until it can be executed at game speed. Once they are shooting at game speed, those shots become indicative of what will happen during a game. The more times they do it, the better they should be at it. Players that do not shoot at game speed during practice are not going to improve their shooting percentage throughout the season. It may be that some players are naturally great shooters, so their percentage will stay consistent, but coaches love to see improvement. There is always room for improvement with any team in every area of shooting.

The drills in this chapter will address the basic concepts of shooting, such as hands ready, butt down, feet and shoulders square to the basket, as well as shooting off the dribbling and coming off a screen. Any player can catch and shoot, but the best players can shoot off the catch and off the dribble.

The shooting drills in this chapter contain drills with one player and one ball, or up to four or five players with

COACHING KEYS

- Make sure each player practices at the same speed he will go during the game.
- Give players the chance to practice the shots they will be taking in the games.
- Always set aside practice time for your team to work on shooting. Make it a priority so that players know how important it is.
- Encourage players to practice shooting on their own, outside of practice time.
- Insist on good form. Watch players and make sure they are shooting properly, especially when they get tired. Make players practice shooting when they are tired.

three balls. That means players can do some of these drills on their own. During practice, these shooting drills should not be "break time" for your players. In some drills there are shooters, rebounders, and passers at each basket. All players should be working hard during the drill. The rebounder is expected to rebound the ball and make a great pass to the shooter. In drills with specific passers, they must concentrate to make each pass to the shooter accurate. A great shot is set up by a great pass.

Individual players may take pride in their shooting. Every player must be willing to put in extra shooting time before or after practice and in the off season because natural ability will only take a person so far. But shooting drills should be included in every practice. As a coach, you may be able to relieve some game-day stress if you adequately practice shooting realistic game shots at practice.

KEY TERMS

Butt down: An athletic stance where the knees are bent and the butt is down so the shooter can catch the basketball and shoot all in one motion.

Game speed: Each drill is done at the speed each player will go during the games.

Hands ready: Both of an anticipated shooter's hands are close together to provide a target for the passer.

Square to the basket: Both feet and shoulders are aligned to face the basket.

3-2 SHOOTING

Difficulty Level: Intermediate

Skills Practiced:
Shooting, rebounding, passing

Number of Players Needed: 3

Number of Basketballs Needed: 2

Ideal Practice Time: Any time

The numbers indicate the order in which the shots should be taken.

INSTRUCTIONS

1. Three players line up at the basket. Two are shooters, with balls, and the third player waits for a pass from either of the two shooters.

2. The coach decides whether the shooting drill will be three, five, or ten minutes in length.

3. The drill begins with both shooters taking bank shots from the block, then rebounding their own shots.

4. The shooter who rebounds his ball first passes it to the third player, who then shoots his bank shot.

5. The second shooter rebounds his own shot and passes the ball to the first shooter.

6. The rotation continues as the shooter rebounds his own shot each time and fires a good pass to the extra player without a ball.

TIPS

This can be an excellent way to get loose and get some shooting done at the beginning of practice. The shot selection can be whatever desired; it does not have to be shots from the block every time.

Beginner: Perform the drill with shots inside a certain range so each player has a realistic shot of getting the ball to the basket. The drill can be done slowly so that there isn't confusion.

Advanced: Make sure the shots are taken quickly. Each shooter should be hustling after each shot, made or missed. Make the shot selection more difficult. For example, take shots from the wings, elbow, or even 3-point line. This will add a conditioning element to the drill because players will have to run farther for rebounds and shots.

INSTRUCTIONS

1. Players partner up at each basket with one ball per two players. (If you do not have enough baskets for each pair, you can put more than one pair at each basket.)
2. One person from the pair is designated as the shooter and one as the passer.
3. Each shooter has thirty seconds to make as many shots as he can from certain spots on the floor. The drill begins with the shooter shooting at the right wing and then the right

Difficulty Level: Beginner

Skills Practiced:
Shooting, rebounding, passing

Number of Players Needed: At least 2

Number of Basketballs Needed: At least 1

Ideal Practice Time: Any time

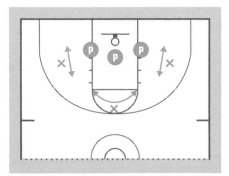

corner, alternating from those two spots for the entire time.

4. The passer must rebound and make a good pass to the shooter after every shot. The balls should not be going all over the gym.
5. After thirty seconds, the players switch positions. Then the drill repeats from the left side of the floor. It repeats again from the right wing to right elbow, then left wing to left elbow, and finally elbow to elbow.

TIPS

Have each player go twice at each spot or have the drill last for one minute instead of thirty seconds. The drill can be made into a shooting competition between the two players with the loser having to run or do a certain amount of push-ups or sit-ups.

Beginner: Perform the drill with shots inside a certain range so each player has a realistic chance of getting the ball to the basket. For example, the shots might be taken from a step or two outside the block. For young athletes, make sure players are using proper shooting technique and not just throwing the ball at the basket.

Advanced: Make sure players take shots quickly. Demand that certain players shoot 3-point shots instead of taking shots inside the arc.

3-2 TO 55 SHOOTING

Difficulty Level: Intermediate

Skills Practiced: Shooting, rebounding, passing

Number of Players Needed: 3

Number of Basketballs Needed: 2

Ideal Practice Time: Any time

INSTRUCTIONS

1. Three players are each assigned a job for the drill: one shooter, one passer, one rebounder. Their roles do not change for the fifty-five seconds the drill takes. Two basketballs are used to keep the drill moving quickly.

2. The shooter begins by taking shots from the right corner with the passer at the right elbow and rebounder at the opposite weak-side block.

3. The shooter shoots as many shots as he can for fifty-five seconds. After each shot, he takes one or two steps toward the basket, then pops back out to the corner and the passer immediately feeds him another ball. The shooter should not be stationary during the drill.

4. The rebounder is responsible for rebounding all shots—makes and misses. He also passes the basketball to the passer, who is responsible for passing the ball directly to the shooter. The passer might have to help rebound as well.

5. After the first shooter is done, the passer becomes the shooter, the rebounder becomes the passer, and the shooter becomes the rebounder.

6. Each player shoots from right corner, left corner, right wing, left wing, right elbow, left elbow, and the free-throw line.

TIPS

It is very important for players to rebound the ball and throw a good pass every time to the shooter. The basketballs should not be going all over the gym.

Decide whether you would like to have each player go twice at each spot. It can be a shooting competition among the three players with the loser having to run or do a certain amount of push-ups or sit-ups.

Beginner: Perform the drill with shots inside a certain range so each player has a realistic shot of at least getting it to the basket. For example, the shots might be taken from a step or two outside the block and no farther. For younger athletes, a focus should be placed on shooting the ball instead of on passing. It may be best to have a coach in the passer position to ensure that all passes to the shooter are accurate.

Advanced: Make sure players know that the shots must be taken quickly but without "hurrying the shot." You might demand that certain players shoot 3-pointers instead of shots inside the arc.

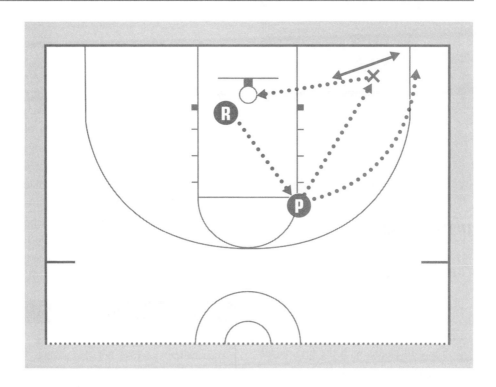

ONE-BALL SHOOTING

Difficulty Level: Intermediate

Skills Practiced: Shooting, dribbling

Number of Players Needed: At least 2

Number of Basketballs Needed: At least 2

Ideal Practice Time:
Beginning or end

INSTRUCTIONS:

1. Players form two lines, one at each block, facing the basket. The lines have the same number of players. If you have enough basketballs, each player has a ball.
2. The drill begins with the first player in each line shooting a bank shot from the block.
3. Once players rebound their own shot, they dribble the ball into the opposite line and shoot a bank shot from the other block.
4. After completing bank shots from the block, players move to other spots on the court and the drill continues from each new location. The first person in each line is responsible for forming the new lines in the correct spots. Players dribble the ball to each new spot on the court.
5. After the first two bank shots on the blocks, the remaining shots come from the following areas on each side of the court: elbow, short corner, wings inside the 3-point arc, off the dribble from corner to elbow, off the dribble from elbow to corner, off the dribble from the wing, and finally back to the bank shots from the block.
6. To end the drill, each player shoots a free throw for a total of fifteen shots.

TIPS

The drill can be used at the beginning of practice for a warm-up drill, and you can decide whether to expand the amount of shots at each spot or continue the rotation for a certain amount of time. Reward the player with the most makes or have a consequence for the players who did not make the most shots.

Beginner: Perform the drill with shots inside a certain range so each player has a realistic shot of at least getting it to the basket. For younger athletes, a focus should be placed on proper shooting form.

Advanced: When dribbling the ball corner to elbow or elbow to corner, Make sure players look at the basket instead of the ball. They should have their heads up at all times and get into the habit of not having to look at the ball when they dribble.

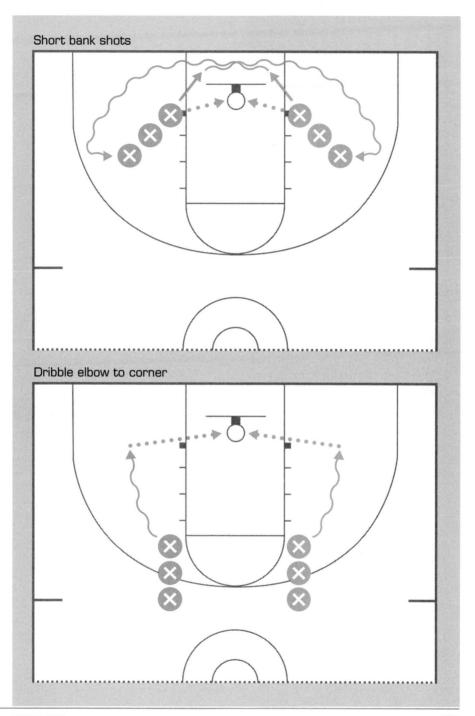

Short bank shots

Dribble elbow to corner

TWO-LINE UNDERNEATH SHOOTING

Difficulty Level: Intermediate

Skills Practiced:
Shooting, rebounding, passing

Number of Players Needed: At least 6

Number of Basketballs Needed: At least 2

Ideal Practice Time: Any time

INSTRUCTIONS

1. Players form two lines underneath the basket, where the lane line meets the baseline.

2. There are two basketballs in each line. The first player in one line does not have a basketball.

3. The player without the ball cuts to the low block on the opposite side of the lane and receives a pass from the first person in the other line. He then shoots a lay-up, rebounds his own ball, and goes to the end of the other line.

4. Immediately after his pass, the passer cuts to the low block opposite of his line, receives the pass, and shoots a lay-up.

5. The rotation continues until a shooting goal is met or time has run out on the drill.

6. Other shots can be included in this drill, including short bank shots from the block, shots from the elbows, and 3-point shots from the wings.

TIPS

The drill can be a certain amount of time, or the players can continue with a certain amount of shots made or made in a row. For example, a goal could be ten shots made at each spot before the team moves on to the next shot.

Beginner: Perform the drill with only one basketball in each line so the drill moves more slowly. Only take shots inside a certain range.

Advanced: Incorporate shots off the dribble.

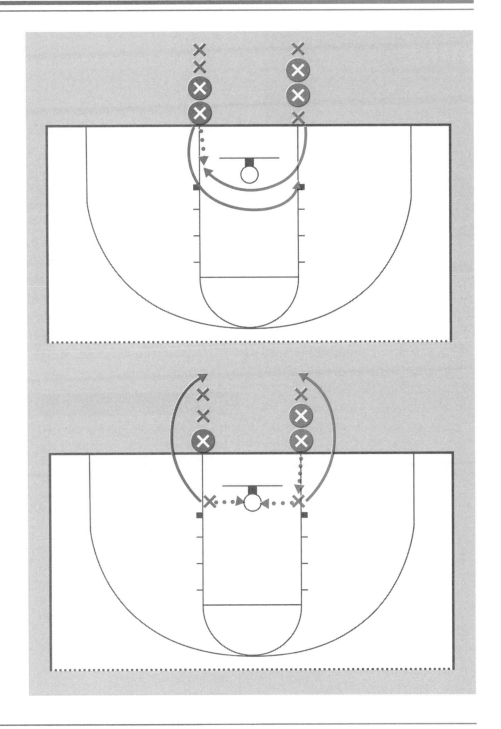

TWO-LINE VICTORY SHOOTING

Difficulty Level: Intermediate

Skills Practiced:
Shooting, rebounding, passing

Number of Players Needed: At least 4

Number of Basketballs Needed: 4

Ideal Practice Time: Any time

INSTRUCTIONS

1. Players form two lines behind the 3-point arc where the free-throw line extended meets the arc.

2. There are two basketballs in each line. The first player in one of the lines does not have a ball.

3. The first player without a ball cuts into the lane, puts one foot in the paint, and finishes her cut around the free-throw line. (This is known as a "victory" cut because it forms a letter "V"; it can be remembered by thinking that making V-cuts will produce many victories.)

4. The player catches a pass from the first player in the other line and shoots a free-throw line jump shot, preferably right in the middle of the foul line.

5. Immediately after throwing the pass, the passer makes her own V-cut, catches a pass at the free-throw line, and shoots.

6. After rebounding their own shots, players fill in at the end of the opposite line.

7. After a certain amount of time or certain amount of shots are made, the two lines can move from the wings to one line in the corner and the other at the top of the key. When the lines are in these spots, the shots are taken at the wings instead of the foul line.

TIPS

This can be a shooting competition drill between two groups, one group on one basket and the other group at the opposite end. The winning group either makes more shots in the time allotted or is the first to a certain number of made shots.

Beginner: Perform the drill using only one basketball in each line, with an emphasis on shots inside a certain range so each player has a realistic chance of at least getting the ball to the basket.

Advanced: Have shots taken off the dribble or have them follow either a ball fake or a shot fake.

BASKETBALL DRILLS, PLAYS, AND STRATEGIES

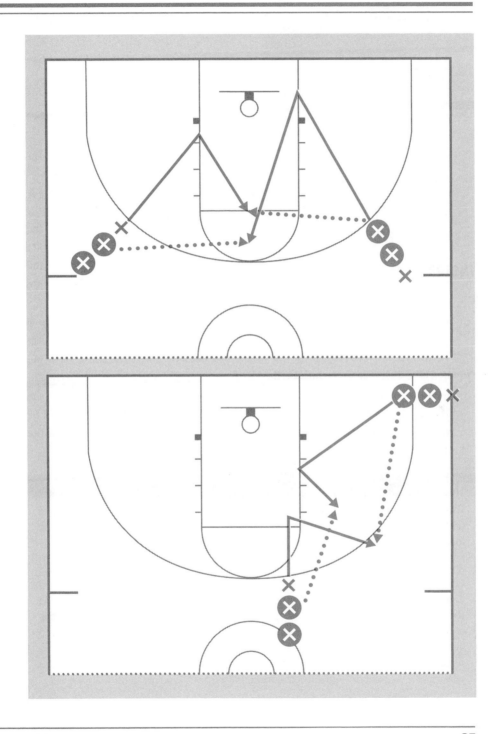

TWO-LINE FLARE SHOOTING

Difficulty Level: Intermediate

Skills Practiced:
Shooting, rebounding, passing

Number of Players Needed: At least 4

Number of Basketballs Needed: 4

Ideal Practice Time: Any time

INSTRUCTIONS

1. Players form two lines at the top of key, where the extended lane line meets the 3-point arc.
2. There are two basketballs in each line. The first player in one of the lines does not have a basketball.
3. The first player without a ball cuts toward the free-throw line and makes a flare cut to the wing. The player cuts as if he is coming off a flare screen (see page 98) around the top of the key.
4. He catches the skip pass from the first player in the other line and shoots a wing jump shot, preferably right inside the 3-point arc.
5. Immediately after throwing the pass, the passer makes his own flare cut, catches the skip pass from the opposite line inside the 3-point arc, and shoots.
6. After a certain amount of time runs out or a certain amount of shots are made, the two lines move from the top of the key to one line in the corner and the other at the top of the key. In this case, the shots should be taken at the corners and top of the key instead of at the wing.

TIPS

This can be a shooting competition drill between two groups, one group on one basket and the other group at the opposite end. The winning group either makes more shots in the time allotted or is the first to a certain number of made shots.

Beginner: Perform the drill using only one basketball in each line, with an emphasis on shots inside a certain range so each player has a realistic shot of at least getting it to the basket. For example, the shots might be taken from a step or two inside the foul line. Emphasize staying within a player's range. For younger athletes, a focus should be placed on shooting the ball instead of throwing the ball. It is important to get repetitions shooting the basketball, not throwing it.
Advanced: The shots off the dribble can follow either a ball fake or a shot fake. Give the players who can shoot 3-pointers the freedom to shoot 3-pointers off the flare cut.

BASKETBALL DRILLS, PLAYS, AND STRATEGIES

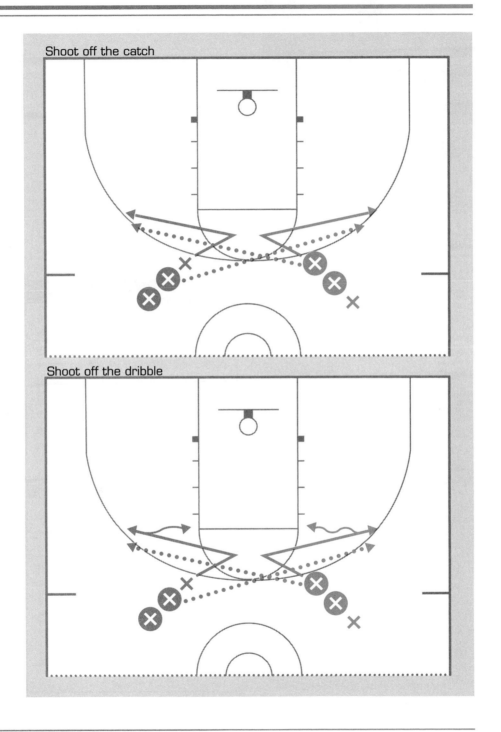

Shoot off the catch

Shoot off the dribble

MACHINE SHOOTING

Difficulty Level: Intermediate

Skills Developed:
Shooting, rebounding, passing

Number of Players Needed: At least 3

Number of Basketballs Needed: 2

Ideal Practice Time: Any time

INSTRUCTIONS

1. Players form one line of at least three players behind the free-throw line. The first two players in line have a ball.
2. The first player shoots the basketball. The second player in line shoots immediately after the first player.
3. The shooters rebound their own shots and pass the ball back to the next player in line without a ball. Each shooter only shoots one shot. Whether she makes or misses it, she rebounds the shot and passes it to the next player in line.
4. The rotation continues with each shooter rebounding her own shot and passing the basketball to the next player in line who does not have a ball.
5. After shooting from the free-throw line, shooters can line up on the wings, baseline, or any position, in front of or behind the 3-point arc.

TIPS

This can be a shooting competition drill between two groups, one group on one basket and the other group at the opposite end. The winning group either makes more shots in the time allotted or is the first to a certain number of made shots. Once a line has more than five or six players, you might have to add another basketball to each line. This drill is a great way to have some fun at the end of practice.

Beginner: Make sure players are performing the drill correctly before the expectations of the drill are raised. This may require some patience.

Advanced: The shots must be taken quickly without hurrying their shots. You might make a conditioning drill a consequence to make the drill more competitive. The group that makes the most shots in a certain amount of time wins and does not have to do the conditioning.

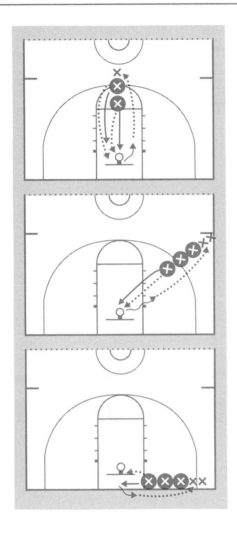

KNOCKOUT

Difficulty Level: Beginner

Skills Practiced:
Shooting, rebounding, passing

Number of Players Needed: At least 3

Number of Basketballs Needed: 2

Ideal Practice Time: Any time

INSTRUCTIONS

1. Players form one line of at least three players behind the free-throw line. The first two players in line have a ball.

2. The first player shoots the basketball. The second player in line shoots immediately after the first.

3. Both players follow their shots. If they miss their shots, they rebound and keep shooting until they make a basket. Follow-up shots are usually lay-ups, but they can be taken from any spot on the floor.

4. The first shooter must make his shot before the second shooter. If he does, he passes the ball to the third person in line, who tries to make his shot before the second shooter.

5. If the second shooter makes the shot before the first shooter, the first shooter is out of the drill and the basketballs are passed to the third and fourth players in line.

6. The drill continues until there is only one shooter remaining.

TIPS

This is a very common game at summer camps that can be used for players of all ages. The drill provides each player with an opportunity to make shots in a pressure situation. This shooting drill is a great way to end practice every day because kids think it is fun.

Beginner: Have players start closer to the basket so that the first shot is easier.

Advanced: Use other shots, such as 3-point shots at the top of the key, corner, wing, or elbow shots.

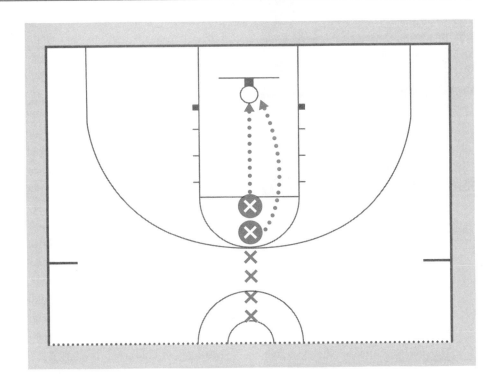

ROCKET SHOOTING

Difficulty Level: Intermediate

Skills Practiced:
Shooting, rebounding, dribbling

Number of Players Needed: 1

Number of Basketballs Needed: 1

Ideal Practice Time: Any time

INSTRUCTIONS

1. A player shoots a total of fifty shots without taking a break for water or rest. After each shot, he rebounds and dribbles the basketball with his weak hand to the proper spot on the court.

2. The player starts by shooting five free-throw line jump shots off the right-hand dribble and five off the left-hand dribble, using either a ball fake or a shot fake.

3. The player then goes directly to the free-throw line, shot fakes, and shoots five jump shots without any dribbles.

4. The player then shoots five elbow jump shots, alternating which side of the court he's on each time. The player spins the ball to himself (to simulate a pass) and shoots without any dribbles.

5. The player then takes five corner jumpers exactly like the elbow jumpers, alternating sides and spinning the ball to himself.

6. The player then takes five jump shots off the dribble from corner to elbow.

7. The next set of shots is five jumpers off the dribble from elbow to corner.

8. Then the player shoots five 3-point shots from the top of the key after spinning the ball and shooting without any dribbles.

9. The player then shoots five 3-point shots from the wing. He alternates from wing to wing for each shot.

10. Finally, the player shoots five 3-point shots from the corner. He alternates from corner to corner between each shot.

TIPS

This drill can be used for players to perform during individual workouts within practice or in the off-season.

Beginner: Place an emphasis on getting somewhere with the dribble. Players should use the dribble to separate from a defensive player. Offensive players need to have this mindset in practice so that it's second nature during game situations.

Advanced: Keep track of the shots made publicly so each player can see where he stacks up compared to the other players in the program. This could provide motivation to individuals to work harder.

BASKETBALL DRILLS, PLAYS, AND STRATEGIES

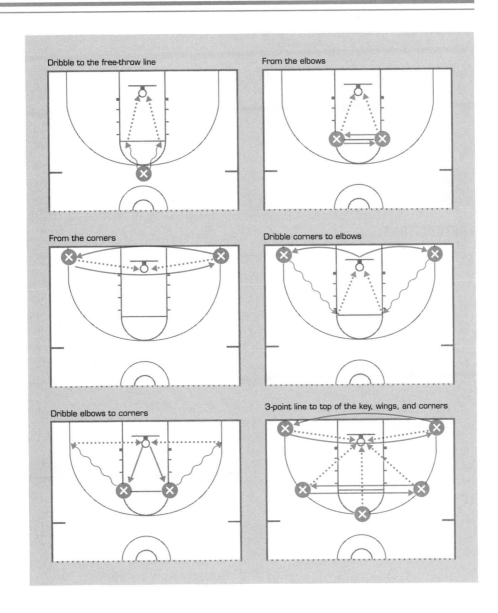

Dribble to the free-throw line

From the elbows

From the corners

Dribble corners to elbows

Dribble elbows to corners

3-point line to top of the key, wings, and corners

NBA SHOOTING

Difficulty Level: Intermediate

Skills Practiced: Shooting, rebounding, passing

Number of Players Needed: At least 3

Number of Basketballs Needed: At least 2

Ideal Practice Time: Any time

INSTRUCTIONS:

1. This drill goes for fifty-five seconds. One player is a shooter and two players act as both passers and rebounders.

2. The passer starts at the right elbow and the rebounder is at the opposite weak-side block (but they will move around as the drill progresses).

3. The shooter begins in the right corner behind the 3-point line, where he takes his first shot. He moves around the court taking shots from the following places: shot two—inside the 3-point line, between the wing and corner; shot three—the wing behind the 3-point line; shot four—inside the 3-point line at the right elbow; shot five—a 3-pointer at the top of the key; shot six—inside the 3-point line at the left elbow; shot seven—3-pointer on the left wing; shot eight—inside the 3-point line between the wing and corner; shots nine and ten—two 3-pointers in the left corner.

4. The shooter does the entire arc again going in the other direction until he gets back to the right corner.

5. The passers and rebounders must quickly rebound balls to keep them out of the shooter's way. They must also feed passes to the shooter, anticipating where he will be going next. There should be no lull in the rhythm of the drill.

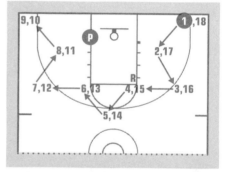

TIPS

It is very important for the passer and rebounder to communicate so the shooter can get to all the shots within the fifty-five seconds. The shooter must go hard the entire time or she will not be able to finish the drill.

Beginner: Perform the drill only going around the arc once and shooting all the shots inside the 3-point line.

Advanced: Set goals for each player to make a certain amount of shots, and be sure the drill is done at game speed.

INSTRUCTIONS

1. Two players and one ball are needed at each basket. One player is a shooter and the other is a rebounder.
2. The coach decides which spot on the floor the shooter will shoot from and how long the drill will last.
3. The shooter shoots from the same spot for the entire drill. He receives 1 point for a make but loses 2 points for a miss.
4. The rebounder rebounds the ball and passes it back to the shooter. He also keeps score.
5. The goal for each shooter is to end up with a positive number and make "money."

MONEY

Difficulty Level: Intermediate

Skills Practiced:
Shooting, rebounding, passing

Number of Players Needed: At least 2

Number of Basketballs Needed: At least 1

Ideal Practice Time: Any time

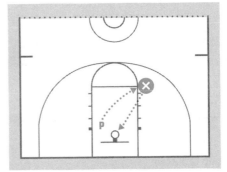

TIPS

Decide how long the drill should last; it can range from thirty seconds to two minutes. This is a good drill to provide players with a realistic evaluation of where their range ends. For example, if a player thinks he is a 3-point shooter, but ends up with -10 when shooting from a spot behind the 3-point line, it might provide the coach (and player) with evidence on why he should be an inside player.

Beginner: Perform the drill with an emphasis on shots inside a certain range so each player has a realistic shot of at least getting it to the basket. For younger athletes, a focus should be placed on shooting the ball instead of the throwing the ball.

Advanced: Make sure shots are taken quickly, at game speed. Incorporate shooting off the dribble, either off a shot fake or ball fake. When players are shooting off the dribble, emphasize that they keep their heads up when dribbling. Also, it is a great idea to use a chair on the floor to simulate a player using a ball screen to create his own shot.

4 Rebounding

I n a basketball game, the team that controls the boards will usually be the team that walks off the court with a victory. Great rebounding not only limits the amount of shots your opponent takes throughout a game, it also increases the number of shot attempts your team will take. Both offensive and defensive rebounding can lead to high-percentage shots. Offensive rebounds often lead to short lay-ups from your center or forwards, while defensive rebounds, along with good outlet passes, can lead to quick lay-ups from guards and forwards. Rebounding is not always about the size of the re-bounder, it is more about the attitude of the rebounder. By teaching good technique and instilling a tough attitude in your players, you can dramatically increase your team's chances of winning.

COACHING KEYS

- Rebounding is a battle of leverage. Players need to be in a strong, low position and move their opponent out of rebounding position using their bodies while keeping both hands up in the air.
- Players should attempt to rebound the ball at its highest point.
- Rebounding is all about effort. Many smaller players can be great rebounders if they are tough and want the rebound more than taller players. By boxing out, smaller players can also cause taller players to go over their backs.
- Players should always know where they are in relation to the basket. If they are closer to the basket, they may want to use their bodies to push their opponent underneath the rim.
- Players should also be aware of what kind of shot has been taken. For example. 3-point shots often lead to long rebounds.

Positioning is the most important as-pect of rebounding. Once a shot goes up, all of your players should quickly read the flight of the ball so that they will know which direction to work their opponent. If it's going to be a long rebound, they can box their opponent toward the rim. If it's going to be a short rebound, they can box their opponent out of the lane. While your players are reading the flight of the ball, they should be positioning their feet to form a strong base. A strong base is typi-cally made by having their feet shoulder-width apart and their knees bent, while driving the opponent in the direction they wish with their bodies rather than their hands. Your players' hands should always be up and ready to catch the ball. By hav-ing good position, your players are more likely to rebound the ball or increase the chances of taller offensive opponents going over their backs and being called for a foul.

The player can then explode to the ball and try to catch it at its highest point. When the player comes down with the ball, she must protect it, either chinning the ball or keeping it high above her head. Once the rebound is secure, it is important that the player looks to make an outlet pass to one of her teammates. If you run a fast-break offense, this quick outlet pass helps get the ball down the court before your opponents can get set up in their defense. On the other hand, if you run a methodical half-court offense, this quick outlet gets the ball to your most reliable ball handler faster.

Note: In this chapter, the perpendicular line (———|) symbolizes boxing out.

KEY TERMS

Box out: Pushing an opponent out of rebounding position to getting into a good rebounding position. Boxing out is a battle of leverage, so a player's knees should be bent, her feet should be shoulder-width apart, and her hands should always be up in the air to catch the ball at its highest point.

Chinning the ball: Grabbing the rebound and securing it strongly in front of the chin with the elbows out, being careful not to swing the elbows. This helps to strongly secure the rebound and keep possession until the rebounder is ready to pass to another player.

Close-out: When a defensive player sprints toward a shooter. The defensive player should have her hand up to contest a shot, but be under control, to not allow dribble penetration if the offensive player shot fakes.

AROUND THE WORLD REBOUNDING

Difficulty Level: Beginner

Skills Practiced: Rebounding

Number of Players Needed: At least 7

Number of Basketballs Needed: 1

Ideal Practice Time: End

INSTRUCTIONS

1. Six shooters line up around the 3-point arc and one rebounder starts in the middle of the lane.
2. The rebounder passes the ball to the first shooter and sprints to that player using a good close-out. Once the shooter shoots, the rebounder boxes out that shooter and gets the rebound.
3. If the rebounder gets the rebound, he passes it to the second shooter and moves to close out and box out that shooter.
4. The rebounder continues this drill until he gets six rebounds in a row. Once this is accomplished, the rebounder becomes the first shooter and the sixth shooter becomes the rebounder.

TIPS

It is important that rebounders use good close-out techniques.

Beginner: Rotate after six rebounds instead of six in a row.

Advanced: Allow shooters to either shoot or penetrate. This keeps the defensive player honest when closing out.

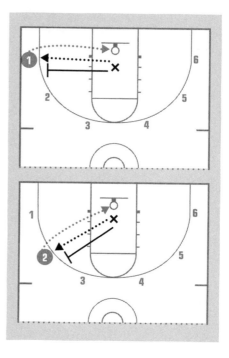

INSTRUCTIONS

1. A coach stands with a ball on the baseline underneath the basket. Three offensive players stand along the 3-point line with one player on each wing and one player at the top of the key.
2. Two defensive players stand on the blocks with their backs to the ball.
3. The coach tosses the ball to one of the offensive players, who shoots and does not run in for the rebound.
4. The two defensive players box out the two nonshooters and secure the rebound.
5. When the defensive players get three rebounds in a row, they go to offense.

Difficulty: Beginner

Skills Practiced: Rebounding, boxing out

Number of Players Needed: At least 5

Number of Basketballs Needed: 1

Ideal Practice Time: Beginning

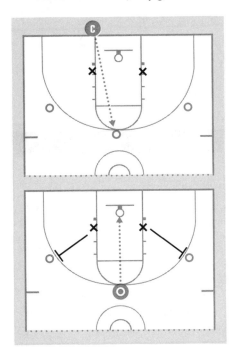

TIPS

Offensive rebounders should be working for the rebound, but they shouldn't push the defensive rebounders in the back.

Beginner: Start defensive players in front of the two offensive players who are not going to shoot the ball.

Advanced: Insist that defensive players must get five rebounds in a row before they can rotate to offense.

4-ON-4 REBOUNDING

Difficulty Level: Intermediate

Skills Practiced: Rebounding, boxing out

Number of Players Needed: 8

Number of Basketballs Needed: 1

Ideal Practice Time: Beginning

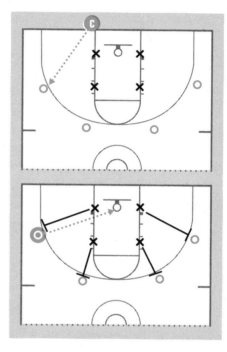

INSTRUCTIONS

1. A coach stands on the baseline with one basketball. Four offensive players stand outside of the 3-point arc, and four defensive players line up with one foot inside the lane.

2. On the coach's signal, the four defensive players get in a defensive stance and chop their feet (quickly move them up and down). The coach then passes the ball out to one of the offensive players, who immediately takes a shot.

3. The defensive players each quickly find their assigned player and box out that player with their hands up.

4. If the defense stops the offense from getting a rebound four times in a row, the defense goes to offense. And offense goes to defense.

TIPS

1. Work with players on boxing out with their hands up.

2. Teach players to find their man, and then find the ball.

Beginner: Set up players next to the player they will be boxing out.

Advanced: Make a rule that to get a stop, the defensive team has to let the ball hit the ground without an offensive player touching it.

THUNDERDOME

INSTRUCTIONS

1. Set one ball at center court.
2. Player 1 stands with his heels on the outer line of the center circle, while player 2 stands between the ball and that player.
3. On the coach's whistle, player 2 boxes out player 1 and prevents him from touching the ball in the middle.
4. If player 2 can keep player 1 from the ball for five seconds, he is the king of the thunderdome. If player 1 gets the ball, player 1 must defend the thunderdome from the next challenger.

TIPS

1. Players may not dive for loose balls in this drill.

2. Make sure players are evenly matched up with like-size players.

3. Use both free-throw lines and the center of the court to have three groups going simultaneously. At the end of the period, have the two players with the best records battle it out for that day's champion. The winner is allowed to pick what the conditioning will be at the end of practice or is given an extra water break.

Beginner: Decrease the amount of time player 2 must box player 1 out.
Advanced: Allow player 1 to push, pull, or spin to get the ball.

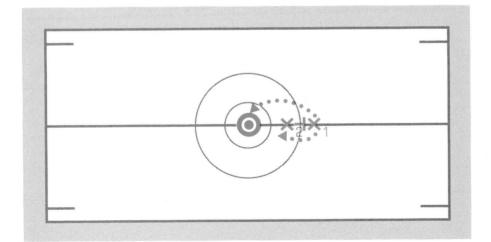

TRIANGLE BOX-OUT

Difficulty Level: Advanced

Skills Practiced: Rebounding

Number of Players Needed: At least 6

Number of Basketballs Needed: 1

Ideal Practice Time: Beginning

INSTRUCTIONS

1. Three offensive players take position around the 3-point arc, one player on top of the key and one player on each wing. One defensive player lines up on the free-throw line while two other defensive players stand near the blocks.

2. A coach takes a shot from anywhere on the floor.

3. When the shot goes up, the defensive players call it out and box out a player. The player on the free-throw line boxes out the player on the left wing, the defensive player on the right block boxes out the player on the top of the key, and the player on the left block boxes out the player on the right wing.

4. The defense must get three rebounds in a row to rotate to offense.

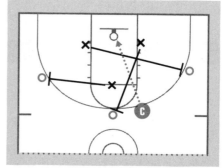

TIPS

1. Players need to sprint to box out a player in their zone.

2. Players need to talk and communicate for the drill to run smoothly.

Beginner: Allow defensive players to box out the player standing closest to them.

Advanced: Allow offensive players to move before the shot. Defensive players must box out and let the ball hit the floor before they can touch it, forcing them to box out their player longer.

INSTRUCTIONS

1. Two players line up about two feet in front of the rim. You can have these two players hold hand-held contact pads if you like, but it's not necessary.

2. A rebounder stands about three feet from the rim in between the other two players.

3. The rebounder throws the ball off the backboard and goes up strong to get the rebound.

4. The rebounder comes down with strong control of the ball, keeping it high and protected. While he is doing this, the two defensive players bump the rebounder with their pads, forcing the rebounder to go strong to the basket. He explodes to the basket to put the ball back in for a lay-up.

TIPS

Players should be watched closely to make sure they do not get too rough while pushing the rebounder.

Beginner: Start with only one defensive player with a pad to give resistance to the rebounder.

Advanced: Allow the defenders to bump the rebounder while he is going up for the rebound.

POWER REBOUNDING

Difficulty Level: Intermediate

Skills Practiced:
Rebounding, scoring in traffic

Number of Players Needed: At least 3

Number of Basketballs Needed: 1

Ideal Practice Time: Beginning

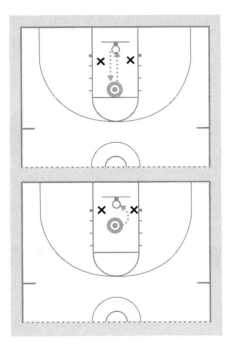

1-ON-1 CLOSE-OUT AND BOX-OUT

Difficulty Level: Intermediate

Skills Practiced: Rebounding, defense

Number of Players Needed: 2

Number of Basketballs Needed: 1

Ideal Practice Time: Beginning

INSTRUCTIONS

1. One offensive player stands on the free-throw line while defensive player stands underneath the basket with a ball.
2. When the defensive player is ready, he passes the ball to the offensive player.
3. The offensive player shoots the ball as soon as he receives it and then follows his shot.
4. The defensive player immediately sprints to the offensive player using a good close-out technique.

5. The defensive player must turn, box out the shooter, and get the rebound.

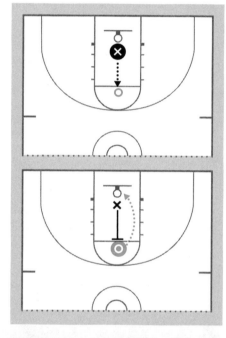

TIPS

1. The rebounder should box out with his hands up and explode to the ball, catching it at its highest point.

2. This is a great drill for players to compete and work hard at boxing out. You can have the defensive player run or do push-ups if he does not get the rebound.

Beginner: Don't allow the shooter to attempt to get the rebound. Make sure the defensive player focuses on getting into the right position.

Advanced: Allow the offensive player to make a shot fake and take two dribbles. This makes sure the defensive player closes out properly and looks to take away both the shot and dribble penetration.

REBOUND AND PUTBACK

Difficulty: Intermediate

Skills Practiced: Rebounding, conditioning

Number of Players Needed: 3

Number of Basketballs Needed: 1

Ideal Practice Time: Beginning

INSTRUCTIONS

1. One player stands in front of the rim while two passers stand on the baseline, on each side of the backboard. The coach stands one step in front of the free-throw line.
2. The coach throws the ball to one side of the backboard and the player rebounds the ball and puts it back into the basket.
3. The passers are there to get the ball as it goes through the net and pass it back to the coach.
4. The player does this drill for one minute or ten baskets at the coach's discretion.

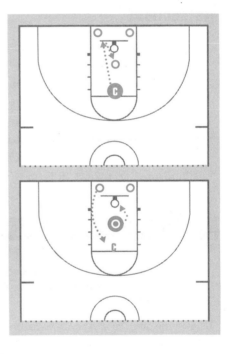

TIPS

The player should always land with the ball high and protected.

Beginner: Emphasize that the player should keep the ball high over her head and put it directly back to the basket.
Advanced: Add a player with a pad to bump and "foul" the rebounder.

BIG 10 REBOUNDING

Difficulty Level: Advanced

Skills Practiced: Rebounding, scoring in traffic, toughness with the ball

Number of Players Needed: At least 5

Number of Basketballs needed: 1

Ideal Practice Time: Before any water break or before shooting free throws

INSTRUCTIONS

1. Players all stand inside the lane. Once the coach starts play, no player may be allowed out of the lane or the low post.

2. To start play, a coach shoots the ball. All players find someone to box out and fight for the rebound. There are no teams; it is every player for himself.

3. If a player gets the rebound, he needs to come down with the ball strong and take it back up and try to score. Other players may do anything they want (within reason) to try to get the ball loose and to prevent that player from scoring

4. No dribbling is allowed.

5. If a player scores, the ball is tossed back to the coach, who puts it back into play.

6. Once a player gets three rebounds and three scores, he may get a drink or shoot free throws at another basket. The last player left must do push-ups or run sprints.

TIPS

1. Watch closely so toughness does not get out of hand. To prevent jumpballs, once someone rebounds the ball, never let other players grab the ball from his hands, but pretty much anything goes as long as players are working to make other players tougher and are not trying to hurt anyone.

2. Split the team up and have smaller or younger players play against players their size, while older or stronger players play against players their size.

Beginner: After a player has rebounded the ball, have the defensive players only stand with their arms straight up. Do not let them foul or push.

Advanced: Have an offensive team play a defensive team inside the 3-point arc. No dribbling is allowed and just about anything goes.

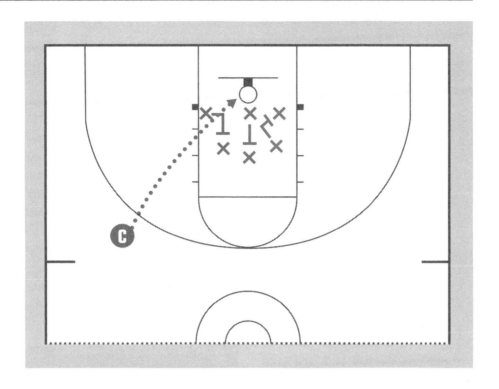

CUTTHROAT REBOUNDING

Difficulty Level: Advanced

Skills Practiced: Rebounding, team defense

Number of Players Needed: At least 12

Number of Basketballs Needed: 1

Ideal Practice Time:
End or before a water break

INSTRUCTIONS

1. Divide players into four teams of three or four. Each team should have a different jersey or shirt.

2. Two coaches stand on the perimeter and pass the ball back and forth to make sure the defensive team is showing ball-side and help-side positions. Either coach may shoot the ball to begin play.

3. Team 1 starts closest to the basket and will be the defensive rebounders as long as they can control the ball. Team 1 gets 1 point for every rebound they get.

4. Team 2 starts behind team 1 and will be the offensive rebounders. If team 2 gets the rebound, they are awarded 1 point. If team 2 puts the ball into the basket off a rebound, they are awarded another point.

5. If team 2 scores, they become the defensive rebounders and team 3 becomes the offensive rebounders.

6. The teams keep rotating depending on which team scores. When a team is scored on, they line up outside of the 3-point arc near the half-court line and wait for their next turn.

7. The winning team may choose what type of conditioning drill the losing teams will run at the end of practice, or they may get a drink while the other teams run.

TIPS

1. Reward hustling plays (such as diving for loose balls).

2. Watch to make sure players are boxing out with their hands up.

3. Decide if you want players to do the drill for a certain amount of time or if you want to set a goal of points to be reached.

Beginner: Have defensive players start in front of offensive players, and have just one coach at the top of the key. Make sure players focus on getting into good rebounding position.
Advanced: Allow offensive players to move the ball and run plays to score to help players focus on rebounding in a game-like situation.

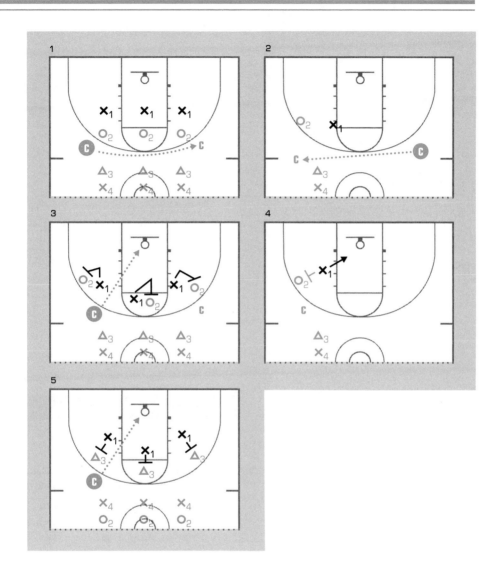

1-ON-1 HELP-SIDE AND BOX-OUT

Difficulty Level: Advanced

Skills Practiced:
Rebounding, boxing out, team defense

Number of Players Needed: At least 4

Number of Basketballs Needed: 1

Ideal Practice Time: End

INSTRUCTIONS

1. One offensive player stands at the top of the key with a ball, another offensive player stands on the wing, and a third offensive player stands on the opposite block.
2. One defensive player guards the offensive player on the block in a three-quarter front denial stance (see page 213).
3. The offensive player at the top of the key passes to the player on the wing.
4. The defensive player sprints to good help-side position.
5. The player with the ball tries to penetrate from the wing and take a shot.
6. The defensive player attacks the penetrator once the ball hits the floor. If the offensive player is stopped outside of the lane, he must take a jump shot. Then the defender sprints back and boxes out the player he originally covered. If the shooter gets to the block or the lane, the defensive player stays on that player, looking to take a charge or box him out after a shot.

TIPS

1. Explain to players that their teammates on defense should rotate down to pick up the player that was left to guard the penetrator.

2. Explain that it is very important to cut off the baseline so that the offensive player cannot get straight to the basket from the baseline.

Beginner: Teach and walk through help-side fundamentals before running this drill.

Advanced: Allow ball reversals to make the defender move in and out of help-side defense and find his player to box out.

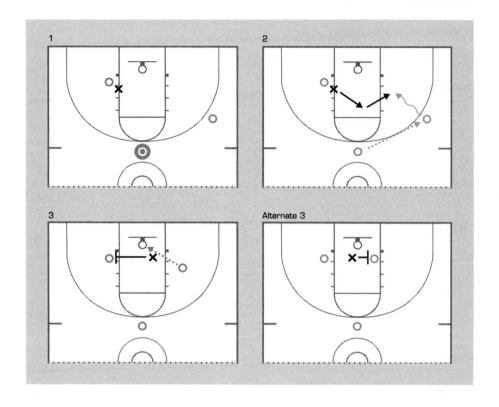

SHELL REBOUNDING

Difficulty Level: Advanced

Skills Practiced:
Rebounding, defense, boxing out

Number of Players Needed: 8

Number of Basketballs Needed: 1

Ideal Practice Time: Beginning

INSTRUCTIONS

1. Two defensive players line up on each side of the key with one foot in the free-throw lane, while four offensive players take position around the 3-point arc.
2. On the coach's signal, defensive players get in a good defensive stance and chop their feet (quickly move them up and down). The coach then passes the ball to an offensive player.
3. When the defensive players see the ball passed, they sprint to their help-side, deny (see page 128), or on-the-ball positions, depending on who the ball is passed to.
4. The offensive players then pass the ball around the 3-point arc, forcing the defenders to switch defensive positions.
5. On the coach's signal, the offensive team takes a shot and the defensive players box out the player they are guarding.
6. When the defensive team gets four rebounds in a row, they move to offense, while the offensive team either moves to defense or waits for their next turn.

TIPS

1. Before you can do this drill you must work on the fundamentals of defense (help-side, deny, and on-the-ball defense [see pages 215–218]).

2. Defensive players need to talk and keep their hands up when boxing out.

Beginner: Make the offense slow the ball down by having each player hold the ball for at least a four-second count to let the defensive players get to their positions.

Advanced: Allow the offense to pass and screen away, making the defense move and search for their man when boxing out. Also have the offense use a penetrating dribble to try and score, making the defense work on eliminating dribble penetration and rebounding shorter shots.

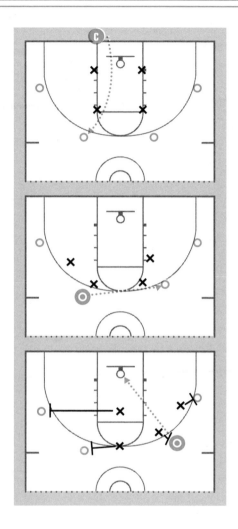

SUPERMAN

Difficulty Level: Advanced

Skill Practiced: Rebounding, conditioning

Number of Players Needed: 1

Number of Basketballs Needed: 1

Ideal Practice Time: Beginning

INSTRUCTIONS

1. One player stands on the block with a ball.
2. The player bounces the ball off the backboard to the opposite block.
3. The player is allowed one step, and then jumps to the opposite block while grabbing the rebound at its highest point.
4. The player lands keeping the ball up and protected, and explodes back up to the basket and makes a lay-up.
5. The player gets her rebound and returns to the block to repeat the drill until she makes twelve lay-ups in a row.

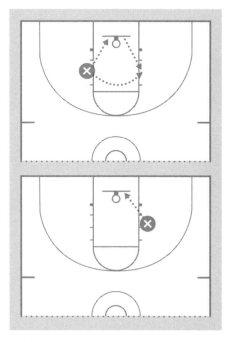

TIPS

The player should always catch the ball at its highest point and land with the ball high and protected.

Beginner: The player may start on one block and a coach can bounce the ball off the backboard to her. Instead of twelve lay-ups in a row, players may participate in the drill for one minute.

Advanced: A coach or player can stand in the lane and offer resistance or try to strip the ball from the player while she is rebounding and shooting.

CHAPTER 5

Offensive Drills

Every time a team has possession of the basketball, the goal should be to score. As a coach, your responsibility is to position your players on the court to enhance their ability to put the ball in the basket. It is impossible to score every possession; however, the offensive drills in this chapter will enable your team to improve its chances of scoring. The following drills should be described to the players before actually practicing them so the players will begin to understand the different game-like scenarios. Also, players should first walk through the drill, and then build up to game speed. A team that does not practice at game speed will not play at game speed in a game.

The drills in this chapter will address not only the basic concepts of offense, such as dribbling, shooting, and passing, but also advanced concepts, like screening nad proper spacing. The biggest priority on offense is to value the basketball, which means limit the number of turnovers. This sounds like a simple concept; however, many players try to force passes, or get flustered while being pressured and turn over the ball. If your team at least takes shots every possession, the odds of scoring points will increase.

The easiest way to increase the odds of your team scoring is to beat the defense down the floor in transition. Any time your team can advance the basketball, do it. This will give your team chances to have advantages such as 3-on-2 or 2-on-1. If your team has a 3-on-2 advantage, the basketball should be centered, with each player on the wing following the ball. If a team has a 2-on-1 advantage, the ball should not be centered—it should be on one side of the court. The reason the ball should not be centered is because the two offensive players can't let one defender guard them both. If the offense is spread out, it is more difficult for the defender to guard both players.

A team may push the ball down the court, and then realize they do not have a good shot. Therefore, the team must have a good half-court offense. Each of the players on offense should be delegated a role, either as a screener or a cutter. Screeners

COACHING KEYS

- Limit turnovers by stressing to players that they secure the ball.
- Practice good shot selection. Emphasize being patient until a good shot is available.
- Insist on good spacing, with a balance of screeners and cutters on each side of the court).

are players who are not consistent shooters, or who cannot beat their players off the dribble. More than likely, your post players will be screeners. Conversely, your cutters will use the screeners to free themselves up, enabling them to get open shots. As a general rule, there should be a mix of screeners and cutters on the floor at all times.

Screening is a very important part of offense. A screen (sometimes called a "pick") is a move in which an offensive player blocks a teammate's defensive player, freeing up the offensive player for a pass or shot. A screener runs to the point where the screen is to be set, but then must be stationary before the defender makes contact with him. Otherwise, he is guilty of a moving screen, which is a foul. It is the cutter's responsiblity to run off the screen (rub shoulders with his teammate), setting up the defender to be stopped by the stationary screener. There are several types of screens: pin screen, back screen, flare screen, ball screen, double screen, flex screen, and down screen (explained in key terms). Players should know what each screen is and what the appropriate time is to use a particular one.

No matter if your team is in transition or in half-court offense, the team should be patient until a good shot is available. Think of it this way: It is much easier to play defense for five seconds than for thirty seconds. If a team is patient, the defense will probably break down and a good shot will become available. By screening, cutting, reversing the basketball, and penetrating the lanes, the offense will improve their shot selection.

KEY TERMS

Back screen: A screen set by a player moving away from the basket so that the cutter can cut toward the basket (i.e., cut to the block).

Ball screen: A screen set for the player with the ball so that she can drive around a defender.

Double screen: When two players simultaneously screen one defensive player, making it extra difficult for her to slide past the screen.

Down screen: A screen set by a player who moves from outside the 3-point arc (most likely the top of the key) to screen for a player down on the blocks.

Flare screen: A screen set from the side so that the cutter fakes moving forward, then cuts to the left or right (whatever side the screen is coming from), leaving him open for a skip pass and jump shot.

Flash: A sudden, quick movement by an offensive player toward the ball.

BASKETBALL DRILLS, PLAYS, AND STRATEGIES

Flex screen: A lateral screen set where the screener moves from the block to set a screen on a defender in the baseline corner (same movement as the screens in the Flex offense on page 200).

Jump stop: A movement where a player stops dribbling the basketball while simultaneously jumping and landing on two feet. A jump stop is used for a dribbler to gain control and avoid charging into the defender.

Outlet: A player, usually a guard, brings the basketball up the court after the ball has been rebounded and passed.

Pin screen: A screen set by a player going toward the basket on a defender positioned near the basket, so the cutter cuts away from the basket (i.e., pops out on the wing).

Screen: When an offensive player jump stops (see page 7) into a defender and remains stationary (moving screens are illegal) in order to get a teammate open for a shot or pass. (Note: Offensive players should rub shoulder to shoulder off screens and remember that the more physical the screen, the better.)

Set-up cut: A preparation cut that is used in anticipation of a screen arriving.

Splitting the defense: A circumstance in which the offense has a 2-on-1 advantage and the ball is on the wing, forcing the defender to choose which offensive player she will guard.

CELTIC FAST BREAK

Difficulty Level: Intermediate

Skills Practiced:
Proper spacing, transition offense, passing, dribble moves, jump stops, shooting

Number of Players Needed: At least 8

Number of Basketballs Needed: 2

Ideal Practice Time: Beginning

INSTRUCTIONS

1. One player with a ball starts under each basket. The remaining players divide up evenly between the two baskets and line up on the sideline at the top of the key extended.

2. The player under the basket passes the ball to the first player in line, who is standing at the top of the key.

3. The player under the basket passes the ball to the player at the top of the key, who is cutting inside the 3-point line to receive the pass.

4. After the player under the basket passes the ball, he sprints down the sideline, while the player that receives the basketball dribbles toward half court. The two players need to keep good space between them.

5. Upon arriving at half court, the player with the ball makes a dribble move (e.g., crossover dribble) and arrives at the free-throw line, where he jump stops and passes to the other player for a lay-up.

6. After shooting the lay-up, the player goes to the end of the line on the opposite side. The player that passed the ball from the free-throw line gets the rebound and passes the ball to the next person in line standing at the 3-point line extended.

TIPS

The player dribbling the basketball must be under control and come to a jump stop at the free-throw line. By coming to a jump stop, the player will learn not to charge into the defender in a game. The player passing the ball for the lay-up should always use a bounce pass. The player receiving the pass should take a 45-degree angle to the rim so he is on a good angle to score a lay-up.

Beginner: Use only two basketballs.
Advanced: Start with two players under each basket and use a total of four basketballs. Using four basketballs will challenge the team's spacing and get more players involved.

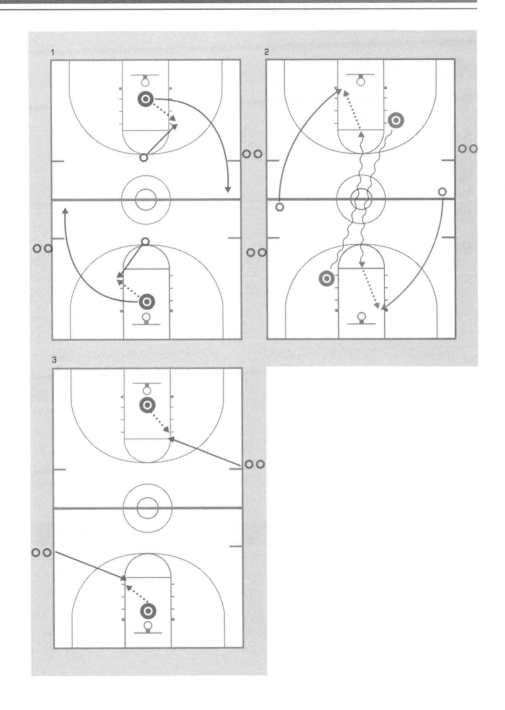

3-ON-3 CHASE

Difficulty Level: Beginner

Skills Practiced:
Making quick decisions in transition

Number of Players Needed: 9–12

Number of Basketballs Needed: 1

Ideal Practice Time:
Middle or before any 5-on-5 drill

INSTRUCTIONS

1. Begin the drill with two defensive players under a basket, three offensive players on the other side of half court, one defensive player on the sideline at half court, and three players off the opposite sideline at half court.

2. The three offensive players advance the ball down the court. As soon the ball passes half court, the player on the sideline sprints to the middle of the court and then becomes the third defensive player. Therefore, for a short amount of time, the offense will have a 3-on-2 advantage; they should use this advantage to get a shot off before the third defender arrives.

3. After the offense shoots the ball, the defense becomes the offense and plays at the other end of the court. Also after the offense shoots, two of the three players on the sideline play defense at the other end of the floor. The last player on the sideline runs to the middle of the court and becomes the third defensive player after the ball passes half court.

4. After the offense shoots the ball, the players go to the sideline where they will eventually get in the drill again as defensive players.

TIPS

When having a 3-on-2 advantage, the last thing an offensive team wants is to let the two defenders guard three offensive players. The player with the ball should always try to score before the defense guards him. By trying to score, he puts pressure on the defense.

Beginner: Emphasize keeping good spacing (when having a 3-on-2 advantage, the offensive team should have the ball in the middle of the floor near the top of the key to spread out the defense).

Advanced: Keep score and penalize the offensive team for a turnover.

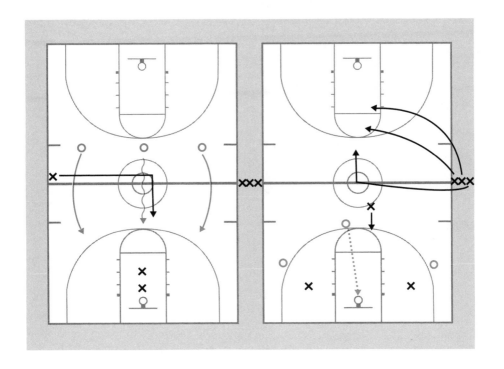

2-ON-0 CUTS

Difficulty Level: Beginner

Skills Practiced: Making sharp cuts, screening, reading screens, passing, shooting

Number of Players Needed: At least 6

Number of Basketballs Needed: 4

Ideal Practice Time: Beginning

INSTRUCTIONS

1. This drill requires two passers and two lines of shooters. One line is designated as a screener line, and the other line is designated as a cutter line.

2. The shooting lines are on the same side of the court. For example, if the line of cutters is in the right corner, and a line of screeners is on the right block.

3. The cutter uses one of four "set-up" cuts (e.g., straight, basket, flare, or back). The cutter has the freedom to choose the type of cut. The type of cut used is usually a spontaneous decision depending on how the defender is guarding. The screener adjusts to the type of cut accordingly and sets an appropriate screen (e.g., flex, up, fade, or back) and then rolls back to the ball. After screening, it is vital that the screener rolls back (or looks for the ball) because

if a solid screen is set, the screener may be open if the defense does not communicate.

4. Both the cutter and the screener receive passes from the passers, and then they shoot, get their rebounds, and become the next two passers. The passers go to the end of the line they just passed to.

TIPS

Make sure players take turns as screeners and cutters. Have a balance of screeners and cutters on the court at the same time to help the continuity of the offense. When a screen occurs, the players should concentrate on going "shoulder to shoulder" next to each other, which makes the screen more difficult to defend.

Beginner: Use only two basketballs. Tell the cutter which type of screen she should use, and tell the defender how he should guard the offense.

Advanced: Use four basketballs and encourage offensive players to use fakes to try and confuse the defense.

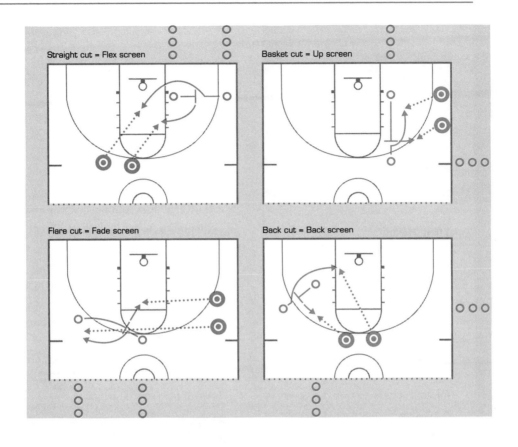

FULL-COURT V-CUTS

Difficulty Level: Intermediate

Skills Practiced: Dribbling, cutting, shooting, coming to the pass

Number of Players Needed: At least 8

Number of Basketballs Needed: At least 2

Ideal Practice Time: Beginning

INSTRUCTIONS

1. One player lines up outside of the 3-point line at each free-throw line extended, for a total of four players.
2. One player starts with a ball.
3. The first player dribbles to half court and does a pull-back crossover (see page 10) to avoid the oncoming trap. (Note: There is no trap; however, by practicing a pull-back crossover, a team is anticipating a trap in a game situation.)
4. After the pull-back crossover is complete, the other player on that end of the court runs to half court and does a V-cut to the top of the key, where he receives a pass from the player with the ball.
5. That player then dribbles across half court to make a pass to the player on the opposite wing at the other end of the court, who is doing a V-cut (running toward the block and finishing at the top of the key) before receiving the pass.
6. As that player is receiving the pass, the other player on his end of the court is doing a V-cut (running toward the block and finishing on the wing). The player with the ball then passes to the cutter.
7. That last player drives and shoots a lay-up or a jump shot, rebounds his ball, and then passes it to the next player in the starting position of the drill.
8. After each player passes the basketball, he goes to the end of the line to which he passed the ball.

TIPS

The offensive players must always meet their passes, especially versus a press. The defense will steal the pass if the offense does not aggressively meet their pass.

Beginner: Use only one basketball.
Advanced: Use many basketballs by having the next player in line begin as soon as the player in front of him has started the drill. Have the players shooting the ball at the end of the drill mix up their cuts.

BASKETBALL DRILLS, PLAYS, AND STRATEGIES

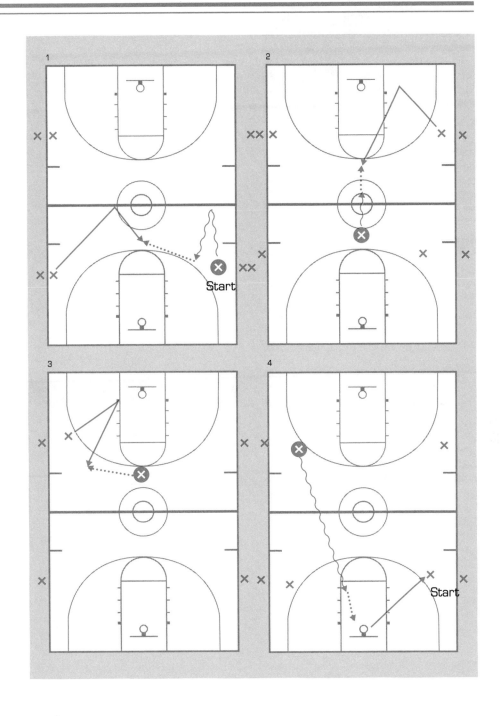

CORRAL

Difficulty Level: Intermediate

Skills Practiced: Splitting the defense, pull-back crossover

Number of Players Needed: At least 3

Number of Basketballs Needed: 1

Ideal Practice Time: Middle

INSTRUCTIONS

1. A player with a ball stands at the free-throw line. A defensive player lines up as if it is a real free throw and stands ready to box-out at the free-throw line. A third player stands at half court.

2. After the player shoots the free throw, the defensive player gets the rebound and plays 1-on-2 against the other players to try to score at the other end of the court.

3. The coach may say "change." If so, the one offensive player then drops the ball and plays defense against two players going back toward the other basket.

TIPS

The offensive player should not pick up her dribble or dribble into prime trapping locations, such as corners. The offensive player may use a pull-back crossover dribble to avoid an on coming trap.

Beginner: Only use three players.
Advanced: Use five or even seven players.

Allow the offensive player who starts the drill to shoot from anywhere, not just the free-throw line.

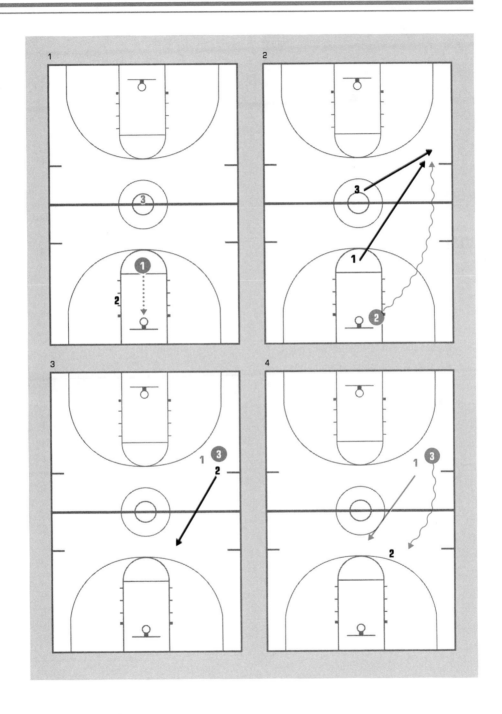

THREE BALL

Difficulty Level: Intermediate

Skills Practiced: Passing, guards relocating, shooting vs. a zone defense

Number of Players Needed: At least 4

Number of Basketballs Needed: 3

Ideal Practice Time: Beginning

INSTRUCTIONS

1. Player 1 takes up position with a ball on the wing. Player 2 (a post player) lines up on the low block on the same side. Player 3 lines up between the top of the key and player 1. Player 4, also with a ball, lines up out of bounds under the basket. A coach with a ball lines up directly parallel to player 1 on the other side of the court.

2. Player 1 makes an entry pass to player 2 and then spots up (looks for a pass) in the corner. Player 1 receives a pass from player 4, and then shoots the ball from the corner.

3. After passing the ball into the post, player 3 cuts to the opposite wing and receives a pass from player 2. He then shoots the ball.

4. After player 2 passes the ball, he should "flash" to the opposite elbow, where he'll receive a pass from the coach. Player 2 shoots an elbow jump shot.

TIPS

Guards should relocate any time a ball is passed into the post. This is because many times the defense will double team the low post, and if the perimeter players (guards) relocate to a different spot on the floor it is more difficult to defend.

Beginner: Go slowly and make sure players concentrate on shooting form. Stop the drill and correct them when needed.

Advanced: Speed things up and have players do quicker repetitions of the drill so that they are going at game speed.

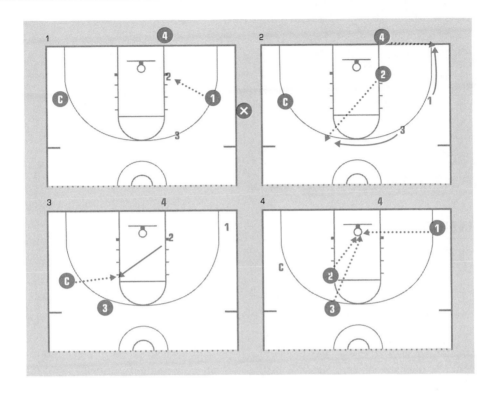

TEN PLAYER

Difficulty Level: Beginner

Skills Practiced:
Passing, dribbling, transition

Number of Players Needed: At least 10

Number of Basketballs Needed: 1

Ideal Practice Time: Beginning or middle

INSTRUCTIONS

1. Three offensive players spread out at half court. Two defensive players line up in the lane at each end of the court. The remaining players form four equal lines on each sideline out of bounds at the top of the key extended.

2. The offensive players take the ball against the two defenders on one end of the court.

3. The offensive team has a 3-on-2 advantage and they get only one shot.

4. After the offensive team shoots the ball, whichever player (offense or defense) rebounds the ball throws an outlet pass to one of the players on the sideline. The rebounder stays in the drill as an offensive player at the other end of the court, playing with the person who received the outlet pass and the player lined up on the opposite sideline. (If the offense turns the ball over, whichever player steals the ball throws the out-let pass and plays on offense going to the other end.)

5. Two players stay to play defense when the ball comes back to their end of the court. The last remaining person fills in one of the outlet lines.

6. This is a continuous drill. Theoretically, a player could remain in the drill the entire time if he continues to rebound the basketball.

TIPS

This is a team drill with an individual concept. The team is trying to score, but the individual (offense or defense) who gets the rebound remains in. The rebounder can play as many possessions as he earns.

Beginner: Allow as many shots as necessary or only allow the defense to rebound the basketball.

Advanced: Limit the number of passes the offense can make while having the 3-on-2 advantage. Make the drill into a competition and challenge players to stay in the drill.

BASKETBALL DRILLS, PLAYS, AND STRATEGIES

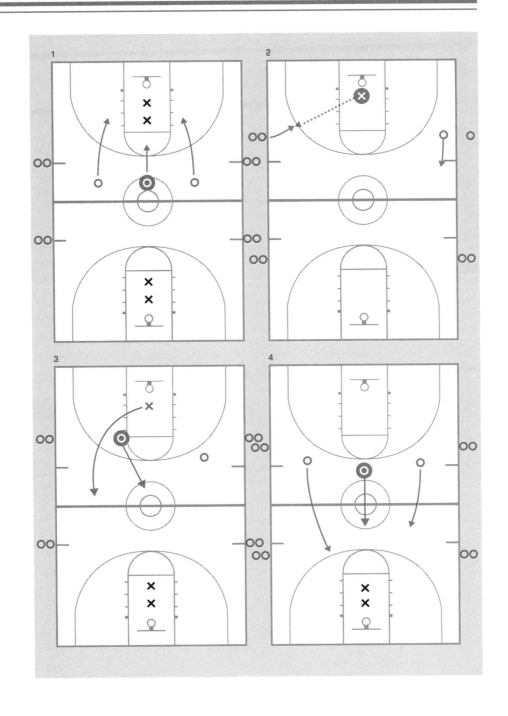

MAKE IT, TAKE IT

Difficulty Level: Intermediate

Skills Practiced: Team half-court offense/defense, transition offense/defense, communication

Number of Players Needed: At least 9 (preferably 15)

Number of Basketballs Needed: 1

Ideal Practice Time: End

INSTRUCTIONS

1. Create three teams with five players on each team (this can be done with three teams of three if necessary).

2. Team 1 is on offense; team 2 is on defense.

3. Team 3 is at half court, just out of bounds, waiting for their turn to play (represented by triangles in the diagram).

4. Teams 1 and 2 play a regular game format (meaning they can use the entire court), but when a team scores, that team gets to stay on offense and play at the other end of the floor. The team that gets scored on must go off to the side, and the team that was on the sideline then comes in on defense.

5. If the offensive team misses a shot and the defense rebounds (or gets a steal), the two teams play full court like a regular game. The defense becomes offense and the two teams remain on the court. The only time new defense comes in is when the current defensive team is scored on.

TIPS

This is a great drill to use when a team struggles playing defense. The team that scores gets to remain on offense. The drill forces the defensive team to get a stop if they want to play offense. The team that is scored on must sit out until another team scores.

Beginner: Only play half court.
Advanced: Play full court for competition. There should also be regulations or stipulations. For example, a team cannot shoot the ball until five passes have been made.

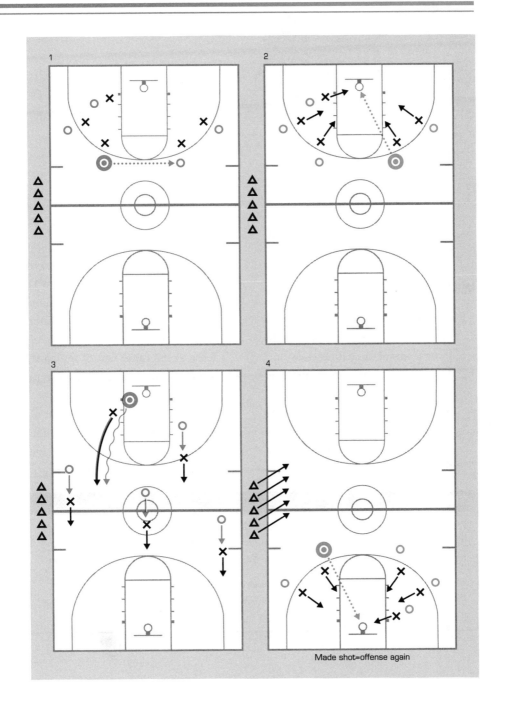

Made shot=offense again

5/55 (FIVE/FIFTY-FIVE)

Difficulty Level: Beginner

Skills Practiced: Team half-court offense/defense, communication

Number of Players Needed: At least 9 (preferably 15)

Number of Basketballs Needed: 1

Ideal Practice Time: End

INSTRUCTIONS

1. Create three teams with five players on each team (this can be done with three teams of three if necessary).
2. Team 1 is on offense; Team 2 is on defense. These two teams play against each other in the half court.
3. Team 3 (triangles in the diagram) is at the other end of the court waiting to play defense against team 2.
4. Unlike make it, take it (see page 114), the team that scores (team 1) does not keep the ball. The team on defense (team 2) gets the ball after a make or miss, and then plays offense at the other end of the court against team 3 who is waiting to play defense.
5. The drill is continuous, with the offensive team always staying as the defensive team the next time the ball comes to their end of the court.

TIPS

The defensive team can mix up the types of defense they play on each possession. For example, a defensive team may play zone on one possession, and man-to-man on the next. This forces the offense to recognize the type of defense in a game situation.

Beginner: Stop between possessions to help players understand the flow of the drill.
Advanced: Keep track of points using a system. For example, you may give +2 for a basket and -1 for a turnover or for giving up an offensive rebound.

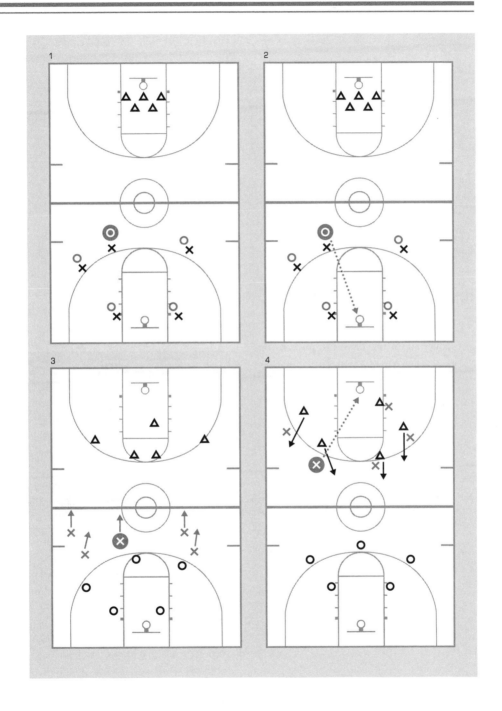

FULL-COURT FOUR CORNERS

Difficulty Level: Intermediate

Skills Practiced: Proper positioning vs. press, meeting the pass

Number of Players Needed: At least 10 (preferably 15)

Number of Basketballs Needed: 1

Ideal Practice Time: Middle or end

INSTRUCTIONS

1. There is a player in each corner of the court and a player in the middle of half court. There is a defensive player guarding each one of these players.
2. A coach with a basketball stands at half court.
3. If there are fifteen players, there should be a player waiting out of bounds in each corner and at half court ready to play offense next turn. The rotation of players is offense to defense, and defense out.
4. The defensive team is prepared to press and has a press predetermined (usually decided by the coach).
5. The coach throws the ball randomly to one corner of the gym.

6. Upon receiving the pass, the offense first recognizes what press they are facing and then tries to break the press. The offense moves the ball toward the basket opposite from the direction the coach threw the first pass.

TIPS

The ideal scenario with the full-court four corners drill is to have three teams of five, with each team wearing a different color uniform. (This will help the team play against a variety of players, not the same each time.)

This drill focuses on proper positioning for the offense when breaking a press.

Beginner: Only use a man-to-man press and have guards at the same end of the court. The coach always throws to a guard.

Advanced: Mix up the type of press the defense uses each time. Have a guard or forward at each end. Finally, throw the ball to a forward to help her understand all the proper positions when breaking a press.

BASKETBALL DRILLS, PLAYS, AND STRATEGIES

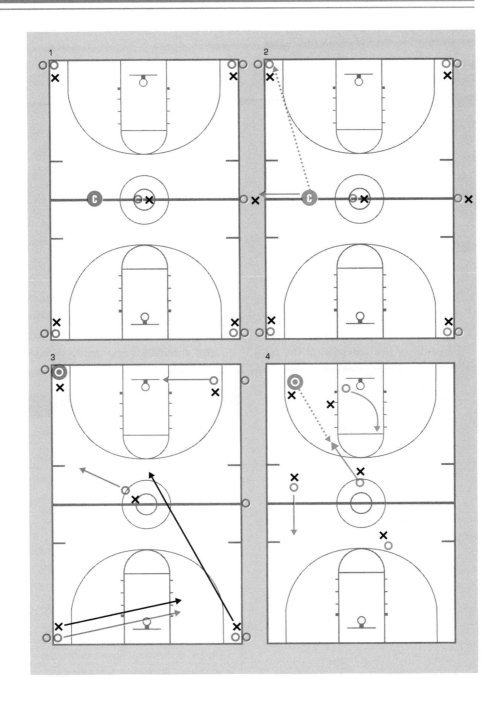

BLUE DEVIL RECOGNITION

Difficulty Level: Intermediate

Skills Practiced: Reading the defense

Number of Players Needed: At least 12

Number of Basketballs Needed: 1

Ideal Practice Time: Middle

INSTRUCTIONS

1. This drill has four offensive players at half court, four defensive players in the lane, and four defensive players standing out of bounds at the free-throw line extended at the opposite end of the defense.

2. Two coaches stand out of bounds on the same side as the players at each free-throw line extended.

3. The four offensive players attack the basket and try to score. Once the offense scores or turns the ball over, the defense becomes the offense and the offense leaves the court.

4. The coach at the opposite end of the court tells the players out of bounds how many of them should go in and play defense. For example, in the third diagram on the next page, the coach sends three defenders. The offense must recognize how many defenders are on the court. The coach can send anywhere from one to four players in on defense.

5. Upon rebounding the ball, the defensive team becomes the offense, with three players going to the other end of the court. The coach at that end determines how many defenders to send in.

TIPS

The following offensive advantage situations may occur, and the ball should be advanced on the court accordingly:

3-on-2 = in the center of the court

2-on-1 = on the wing that will split the defender

4-on-3 = around the elbow area, with a post player trailing the play next to the ball (this will keep good spacing)

Beginner: Always send the same number of defenders onto the court.
Advanced: Mix up the number of defenders; sometimes have fewer offensive players than defensive players.

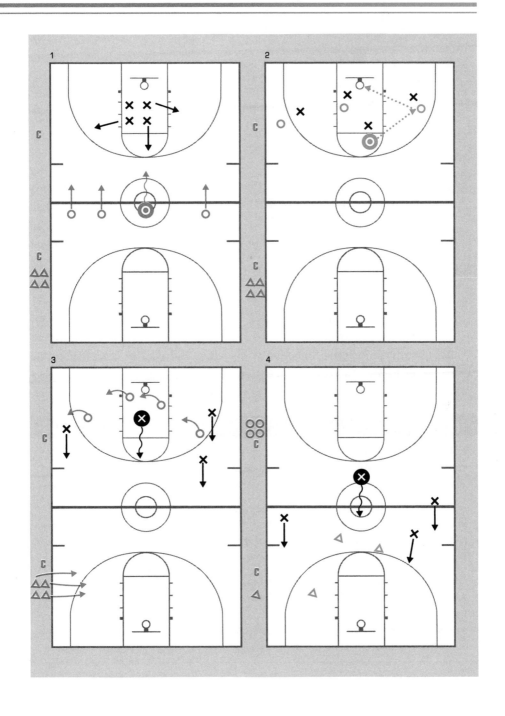

3-ON-3 SHORT COURT

Difficulty Level: Intermediate

Skills Practiced: Making quick offensive decisions, proper spacing, passing

Number of Players Needed: 6

Number of Basketballs Needed: 1

Ideal Practice Time: Middle

INSTRUCTIONS

1. This is a half-court drill. Three offensive players start with one foot inside the 3-point line and three defensive players start in the lane under the basket. The coach has the ball and is under the basket.

2. The coach throws the ball to one of the offensive players on the perimeter.

3. The defender guarding the ball sprints and purposely closes out poorly, allowing the offensive player to penetrate past her into the lane. Then the defender recovers back to the player that is penetrating.

4. For a brief period of time, the offensive team has a 3-on-2 advantage and tries to score before the third defender recovers back into the drill.

TIPS

1. The object of the drill is to make quick decisions in a small area before the defense can recover. The drill is very effective for good shooting teams because poor close-outs are more likely to occur.

2. The offensive team should attack to the basket when having the brief 3-on-2 advantage. If the offensive team must pass the ball, they should use a bounce pass, not a chest pass. The offensive team should realize the number of passes is limited because eventually the third defender will be back in the drill.

Beginner: Walk through the drill first and explain help defense so players understand why they need to help and when it is important to do so. Emphasize communication between the players.

Advanced: Throw the ball to different players on the court so that the help defense must come from varioius positions instead of having the wings always helping in the lane.

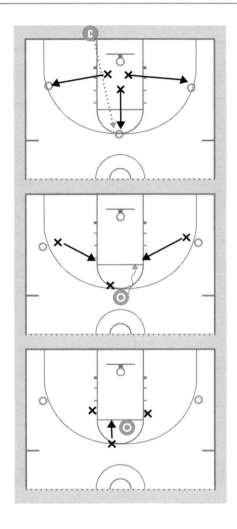

ELEVEN-PLAYER UP-TEMPO

Difficulty Level: Advanced

Skills Practiced:
Passing, shooting, conditioning

Number of Players Needed: 11

Number of Basketballs Needed: 7

Ideal Practice Time: Beginning or end

INSTRUCTIONS

1. Player 1 lines up near the basket with a ball and shoots a lay-up. Player 2 lines up at the elbow with a ball at the same basket and shoots a fifteen-foot jump shot. Player 3 lines up at the top of the key with a ball and shoots a 3-point shot. Players 4 through 11 line up out of bounds at the free-throw line extended in groups of two, so that there are two people at each end of the court on each sideline. The players at the free-throw line extended on the opposite end of the court from the shooters should have balls (players 6 and 7 in the diagram).

2. Players 1, 2, and 3 shoot the balls and get their own rebounds. After his lay-up, player 1 outlets the ball to player 5 at the free-throw line extended and then runs down court to receive a pass from player 7 and shoots a 3-point shot. Players 2 and

3 get their own rebounds and give the balls to the next players in line on the sidelines (players 10 and 11) on their end of the court.

3. As player 5 receives the pass, player 4 (in line on the other sideline) runs down court toward the other basket.

4. Once player 5 receives the outlet pass from player 1, he dribbles to the center of the court and passes the ball to player 4, who is heading in for a lay-up.

5. After player 5 passes to player 4, he continues down court to receive a pass from player 6 (on the sideline) and shoots a fifteen-foot jump shot.

6. If a player has just shot a fifteen-foot jump shot or a 3-point shot, he should fill in the line that he received the pass from.

7. This drill continues as long as the coach desires with a continuous player rotation following the same pattern.

TIPS

One side of the court is always the lay-up side of the court. The lay-up side always passes the ball to the fifteen-foot jump shooter. The other side of the court is always the outlet side. This side always passes to the 3-point shooter.

Beginner: Walk through the drill so everyone understands the progression.
Advanced: Have a time limit and a goal as to how many shots you would like to make as a team.

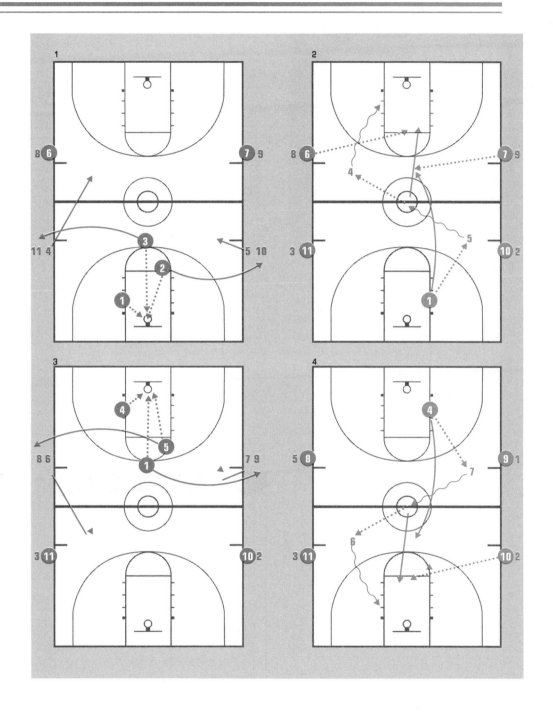

CIRCLE TRANSITION

Difficulty Level: Beginner

Skills Practiced: Recognizing what player is guarding the basketball

Number of Players Needed: 8–10

Number of Basketballs Needed: 1

Ideal Practice Time: Middle or end

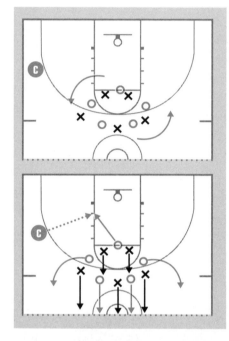

INSTRUCTIONS

1. Players are divided up into two teams.
2. All players form a circle, alternating so that no team members are standing next to each other.
3. The players begin to run in a circle in a counterclockwise direction.
4. The coach drops the ball or shoots and calls a player's name for him to receive the ball, and his team becomes the offense. They will then play half court against the other team.

TIPS

The offensive team should pass or dribble the ball up the court quickly because they will more than likely have a mismatch. For example, a guard may be defending an offensive post player for a short time during the possession.

Beginner: Throw the ball to a player instead of dropping it.
Advanced: Throw the ball out of bounds and let the other team set up in a press.

Defensive Drills

The key to defense is communication. Whether your team is playing man-to-man defense or a zone defense, it is important that all five defense players are communicating at all times. Communication involves players letting their teammates know when the ball is shot, or if a screen is occurring, or if a player is there to help them out if they get beat off the dribble.

The most fundamental concept to defense is for players to be between the ball and their man. This is known as the ball-you-man, or BUM, concept. This will enable players to see all aspects of the court, not just the ball or man. For example, if the opponent the player is guarding is on one side of the court, and the ball is on the other side, the player should be split between the two, leaving equal distance between the ball, the player, and the man he is guarding. This will enable the player to help his teammates if dribble penetration occurs or a lob pass is attempted by the offense.

The player guarding the basketball should have a hand up for the side of the court that is closest to the middle, and he should shade his player to the baseline, but cut her off at the short corner. (The short corner is the area behind the basket between the 3-point line and the lane.) Players not guarding the ball should keep the BUM concept in mind. This may mean that they need to be on the seam or in the center of the court.

> ## COACHING KEYS
>
> - The positioning of defensive players is critical to the success of the team (BUM concept).
> - Players need to understand the rotation necessary for help-side upon dribble penetration. (See page 217.) Always remember that defense involves all five players.
> - Discipline, discipline, discipline! Players need to concentrate on areas such as closing out, boxing out, and limiting false hustle.

This chapter contains drills to improve half-court defense, transition defense, and individual defense. Also, these drills will address proper defensive positioning, defending screens, closing out, blocking shots, and taking charges.

Depending on your preference, your team should either deny passes to the wings or deny reversal passes. Denying a pass means the defender not guarding the ball is between the ball and the player he is guarding. While in between the ball and the player, the defender tries to not allow the pass to get to the player he is guarding. By denying passes to the wing, the opponent will have a difficult time starting their offense; however, the defense will be subject to allowing backdoor passes. By denying reversal passes, the defense enables the opponent to begin their offense but, from that point forward, makes passes difficult. Defensive drills should be completed the same regardless if your team is playing man-to-man or zone defense.

The defense should try to force the offense into the corners. They must protect the high post and try to prevent penetration to the middle of the court or to the baseline. These drills will improve your team's defensive skills. Defense is about attitude and desire. All players can be good defensive players if they are willing to put in the effort.

KEY TERMS

BUM: The single most important individual defensive concept. BUM stands for ball-you-man. The BUM concept means that the player (you) is between the ball and his opponent (man) at all times. This concept also means that a player has one hand pointing at the ball and another hand pointing at the opponent he is guarding, which, in turn, lets him always see both the ball and his man.

Defensive communication: Words or actions used to interact with defensive teammates on the court. Defensive communication allows teams to be in proper position at all times. It entails that defense involves all five players.

Fake and fall: The action taken by a defensive player that is in a situation of disadvantage to put confusion in the offensive player's mind. For example, if a defensive player is in a 2-on-1 situation, the one defensive player might bluff at the basketball to put confusion into the offensive player's mind as to whom the defender is guarding.

Hedge: An action by a player that is not guarding the ball to temporarily guard the ball for a split second until the original defender that was being screened can recover back on his man.

Help-side: The position on the court where a defensive player that is not guarding the basketball is located if dribble penetration occurs.

BASKETBALL DRILLS, PLAYS, AND STRATEGIES

INSTRUCTIONS

1. Two players line up: an offensive player near the sideline on one side of half court; a defensive player near the center of half court, on the opposite side of half court. A coach with a basketball stands between the two players.
2. The coach throws the ball to the offensive player, who starts dribbling toward

Difficulty Level: Beginner

Skills Practiced: 1-on-1 transition defense, faking, taking a charge

Number of Players Needed: 2

Number of Basketballs Needed: 1

Ideal Practice Time: Beginning

the basket, while the defensive player tries to catch up and contain the offensive player so he can't score a lay-up.

3. The defensive player should judge whether he should try to block the shot, take a charge, or simply contest a shot.

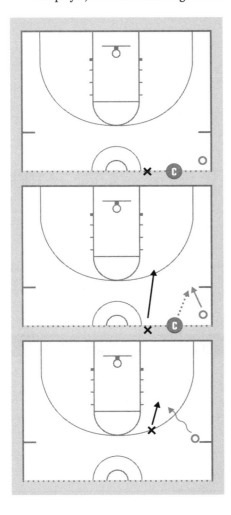

TIPS

It is vital that the defender takes a good angle to stop the offensive player. This requires good judgment on how fast the player with the ball is. The defender should sprint to a spot that she can beat the offensive player to. The farther out from the basket the defender meets the offensive player, the better.

Beginner: Start the defense even with the offense to limit the advantage the offense has.

Advanced: Start the defense even farther behind the offense to make it more difficult to catch up to the offensive player.

TEAM CLOSE-OUT

Difficulty Level: Intermediate

Skills Practiced: Closing out on shooters under control and on balance, help-side defense, transition defense

Number of Players Needed: At least 10

Number of Basketballs Needed: 1

Ideal Practice Time: Middle

INSTRUCTIONS

1. Five offensive players line up around the 3-point arc.
2. A coach stands directly under the basket with a ball.
3. Five defensive players stand under the basket, around the coach, with one hand touching the basketball.
4. The coach throws the ball to a player on the perimeter and the defense must adapt to where the ball is thrown and be in proper position. The defender guarding the person who receives the ball must correctly close out.
5. After being stationary for a second, the offensive player throws the ball back to the coach under the basket.
6. The defense must run back and touch the ball under the basket.
7. After the players touch the ball a second time, the coach throws it to the offense, and then the teams play "live" 5-on-5.

(———| indicates a closeout.)

TIPS

The defender guarding the ball should not jump when a shot is attempted. If the defender jumps, he will not have control of his body, and the shooter will lean into the defender to draw contact, which results in a foul on the defense. This requires discipline by the defense. The four defenders not guarding the ball should be in proper position at all times.

Beginner: Start out playing 3-on-3 or 4-on-4.
Advanced: Have players run out to a different player after touching the ball.

BASKETBALL DRILLS, PLAYS, AND STRATEGIES

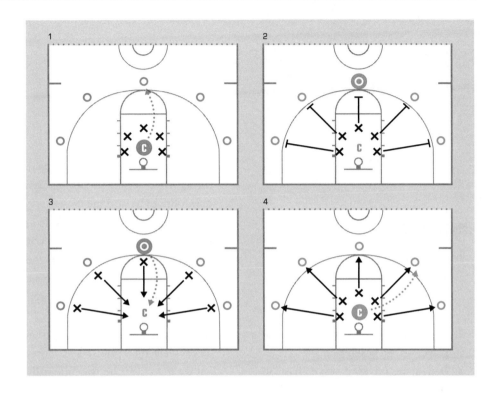

CHARGE

Difficulty Level: Intermediate

Skills Practiced: Defensive stance, defensive position, taking a charge, close-outs

Number of Players Needed: 5

Number of Basketballs Needed: 1

Ideal Practice Time: Middle

INSTRUCTIONS

1. Four offensive players take position around the perimeter, including one player at the baseline who has a ball.

2. One defensive player guards the player on the baseline.

3. Depending on what player has the ball, the defensive player should be in the correct position to see the player he is guarding and stay between him and the ball.

4. The ball is passed to each person on the perimeter as the defender adjusts to each throw. Once the ball gets to the player in the opposite corner from where it began, that player drives toward the basket.

5. The defensive player is help-side at this point and takes a charge outside of the lane. After charging, the offensive player skips the ball back to the player the defender was originally guarding.

6. After taking a charge, the defensive player gets up, sprints, and closes out on the player he was originally guarding, who now has the ball.

7. The defensive player then rotates in for the player he finishes guarding and all the other players rotate on the perimeter to their left. The last player (who committed the charge) becomes the defender.

TIPS

If the ball is in the corner opposite of the defender's man, the defensive player should be in the middle of the court (the seam) between the ball and his man. This is known as BUM (see page 128).

Beginner: Shorten this drill by having players only close-out. Also, offensive players hold the ball for two or three seconds.

Advanced: Have offensive players pass the ball quickly to different positions. This will simulate game speed and situations.

BASKETBALL DRILLS, PLAYS, AND STRATEGIES

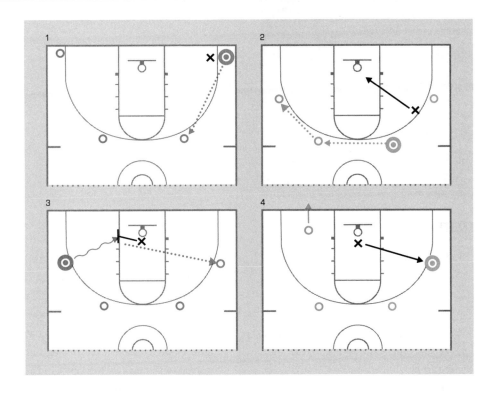

ZIGZAGS

Difficulty Level: Beginner

Skills Practiced: Defensive stance, close-outs, slides, taking charges

Number of Players Needed: At least 1

Number of Basketballs Needed: 0

Ideal Practice Time: Beginning or middle

INSTRUCTIONS

1. Players form a line in one corner of the court on the baseline.
2. The first player faces the basket and slides to the elbow.
3. Upon getting to the elbow, the player open pivots and slides to the half-court sideline.
4. Upon getting to the half court sideline, the player open pivots and slides to the elbow on the other side of half court.
5. The sequence continues around the court.
6. The second player in line starts when the first player reaches the first elbow.
7. Players can also sprint and close out at each elbow. If players are closing out instead of sliding, coaches can stand at each elbow pretending to shoot.

TIPS

Depending on your team's area of defensive weakness, this drill is great for many quick repetitions in a short amount of time. Concentrate on technique before speed.

Beginner: Go through the drill slowly, perhaps even walking through it, so that players can understand the technique.

Advanced: Mix defensive ideas in the same drill by switching between charges, slides, and close-outs.

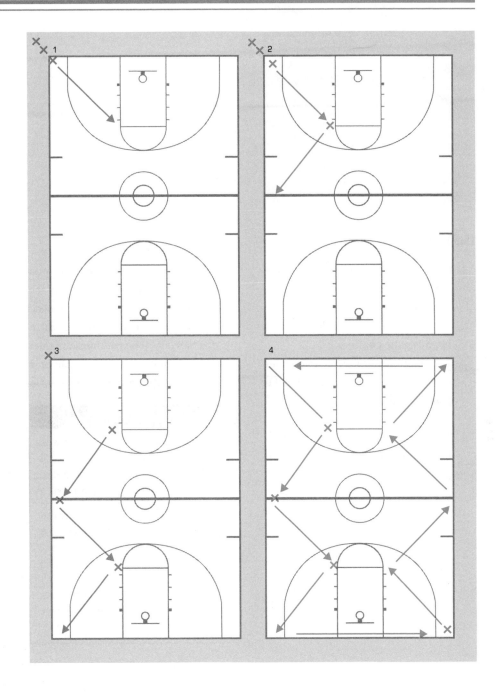

SLIDE REACTION

Difficulty Level: Beginner

Skills Practiced:
Sliding, controlling the ball, backpedaling

Number of Players Needed: At least 1

Number of Basketballs Needed: 1

Ideal Practice Time: Beginning or middle

INSTRUCTIONS

1. One player begins on the low post block facing the baseline in a defensive stance.
2. A coach is on the baseline, out of bounds with a ball.
3. The other players are lined up under the basket ready to step in after the players before them have finished the drill.
4. The player on the baseline slides to the sideline and back to the low-post block.
5. After getting back to the low-post block, the player backpedals until the coach throws the ball near the sideline.
6. The player turns and sprints to catch the ball, and then gets himself under control and dribbles in to shoot a lay-up or a jump shot.

TIPS

Players should backpedal as quickly as possible while you throw the ball to different parts of the court. This will make the drill more random and game-like.

Beginner: Have players concentrate on being balanced when they catch the pass. After catching the ball, players should be in a triple-threat position (see page 7).

Advanced: Run the drill on both sides of the basket by staggering the start on each side.

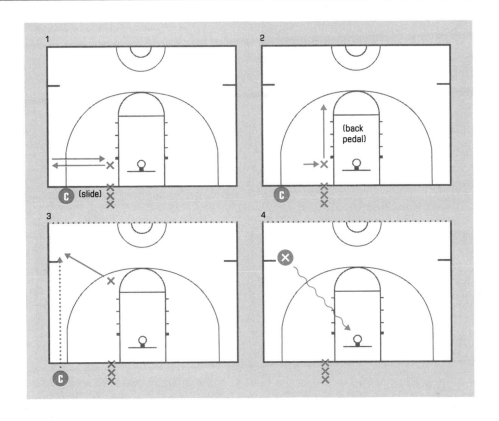

ADVANCED ALLEYBALL

Difficulty Level: Intermediate

Skills Practiced: Defensive 1-on-1

Number of Players Needed: At least 2

Number of Basketballs Needed: 1

Ideal Practice Time: Beginning or middle

INSTRUCTIONS

1. A coach stands at the top of the key.
2. An offensive player and a defensive player start at corner near the baseline.
3. The offensive player has the ball, but he is limited to dribbling from the sideline to the lane line.
4. The defender moves in and plays 1-on-1 with the offensive player.
5. When the offensive player arrives at half court, he passes to the coach at the top of the key.
6. The offensive player tries to get open for a pass from the coach while the defense tries to deny him the ball.
7. After the offensive player gets the ball again, the players play 1-on-1 until the offensive player scores or the defender gets a rebound.
8. The players switch and do the drill again.

TIPS

Stress a good defensive stance and make sure the defender slides his feet without crossing them. The defender should keep the dribbler in front of him. Physical and mental endurance will grow with more repetitions. Also, the defender will gain confidence playing on-the-ball defense.

Beginner: Run the drill without passing the ball to the coach, but still play 1-on-1, which will help the defender concentrate on technique for half-court defense.

Advanced: Have players play 1-on-1 from the start. Also, blow your whistle to have the dribblers pick up the ball and have the defense pressure them forcing the offensive players to be strong. Blow the whistle again to indicate that it's time for the game to continue.

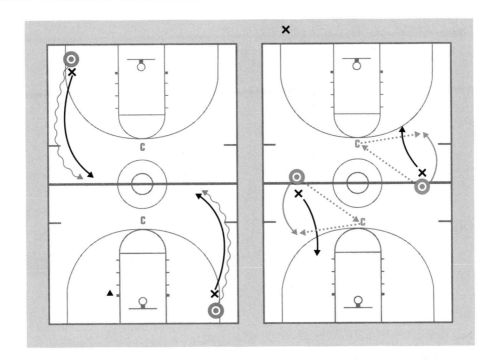

SHELL

Difficulty Level: Intermediate

Skills Practiced: Defensive positioning, defensive communication

Number of Players Needed: At least 6

Number of Basketballs Needed: 1

Ideal Practice Time: Middle or end

INSTRUCTIONS

1. Five offensive players go against five defensive players. The offense remains stationary and passes the ball around the court to each other. Upon receiving the ball, an offensive player holds the ball for three seconds before passing again.

2. As the offense passes the ball, the defense communicates to each other to make sure all of the offensive players are covered.

3. If the ball is in the corner, the defensive players on the opposite side of the court are in the middle of the court—on the seam between the ball and their man.

4. After the ball has been rotated around the corner several times, and the defense understands the concept, the coach can call "play" to initiate live play.

5. Change up the offensive positioning. See the drill illustration for some positions. The charge drill (see page 132) is a good individual drill to help with defensive positioning and rotation.

TIPS

1. Helping and communicating with teammates on defense is crucial.

2. The defense must get between the ball and the opponents they are guarding (see BUM on page 128).

Beginner: Start out playing 3-on-3 and have the players remain stationary to begin the drill.

Advanced: Mix in regulations or sequences. For example, a team may start with the offense stationary for the first possession, then for the subsequent possessions, they may be able to penetrate; penetrate and skip pass; or have the post players move between the low post and the high post.

While you do not have to have the offensive remain stationary, you can have other regulations, such as limiting their number of dribbles.

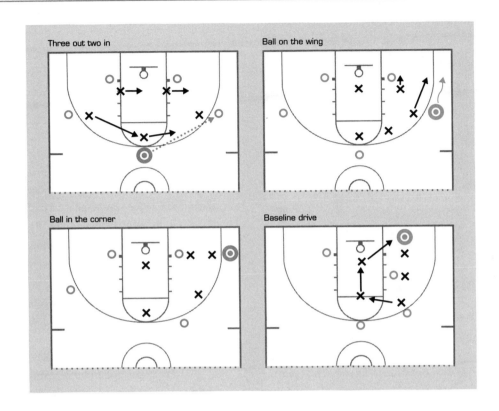

Three out two in

Ball on the wing

Ball in the corner

Baseline drive

GUARDING BALL SCREENS: FOUR TYPES

Difficulty Level: Intermediate

Skills Practiced: Defensive communication

Number of Players Needed: 4

Number of Basketballs Needed: 1

Ideal Practice Time: Beginning

INSTRUCTIONS

Two offensive players play against two defensive players, who practice the four ways to guard ball screens:

1. Go over and under: The player guarding the screener gets even with the level of the ball. The defensive player goes over the screener and under the defender.

2. Trap: The player guarding the screener gets even with the level of the ball. The player getting screened fights over the top of the screen and traps the player with the ball. The players opposite of where the screen takes place help on the screener.

3. Switch: The easiest way, though not the most effective way, to guard a ball screen, is to switch. That is, the defender guarding the screener switches and guards the ball, while the player guarding the ball handler guards the screener. The defenders just switch who they are guarding and stay in the same location on the court.

4. Show and recover (hedge): The player guarding the screen bluffs at the ball for enough time to let her teammate get through the screen.

TIPS

You may know a team sets ball screens if you scout your opponents. Depending on the player using the ball screen, a team may want to defend a specific way. For example, if a team has a good shooter, a defensive team may trap the ball screen.

Beginner: Practice one consistent way to guard screens instead of trying all four.

Advanced: Add a third player to have the teams 3-on-3 and not 2-on-2.

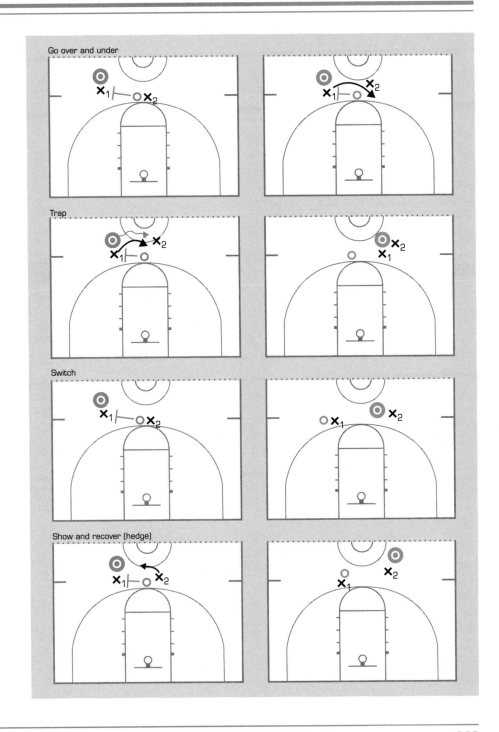

Go over and under

Trap

Switch

Show and recover (hedge)

2-ON-2 GETTING THROUGH SCREENS

Difficulty Level: Intermediate

Skills Practiced: Defensive communication, bumping screens, getting through screens

Number of Players Needed: 4

Number of Basketballs Needed: 1

Ideal Practice Time: Beginning or middle

INSTRUCTIONS

1. Two offensive players, one a screener, and the other a cutter, play 2-on-2 against two defensive players. A coach with the ball stands at the top of the key.

2. The screener screens the defensive player guarding the cutter. The player guarding the screener jumps to the ball (or opens up) and lets the defensive player getting screened have the option of following the screen or going between the screen.

3. The coach passes the ball to the cutter and the two teams play two-on-two.

TIPS

1. This drill will work for all screens except ball screens.

2. Stress to your players to communicate and talk, letting others know a screen may be occurring.

3. If a player is screening, he can put his arm out, or hedge, for a second or two to deter a pass from being made.

4. Communication is the key to defense because if a player can't get through a screen, he and his temmate may need to switch the screen.

Beginner: Walk through the drill so that young players understand the concepts of defending screens.

Advanced: Pass the ball to the offensive player and receive the pass back. After the player passes the ball back to the coach, have the offensive player should screen again. Multiple types of screens and screening angles can be used on the same repetition.

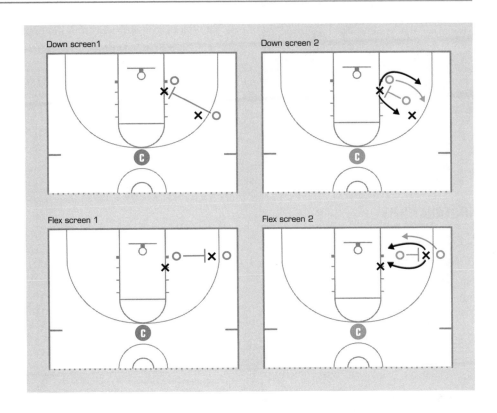

CHANGE

Difficulty Level: Intermediate

Skills Practiced: Defensive communication

Number of Players Needed: 10

Number of Basketballs Needed: 1

Ideal Practice Time: End

INSTRUCTIONS

1. Five offensive players pass the ball around the court while five defensive players guard them.
2. After several passes, the coach says "change." The offensive team sets the ball down and sprints to the middle of the lane. They then become the defensive team and must match up

with a player different from the one who was guarding them.

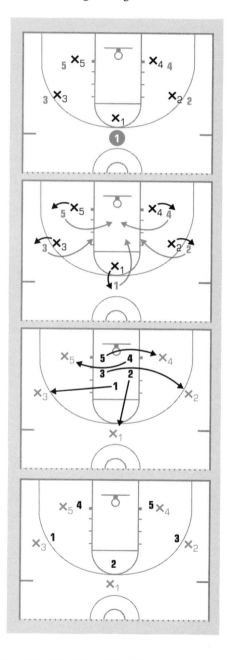

TIPS

Make sure defenders sprint, not jog, into the lane. The purpose of the drill is to adjust quickly to random game situations where the offensive team may have a mismatch, such as a post player defending a guard. Defenders must talk, calling out their responsibilities, such as "deny," "help," or "ball."

Beginner: Keep the drill in the half court.

Advanced: Expand the drill to incorporate the full court. You can also incorporate the switch drill (see page 147) at the same time by randomly calling out "switch" or "change."

INSTRUCTIONS

1. Five offensive players pass the ball around the court while five defensive players guard them. The offensive players can start in a "five-out" set, which means no offensive players are within fifteen feet of the basket.

2. After several passes, the coach says "switch" and the players on defense must touch in the paint and sprint to match up with a different player. When switching to a player, advanced-level players switch to players of similar positions. Beginner-level players switch to any new player.

3. Upon hearing the coach say "switch," the offense tries to score before the defense can get set. Usually, the drill involves only one "switch" sequence.

TIPS

The goal of the drill is to teach defensive players to communicate with each other. The offensive team learns to take advantage of situations with mismatch opportunities (for example, when a guard ends up defending a post player).

Beginner: Offensive players should remain in the same spots.

Advanced: Offensive players may move around the court before the coach shouts "switch" to let the team on offense know to set the ball down.

SWITCH

Difficulty Level: Intermediate

Skills Practiced: Defensive communication

Number of Players Needed: 10

Number of Basketballs Needed: 1

Ideal Practice Time: End

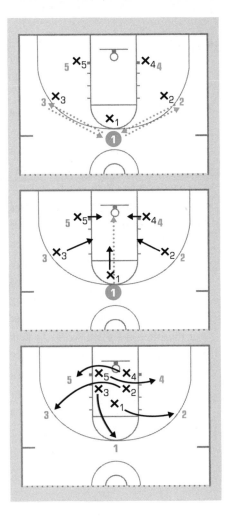

ONE-MINUTE DRILL

Difficulty Level: Advanced

Skills Practiced:
Half-court defensive endurance

Number of Players Needed: 10

Number of Basketballs Needed: 1

Ideal Practice Time: End

INSTRUCTIONS

1. This drill is strictly to be used in the half court.
2. Five offensive players play against five defensive players.
3. The object of the drill is to play for one minute without letting the offense score or get an offensive rebound.
4. The clock stops after each possession. For example, if the offensive team misses a shot and the possession took twelve seconds, the coach stops the clock until both teams are set, and then he starts counting from forty-eight seconds. However, if the offensive team scores or gets a rebound, the clock is reset to sixty seconds. The drill is not over until the defense is successful for sixty seconds, which usually involves multiple possessions.

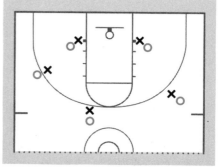

TIPS

Team defense is the key to this drill. All five defenders must guard and box out for several possessions; otherwise, the drill will continue. The better the defense, the sooner the drill will be over. This is a great physical and mental drill that is used to improve your half-court defense.

Beginner: Use fewer stipulations and regulations.
Advanced: Use more regulations to satisfy the one-minute drill. Also, the time for the drill can be increased.

BLOCKING SHOTS

Difficulty Level: Beginner

Skills Practiced: Timing and blocking shots

Number of Players Needed: At least 2

Number of Basketballs Needed: At least 1

Ideal Practice Time: Middle

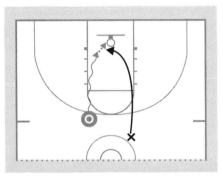

TIPS

Understand that this is the last resort option. Players should try to take charges rather than block shots. However, if your team is tall or athletic, this is a good drill that should limit fouls when attempting to block shots in games.

Beginner: Do not go live; teach technique. Players should initially walk through the drill so they understand concepts.

Advanced: To make the drill more difficult or more like a game situation, put two offensive players in the drill. Also, the drill can be started in different positions.

INSTRUCTIONS

1. An offensive player lines up a couple feet above the top of the key.
2. A defensive player lines up several feet behind the offensive player.
3. The offensive player attempts a layup. Trying to catch the offensive player from behind, the defender blocks the shot with the hand on the opposite side from which the lay-up is being attempted. For example, if the offensive player is on the left side, the defensive player tries to block the shot with his right hand.

Team Drills

A s a coach, your responsibility is to have your team prepared, putting players in situations during practice that they will be in during a game time. You do not want them to face situations during a game that they have never thought through before. The team drills in this chapter vary from passing drills to working on transition and half-court offense. These drills should give you ideas that you can incorporate into your practice plans.

In games, each team has five players on the floor at all times, but there is nothing wrong with playing 3-on-3 or 4-on-4 during practice. The emphasis on offense can then be placed on floor spacing, moving without the ball, and setting screens. While on defense, a coach can demand that each player pressure the basketball, deny one pass away, and be positioned in help-side defense if they are two passes away.

There are many situations throughout a game where it will not be 5-on-5. During the transition from offense to defense, one team might have more players involved in the play than the other. To simulate situations such as these, take a look at the half-court and full-court disadvantage drills (pages 156 and 160) and review the 12345 numbers transition drill (page 164). As much as you hope to have five players back in transition to defend your basket, you usually won't. By having your players practice in a position where they are outnumbered, the better they will handle those situations when they occur in a game.

COACHING KEYS

- Choose team drills wisely. Relate each team drill to your coaching philosophy.
- Be goal-oriented and have high expectations.
- Have rewards for goals accomplished and consequences for when goals are not met.
- Use a variety of drills so your players stay enthusiastic about practicing.

Make communication a key component of these drills. Put them in a position with these drills that they have to communicate. It could be as simple as calling for the basketball or calling out the player's name that they are passing the basketball to. Communication among players can lead to better team chemistry and teamwork.

KEY TERMS

Ball pressure: Pressuring the basketball but staying in front of it, playing tough defense on the offensive player who has the basketball, but not so much that she will drive around the corresponding defender.

Floor spacing: Balance among all players on the offensive end of the floor, where each player is spaced out evenly.

Moving without the ball: Each offensive player setting up her defender by cutting either to the basket or getting ready to use a screen.

One pass away: An offensive player who is a single pass away from the player with the ball.

Setting screens: An offensive player using her body to set up her teammate with an opportunity to score.

Transition: Moving either from offense to defense or defense to offense.

3-ON-3 FULL COURT

Difficulty Level: Intermediate to advanced

Skills Practiced: Team-play offense and defense, conditioning

Number of Players Needed: At least 6

Number of Basketballs Needed: 1

Ideal Practice Time: Middle or end

INSTRUCTIONS

1. The players are divided into two teams of three that will play full court. The drill can go on for a time limit or a certain amount of points. Score can be kept by ones or twos.

2. The drill starts with the coach throwing the ball inbounds from the baseline to the offensive team. The offense tries to move down court against a full-court press. (The defense must pick up in the full court.)

3. If the possession changes either on a turnover or a missed shot and defensive rebound, the other team pushes the basketball as hard as they can down the court to try and take advantage of a 3-on-2 or 3-on-1 transition.

4. On a made basket, the defense picks up full court and the offense tries to beat the press as quickly as possible.

TIPS

The drill can be used to simplify the game with only three players. The coach can focus on floor spacing, screening, and moving without the basketball. The full court allows the players to improve conditioning while playing the game and using the basketball.

Beginner: Perform the drill with evenly matched teams so the players can begin to understand making cuts to get open, setting screens, and moving without the ball. Two evenly matched teams can allow each player to give total effort.

Advanced: Emphasize the importance of the defense staying in front of the basketball. The help-side defenders need to work on staying between the ball and their man. Offensive players should not get caught up in dribbling, but instead should pass the ball and utilize their teammates.

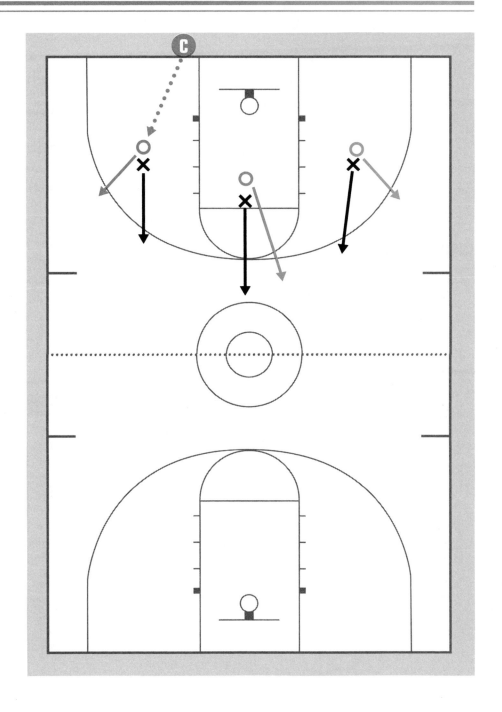

5-ON-5 CATCH UP

Difficulty Level: Intermediate

Skills Practiced:
Passing, dribbling, communication, defensive transition, court awareness, conditioning

Number of Players Needed: 10

Number of Basketballs Needed: 1

Ideal Practice Time: Middle or end

INSTRUCTIONS

1. Five offensive players line up on the baseline: one under the basket, one on each of the sidelines, and one between the middle and sideline players.

2. Five defensive players line up on the free-throw line extended, directly across from the five offensive players.

3. The coach calls out the name of one of the defensive players while passing the basketball to the one of the offensive players.

4. The defensive player called by the coach sprints to touch the baseline where the offense started. The other defensive players play 5-on-4 until he "catches up."

5. The offensive players try to use their number advantage, 5-on-4, for a scoring opportunity by passing the ball ahead or with the dribble.

6. The defensive players try to protect their basket and limit any easy scoring opportunities until the fifth defensive player catches up.

7. After the possession ends, whether on a made shot, turnover, or missed shot and defensive rebound, both teams play a possession 5-on-5 coming back to the end where the drill began.

8. When that possession is over, stop the drill and switch offense and defense. Then repeat the drill.

TIPS

The offensive team should realize that there will be at least one defender trailing the play in a transition situation (see page 151). It is crucial that the offensive players without the ball shout to the ball handler if a defender is coming from behind him. The offense should try to score quickly because they will have a brief advantage until the defense recovers.

Beginner: Use 3-on-3 or 4-on-4 before attempting 5-on-5.

Advanced: Call on two defensive players to touch the baseline so the defense has to play 5-on-3 until the other players catch up.

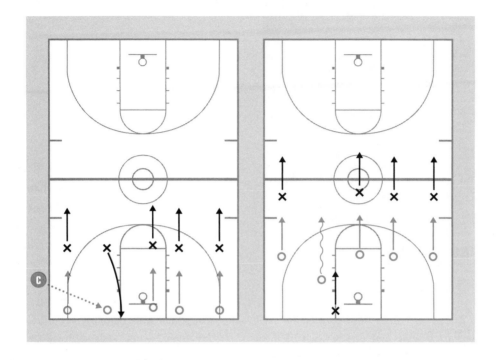

HALF-COURT DISADVANTAGE

Difficulty Level: Beginner

Skills Practiced: Team-play offense, defense, passing, rebounding

Number of Players Needed: 7

Number of Basketballs Needed: 1

Ideal Practice Time: Any time

INSTRUCTIONS

1. The coach stands on the baseline underneath the basket with the ball.
2. The offense has four players, one at each wing and one in each of the corners. The defense has three players, all starting inside the lane.
3. The coach instructs the drill to begin and the defensive team chops their feet.
4. The coach passes the ball to an offensive player, and one of the defensive players closes out the player with the ball.
5. The offensive team passes the ball around, searching for a good look at the basket, while the defensive team works on communicating and help defense.
6. Each defensive player cannot guard two passes in a row, meaning that with every pass made by the offensive team, a new defender will be guarding the ball. Therefore, all three players have to be alert and willing to play hard to get out to the shooter.

TIPS

Emphasize the importance of communication on the half court defensive end. The players will learn to help each other and communicate so that only one of them is running out to shooters.

Beginner: Perform the drill with a stationary offense, where the offensive players can only pass or shoot and all four offensive players are inside the 3-point line.

Advanced: Advance the drill to the point where the offensive players can move and dribble between passes.

BASKETBALL DRILLS, PLAYS, AND STRATEGIES

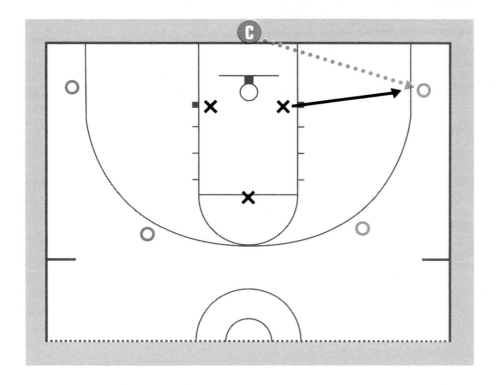

DOMINO

Difficulty Level: Intermediate

Skills Practiced: Passing, dribbling, lay-ups, conditioning

Number of Players Needed: At least 8

Number of Basketballs Needed: 2

Ideal Practice Time: Beginning or end

INSTRUCTIONS

1. One player with the basketball stands on the baseline directly underneath the basket, facing half court. A second player stands on the right sideline at the free-throw line extended. Another player is at half court, outside the inner circle. A fourth player is on the sideline at the free-throw line extended at the other end of the court. The same set-up of four players occurs on the opposite side of the court.

2. The two players with balls (on the baselines) pass to the players on the sideline. While the pass is in the air, the passer sprints up the floor and receives the pass back from the sideline player. He then passes to the player at half court.

3. The player continues to sprint up the floor, receives the pass back from the player at half court, and then passes the ball to the player on the opposite sideline.

4. The player on the sideline receives the pass and then throws a bounce pass to the sprinting player, who shoots a lay-up. The player who throws the bounce pass then rebounds the shot and continues the drill up the other side of the floor. The shooter fills in at the sideline on the side opposite of where he took the shot.

TIPS

The drill can be used for conditioning purposes at the end of a practice or as a warm-up drill at the beginning. Players must throw a good pass and provide a target with their hands to let their teammates know where they want the ball.

Beginner: Perform the drill for only a minute or so and focus on doing the drill right instead of fast.

Advanced: Put two minutes on the clock and see how many lay-ups the team can make. After the first two minutes are up, put the same amount of time on the clock but switch sides so players are using the opposite hand.

BASKETBALL DRILLS, PLAYS, AND STRATEGIES

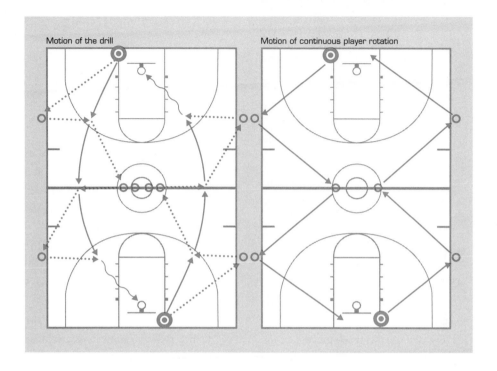

Motion of the drill

Motion of continuous player rotation

FULL-COURT DISADVANTAGE

Difficulty Level: Intermediate

Skills Practiced: Team offense, defense, transitioning, conditioning

Number of Players Needed: At least 10

Number of Basketballs Needed: 1

Ideal Practice Time: Any time

INSTRUCTIONS

1. There are five offensive players and one coach with the basketball on one end of the court.
2. The defense has three players on the other end of the court waiting for the offense.
3. The defense also has one player at each sideline at half court. These two defensive players are not able to sprint into the drill until the offensive team takes the ball across half court. Then they must sprint into the inner circle at half court and get into the play.
4. The coach begins the drill by shooting the ball. One of the offensive players rebounds, and the team quickly moves the ball up the court.
5. The offensive team tries to score as quickly as possible using the 5-on-3 advantage. The defense tries to keep the offense from scoring until the other two players join them.
6. The possession plays out and the defensive team then brings the ball back to the other basket, playing 5-on-5 for one possession.
7. After that possession is over, the teams switch offense and defense and repeat the drill.

TIPS

Emphasize the importance of communication in the full court regarding defensive strategy. It is important that the offense get a great shot off quickly when they have a number advantage.

Beginner: Perform the drill 3-on-2 with only one defender coming in at half court, or 4-on-3, with only one defender coming in at half court.

Advanced: Move the two defensive players at half court to the opposite top of the key to make it more difficult on the three defenders to hold up their end with 3-on-5.

BASKETBALL DRILLS, PLAYS, AND STRATEGIES

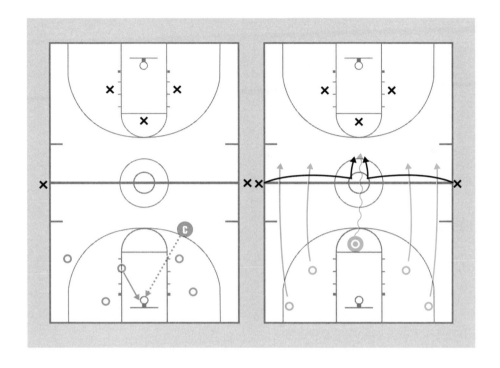

O-D-O

Difficulty Level: Intermediate to advanced

Skills Practiced: Team-play offense, defense, conditioning

Number of Players Needed: At least 10

Number of Basketballs Needed: 1

Ideal Practice Time: Middle or end

INSTRUCTIONS

1. Divide players into two teams of five. Team 1 begins with the ball, running their half court offense versus team 2. This is a full-court drill, but it starts with a half-court possession.

2. The possession plays out with a score, turnover, or missed shot and defensive rebound. Then team 2 becomes offense playing against team 1. The possession continues until a score, turnover, missed shot, etc.

3. Team 1 then takes the ball against team 2, pushing the ball in transition, going from defense to offense. If you run a specific offense, call it out then.

4. The drill stops after the possession is over.

TIPS

The drill can be used for conditioning purposes at the end of practice. Divide the teams evenly in terms of talent, or use a first- and second-string split.

Beginner: Perform the drill with two evenly matched groups and switch which team begins with the ball.

Advanced: Put ten minutes on the clock and let the possessions play out, switching which team plays offense first. Keep score until the time runs out and have consequences for the losing team.

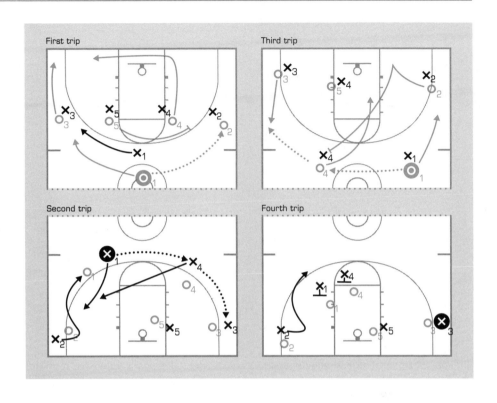

12345 NUMBERS TRANSITION

Difficulty Level: Intermediate to advanced

Skills Practiced: Passing, dribbling, communication, offensive and defensive transition, conditioning

Number of Players Needed: 9

Number of Basketballs Needed: 1

Ideal Practice Time: Any time

INSTRUCTIONS

1. Nine players are necessary, divided into five blue jersey players and four white jersey players. (The colors can be whatever color practice jersey you have to use.)

2. One blue offensive player lines up on the free-throw line, getting ready to shoot a free throw, while two white jersey players line up on the lane lines.

TIPS

The drill can be used to emphasize both offense and defensive transition philosophy.

Beginner: Use 2-on-1 and 3-on-2 situations before trying 4-on-3 and 5-on-4.

Advanced: Emphasize to the new players coming in to the drill to stay behind the baseline before hopping into the drill.

3. The blue player shoots a free throw and immediately begins to sprint (not backpedal) back on defense.

4. Make or miss, the two white players take the ball down on a 2-on-1 situation.

5. When there is a defensive rebound, two more blue players jump in, making it a 3-on-2 situation. The white players sprint back to guard their basket.

6. A defensive rebound on a make or miss brings in two more white players, creating 4-on-3.

7. Again, on a make or miss on a defensive rebound, two more blue players jump in, making it 5-on-4.

8. Finally, on a make or miss on a defensive rebound, one more white player comes in to make it 5-on-5.

9. The drill can then end at the coach's discretion.

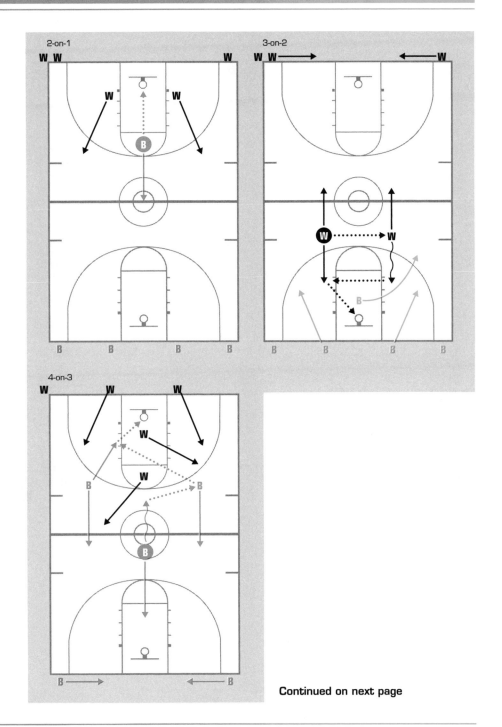

2-on-1

3-on-2

4-on-3

Continued on next page

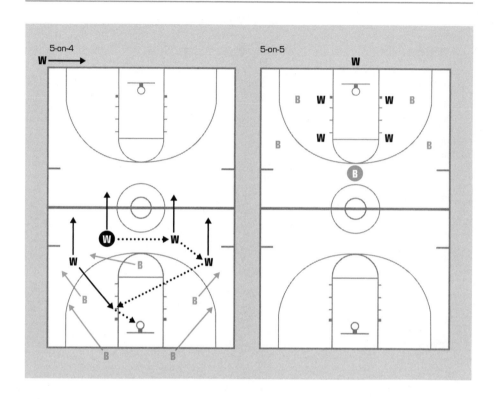

5-on-4

5-on-5

INSTRUCTIONS

1. Three offensive players play against three defensive players on a half court. The offensive team waits for the defensive team to match up accordingly.
2. The offense passes the ball to begin the drill.
3. Each offensive player has a dribble limit of no more than three dribbles whenever she has the ball.
4. If the possession changes, either on a turnover or a missed shot and defensive rebound, the offense must

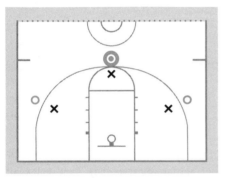

HOOP IT UP

Difficulty Level: Advanced

Skills Practiced: Team-play offense and defense, screening

Number of Players Needed: 6

Number of Basketballs Needed: 1

Ideal Practice Time: Any time

take it back to the 3-point line before the drill proceeds.

5. There can be a time limit or players play to a certain amount of points. Teams change possession after a made shot, or make a regulation that if the offense scores, they get to stay on offense.

TIPS

The drill can be used to simplify the game. With only three players, the coach can focus on floor spacing, screening, and moving without the basketball.

Beginner: Perform the drill with evenly matched teams so the players can begin to understand making cuts to get open, setting screens, and moving without the ball.

Advanced: With the dribble limit, the players should begin to set good screens and read their defender on how they are playing the screens. For example, if the defender is trailing or chasing the screen, the offensive player curls the screens and cuts directly to the basket. The drill can also place an emphasis on the defending screens, either getting through the screen or showing and recovering against the screen.

WARM-UP FAST BREAK

Difficulty Level: Intermediate

Skills Practiced: Passing, lay-ups, ball control, conditioning

Number of Players Needed: At least 6

Number of Basketballs Needed: 1

Ideal Practice Time: Beginning

INSTRUCTIONS

1. Players line up in three lines: one line on the free-throw line (the first player in this line has a ball), and two lines three feet from the sidelines at the free-throw line extended. Once the drill begins, the first player in each line runs toward the opposite basket.
2. The player with the ball passes to the player in the line to the left. As he runs forward, the ball is passed back to him.
3. The player then dribbles up court to pass the ball to the player on the right; once the player receives the pass, he jump stops outside of the lane.
4. The player throws a bounce pass to the player on the left, who shoots a lay-up. The middle player quickly sprints to the sideline to fill in for the player shooting the lay-up.
5. The third player rebounds the shot, takes it out of bounds underneath, and quickly throws an outlet pass to the "middle" player (now the outlet player) who now is on the left side of the floor.
6. The outlet man has his back to the sideline, and after catching the outlet pass, throws a baseball pass to the player on the opposite free-throw line extended.
7. The drill continues with the player on the right passing to the middle player, who passes to the left, then receives the pass back to the middle. The entire drill repeats and is continuous.
8. The first three players rotate to different lines so they experience all three positions of the drill.

TIPS

The drill calls for different types of passes: bounce, chest, baseball, and two-hand overhead passes by the player who has to take the ball out of bounds.

Beginner: Start each group of three with one ball in the middle. The first group goes down the floor. The next group follows and then waits for all the following groups to finish. Then do the same thing in the opposite direction.

Advanced: Set a goal for the team to make a certain number of lay-ups in a row before they move on to a new drill. After a certain number of made lay-ups in a row, have the team make a certain number of short bank shots from the block in a row.

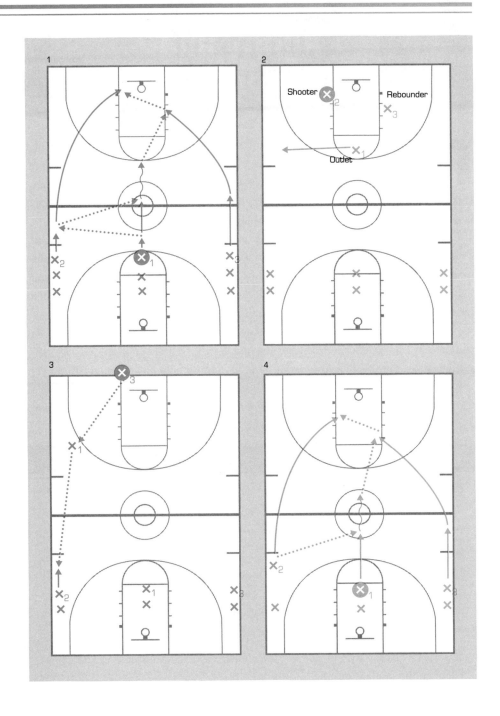

TEAM DRILLS

169

Agility and Conditioning

The demand placed on today's basketball players at the high-school level is much different in comparison to just fifteen years ago. With AAU basketball and spring and summer teams, the level of play, players, and competition continues to elevate year after year. Competition levels can also be attributed to a new type of athlete that is quicker, faster, stronger, and more explosive.

There is an old saying about coaching basketball: "You can't teach height and athleticism." Obviously, that's true. And unless you are at the college level, you can't choose what players are going to be playing for you. However, one thing you can control is your players' conditioning level, which, through the use of the drills in this chapter, can help increase your players' athleticism in this era of competitive basketball.

One of the important steps in increasing your players' athleticism is teaching and emphasizing the significance of stretching and flexibility. It is important for players to stretch before they begin a rigorous workout in order to help prevent injury. But if you are looking to improve the athleticism of your players, it is vital that players stretch at the end of a workout when their muscles are already warm. Studies show that the more flexible an athlete is, the more explosive she will be.

KEY TERMS

Plyometrics: Drills that are used by performing quick, powerful movements to develop muscular power for jumping explosiveness, quick bursts of speed, and swift changes of direction.

Slide: A lateral defensive movement used to prevent an opponent from dribbling around the defense. When performing a defensive slide, a player has a low, wide base, wider than shoulder-width apart. The player keeps his back straight, knees bent, and butt down. When sliding laterally, the player should bring his feet together without letting them cross.

Up-backs: When a player goes "up" the court to a certain destination and comes "back" to the original starting position.

The word "plyometrics" should be added to your coaching vocabulary. (Plyometrics can present negative effects for underdeveloped, out-of-shape, or unconditioned athletes. For this reason, not all the drills have beginner instructions; athletes that are not at least high-school age should not complete the advanced exercises.) In order to see maximum gains, plyometric drills need to be performed at a high-intensity level and with the proper form. Plyometric exercises should be completed over short intervals of time, followed by a proper rest period (a minimum of one minute), and on surfaces that have some give, such as a basketball court. After completing a plyometrics workout, which usually consists of five to seven exercises, players should be given a minimum of forty-eight hours before engaging in another set of plyometrics.

This chapter contains different conditioning drills used to get your players in shape. Superior conditioned teams tend to be successful in close games. That is why it is so important that you challenge your players in the off season through a demanding mix of plyometric and conditioning drills that increase physical performance as well as mental toughness. Remember, winning close games can be the difference between an average season and a great season, so by challenging your players to push themselves in the off season, you are giving them an edge in tough situations.

COACHING KEYS

- Your players' conditioning levels are critical to the success of your team. That is why it is so important to emphasize the value of being in top shape year-round.
- Conditioning is something that takes both physical and mental toughness for players to fight through. But if you challenge your players to a rigorous conditioning regimen in the off season, you will reap the benefits in the W-L column. Conditioning does not only mean putting your players on the line and running them. Use different methods, such as plyometrics or drills.
- Once your team is in season, you may not need to have them run many sprints because if you make practice hard enough and make them give 100 percent effort, they will have plenty of conditioning from the off-season.
- Conditioning brings players together because they are facing mental and physical adversity as a team and getting through it as a team, something you hope carries over into situations during the season.
- Remember, basketball is a long season and players need their legs for the second half and post-season portion of your year. A good coach must find that balance between effectiveness and overkill.

KNEES TO CHEST JUMPS

Difficulty Level: Advanced

Skills Practiced: Jumping explosiveness

Number of Players Needed: No limit

Number of Basketballs Needed: 0

Ideal Practice Time:
End or pre-season conditioning

INSTRUCTIONS

1. The player stands with her feet parallel and spread shoulder-width apart.
2. The player drops her body to a quarter-squat level and quickly jumps straight up without any steps.
3. While in the air, the player brings his knees up to his chest.
4. When she lands (as softly as possible), both feet hit simultaneously and she immediately repeat steps two and three.
5. The player continues jumping for thirty seconds, then rests and repeats.

TIPS

1. It is very important that players bring their knees to their chests to achieve the full effect.

2. Really focus on players exploding up as soon as they hit the floor from the previous jump.

INSTRUCTIONS

1. The player stands with her feet parallel and spread shoulder-width apart.

2. The player begins by bending the knees and jumping straight up without any steps.

3. While in the air at her highest point, the player brings the heels of her feet up to touch her butt.

4. When she lands (as softly as possible), both feet hit simultaneously and she immediately repeats steps two and three.

5. The player continues jumping for thirty seconds, then rests and repeats.

HEELS TO BUT JUMPS

Difficulty Level: Advanced

Skills Practiced: Jumping explosiveness

Number of Players Needed: No limit

Number of Basketballs Needed: 0

Ideal Practice Time:
End or pre-season conditioning

TIPS

1. It is very important that players bring their heels to their butts to achieve the full effect.

2. Really focus on players exploding up as soon as they hit the floor from the previous jump.

SQUAT JUMPS

Difficulty Level: Advanced

Skills Practiced: Jumping explosiveness

Number of Players Needed: No limit

Number of Basketballs Needed: 0

Ideal Practice Time:
End or pre-season conditioning

INSTRUCTIONS

1. The player stands with his feet parallel and spread slightly more than shoulder-width apart (as if performing a weight room squat).

2. He begins by lowering his body in a three-quarter squat position, keeping his back straight. Then he quickly jumps straight up.

3. While in the air, the player visualizes rebounding a basketball at it's highest peak.

4. When he lands (as softly as possible), both feet hit simultaneously and the player imagines he has rebounded the basketball, keeping both elbows high extended at shoulder level (with hands in the middle to protect the basketball).

TIPS

To acheive the full effect, focus on players getting a good deep squat before jumping.

5. The player holds the landing position for two seconds and repeats steps two through four.

6. The player continues the drill for thirty seconds, then rests and repeats.

INSTRUCTIONS

1. Players start on the baseline in two groups. Each player in the first group stands straight up and takes a long stride with her right foot.

2. After planting her right foot, the player bends her right knee forward while driving her left knee close to the floor. The player needs to keep her back straight up and down while pumping her left arm forward and right arm back (as if she were sprinting).

3. Once the player touches her left knee to the ground, she comes back to a standing position with feet parallel.

4. The player now takes a long stride with her left foot, and after planting the foot, she bends her left knee forward while driving her right knee

POWER WALK

Difficulty Level: Advanced

Skills Practiced:
Strength and flexibility in legs

Number of Players Needed: No limit

Number of Basketballs Needed: 0

Ideal Practice Time:
Beginning or pre-season conditioning

close to the floor. The player needs to keep her back straight up and down while pumping her right arm forward and left arm back (as if she were sprinting).

5. Once the player touches her right knee to the ground, she comes back to a standing position with her feet parallel.

6. The player continues to alternate legs until she reaches half court and stops. After the first group has reached half court, the second group will go until they reach half court and stop. Once the second group reaches half court, the first group turns around and completes the steps coming back to the baseline. The second group follows.

7. Players complete the drill one time up to half court and back.

TIPS

This is a great exercise for getting leg muscles loose before starting practice.

Difficulty Level: Advanced

Skills Practiced:
Jumping explosiveness and quickness

Number of Players Needed: No limit

Number of Basketballs Needed: 0

Ideal Practice Time:
End or pre-season conditioning

INSTRUCTIONS

1. Tie two cones together with one piece of string, spacing the cones two to three feet apart (depending on length of string).
2. The player stands on one side of the string with her feet together.
3. She jumps laterally across the string with her feet remaining together, while keeping her body and head erect.
4. After landing with both feet simultaneously, she immediately jumps laterally back over the string, keeping her body and head erect.
5. She continuously repeats steps three and four for thirty seconds.
6. Players complete the drill two times, for thirty seconds each.

TIPS

In order to reach maximum gains, players need to spend as little time as possible on the ground.

INSTRUCTIONS

1. Find a sturdy box for the player to jump on. The advancement of the athlete will determine how tall the box is.

2. The player stands in a position with her feet parallel and spread shoulder-width apart.

Difficulty Level: Advanced

Skills Practiced: Jumping explosiveness

Number of Players Needed: No limit

Number of Basketballs Needed: 0

Ideal Practice Time:
End or pre-season conditioning

3. Standing close to the box, the player slightly drops her body, bending her knees and using her arms to quickly jump forward, propelling herself up and onto the box.

4. After landing on the box, she instantly jumps back down off the box.

5. Once landing on the ground, she immediately repeats steps three and four with a minimal amount of time spent on the ground.

6. Players complete the drill by doing two sets of ten repetitions each.

TIPS

To prevent injury, make sure the jumping surface has some give. A basketball court, track, or similar surface works best. Be sure that the box is secure so it doesn't slide out from under the jumper

LINE JUMPS

Difficulty Level: Advanced

Skills Practiced: Foot speed and quickness

Number of Players Needed: No limit

Number of Basketballs Needed: 0

Ideal Practice Time:
End or pre-season conditioning

INSTRUCTIONS

1. The player stands with her feet together on one side of any line on the basketball court (ex. free throw line).

2. The player jumps laterally across the line with her feet remaining together, while keeping body and head erect.

3. After landing with both feet simultaneously, the player immediately jumps laterally back over the line, keeping her body and head erect.

4. The player continuously repeats steps two and three for thirty seconds, then rests and repeats.

TIPS

1. Make sure players get across the line every time they jump to ensure maximum gains.

2. To mix it up, have players do line jumps with one foot instead of two.

3. The key is quickness from side to side, not the height players get from jump to jump.

INSTRUCTIONS

1. Players line up in equal lines, one on each baseline.
2. On the coach's whistle, the first player in each line sprints to the opposite basket where he jumps up with both arms extended and touches the backboard ten times (if he cannot touch the backboard, he needs to jump to his highest peak).
3. The player then goes to the end of the line on that side of the court.
4. When he is first in line again, he sprints to the opposite basket and touches the backboard nine times.
5. Players continue to do this, dropping one backboard slap per round until they reach one backboard slap, marking the end of the drill.

TIPS

Make sure each player's form doesn't get poor as he gets tired. He should be jumping and reaching as high as possible each time.

Beginner: If players are too short to touch the backboard, you can have them jump and touch a wall at the highest spot they can.

Advanced: Time players and make sure they get all the repetitions done under the specified time.

BACKBOARD SLAPS

Difficulty Level: Intermediate

Skills Practiced: Jumping explosiveness, conditioning, physical and mental toughness

Number of Players: No limit

Number of Basketballs Needed: 0

Ideal Practice Time:
End or pre-season conditioning

FULL-COURT STAR

Difficulty Level: Intermediate

Skills Practiced: Lateral quickness, defensive technique, conditioning

Number of Players Needed: No limit

Number of Basketballs Needed: 0

Ideal Practice Time: Any time

INSTRUCTIONS

1. Set up a cone in each of the following six places: outside the 3-point line at block extended at both ends of the floor and at each side, plus on each sideline at half court.

2. Players start in a single-file line underneath one basket.

3. On the coach's whistle, the first player sprints to half court and touches her foot somewhere in the circle. (Once she touches the circle, the next player goes.)

4. The player sprints to the first cone at block extended. Once she gets close to the cone, she breaks down in a proper close-out position.

5. The player then breaks down in a defensive stance and slides around the cone and continues until she reaches the circle.

6. From her defensive stance, she sprints to the sideline cone at half court. Once again, when the player gets close to the cone, she breaks down in a close-out position.

7. She then breaks down in a defensive stance and slides around the cone and continues until she reaches the circle.

8. From her defensive stance, she sprints to the cone at the next block extended, breaking down in a close-out position.

9. The player continues to repeat the same movements (no stopping) on the opposite side of the floor.

10. After touching the circle for the last time, the player finishes by running through the baseline.

TIPS

Focus on players using proper defensive technique. The more tired they get, the sloppier their technique will get, which will translate into game situations.

Beginner: Condense the drill by putting cones only in the half court for endurance reasons.

Advanced: If one player does not execute the drill properly, have everyone start over. This tests players' mental and physical toughness when they become tired.

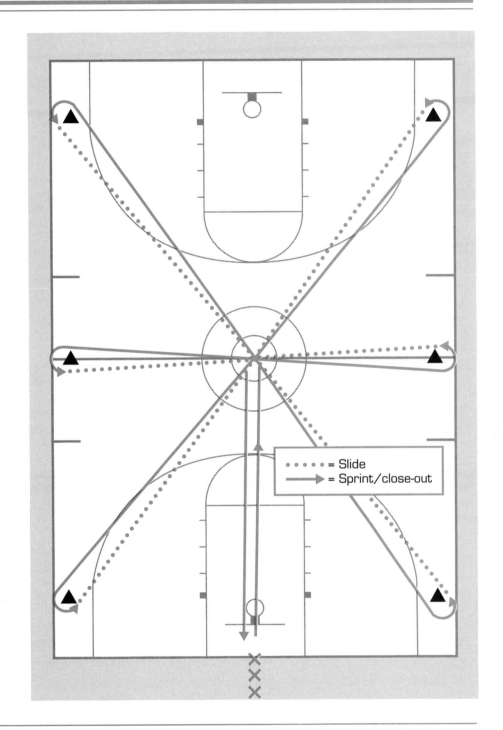

= Slide

= Sprint/close-out

HELP-SIDE AGILITY

Difficulty Level: Advanced

Skills Practiced: Quickness in change of direction, help-side defense

Number of Players Needed: No limit

Number of Basketballs Needed: 0

Ideal Practice Time:
Any time or pre-season conditioning

INSTRUCTIONS

1. A player starts in the middle of the lane with her back to the basket, chopping her feet in a defensive stance.
2. There are four designated spots on the perimeter of the 3-point arc: A, B, C, D.
3. A coach calls out one of the spots.
4. The player sprints to that spot and as she gets closer, she closes out on that spot.
5. Immediately after closing out, she changes direction and sprints back to the middle of the lane, where she continuously chops her feet in a defensive stance.
6. The coach calls out another spot and she repeats steps four and five.
7. This drill is done three times for thirty seconds to simulate a defensive possession in a game.

TIPS

Focus on players not coming out of their stance and staying low when they go from a defensive stance to a sprint. That split second can be the difference between a steal and a clean look for a shooter.

Beginner: Work on players using a proper defensive stance when they slide from line to line in the middle of the lane. It is important that players learn the proper technique in defensive slides before they learn tougher concepts like help-side.

Advanced: Pay attention to close-outs as time winds down. Make sure the players' close-out techniques do not suffer when they get tired. If they do not make a proper close-out during the thirty second span, they must start over.

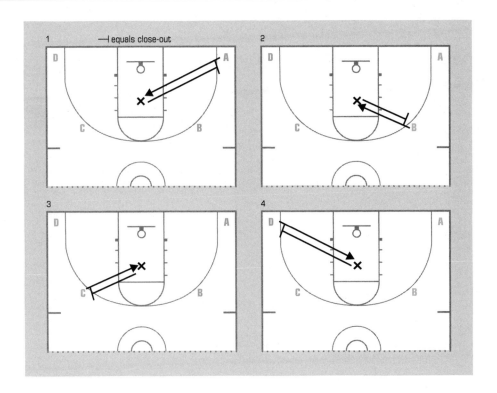

LADDERS

Difficulty Level: Intermediate

Skills Practiced: Conditioning, physical and mental toughness

Number of Players Needed: At least 2

Number of Basketballs Needed: 0

Ideal Practice Time:
End or pre-season conditioning

TIPS

This is a great conditioning drill, especially before the season starts, as it mixes both short bursts of speed conditioning with endurance conditioning.

Beginner: Don't go all the way to five up-backs because younger players cannot handle that much conditioning.

Advanced: Add a ball to make it a dribbling series of ladders to further test their mental and physical toughness.

INSTRUCTIONS

1. Players line up in two groups on the baseline. On the coach's whistle, the first player in eac line runs to the opposite baseline and back (in a set amount of time). Once the first group is finished, the second group goes.

2. After both groups have finished, the first group runs to the opposite baseline and back twice (in a set amount of time). Once the first group is finished, the second group goes.

3. The groups continue to alternate going up to five up-backs.

4. After both groups have progressed to five up-backs, they continue to alternate while they each do four up-backs, followed by three, then two, and one.

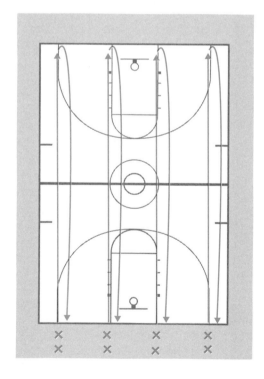

INSTRUCTIONS

1. Players line up on the baseline. On the coach's whistle the players run to the free-throw line and back to the baseline.
2. After touching the baseline, players run to half court and back to the baseline.
3. After touching the baseline, players run to the opposite free-throw line and back to the baseline.
4. After touching the baseline, players run to the opposite baseline and back through the baseline without stopping.

LINE DRILLS

Difficulty Level: Advanced

Skills Practiced: Conditioning, physical and mental toughness

Number of Players Needed: No limit

Number of Basketballs Needed: 0

Ideal Practice Time:
End or pre-season conditioning

(Each spot on the floor shows one progression of the drill.)

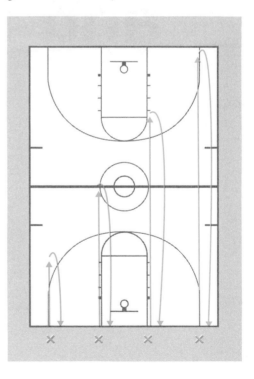

Game Strategies and Plays

CHAPTER 9

Offenses

No matter what offense a team runs, the one goal is to score on every possession. Obviously, though, it doesn't happen that way. As a coach, you need to decide what offense will give your team the most opportunity to score on every possession. When choosing an offense, there are many things you should take into consideration, but most importantly, you need to ask yourself two questions: Can your players run this offense successfully? Can this offense put your players in a position to be successful? If you have a team that has many guards and not a lot of size, you would probably not want to choose an offense based around strong post play. On the other hand, if you have a lot of size and not many great ball handlers, you probably wouldn't want to run a guard-oriented offense. Before you choose any offense, make sure your team is proficient at the fundamentals of any offense, which include passing, cutting, and screening (covered in part 1). The better your team performs these skills, the better your offense will be, no matter which offense you choose.

The two types of offenses described in this chapter are pattern and motion offenses. In a patterned offense, cuts and passes are set up in a prearranged system. While a pattern offense may be scouted easily, if it is run correctly and efficiently, it can be very successful and hard to guard. In a motion offense, cuts and passes are set up by reading and reacting to the defense. Motion offense may be harder to scout and defend, but it takes lots of practice to understand the fundamentals and techniques used to make it successful. However, no matter which type of offense you prefer, it is important to emphasize these four rules of any successful offense to players:

COACHING KEYS

- Emphasize that by spacing out the defense, offensive opportunities open up.
- Teach players to be strong with the ball; they should square up strong and face the basket whenever they receive a pass.
- Take advantage of your team's strengths within your offense.
- Insist that players be patient and move with a purpose. Players often try to do too many things too fast. While it's not good to just stand in one place for too long, it's also not good to move too many places in a short time.

1. Take care of the ball and eliminate turnovers.
2. Take good, smart shots.
3. Move when you don't have the ball.
4. Help teammates get open.

KEY TERMS

Basket cut: Any hard cut to the basket.

High post: The area on the court around and near the free-throw line.

L-cut: A cut made from the perimeter to the lane, up to the elbow of the free-throw line, and back to the perimeter. When drawn, this cut looks like an L. The L-cut is used to get open on the wing without the help of a screen.

Low post: The area around and near the rim and the low blocks.

Motion line: The imaginary line that cuts the court right below the free-throw line. By having guards stay above this line, the offense stays "high and wide," which spreads out the defense.

Paint cut: Any cut through the lane.

Screen away and seal: If a post player screens for the opposite post, as he sets his screen, he may be able to position himself in front of the defensive player he just screened.

Seal: When an offensive post player keeps a defensive player behind her by swinging her leg around the defender while keeping her hands up in order to stay in good positon to score.

Seal the opposite side: If the defense is playing in front of the post while the ball is on the wing, the post player can try to position himself so that he is posting up between the defensive player and the basket. When the ball is reversed to the top of the key, the guard should have an easy pass into the post player because he has sealed his defender to the outside.

Shallow cut: Any cut that loops from the wing back to the top of the key.

V-cut: A cut made from the perimeter into the lane and back to the perimeter (made in the shape of a V). This cut is used to get open on the perimeter without using a screen. The V-cut can also be used to set up a screen.

MOTION OFFENSE

The benefit of running a motion offense is that your team becomes unpredictable and hard to scout. Instead of assigned movements and cuts like in a patterned offense, players in a motion offense learn to read a defense and screen and cut accordingly. Players in a motion offense learn how to play the game while learning how to read the defense, rather than just memorizing plays and running them. Motion offense can also be altered depending on your team's strengths and weaknesses. It can work against any half-court defense that your opponent throws at you.

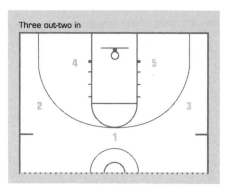

Three out-two in

When running a motion offense you can start your team in many alignments. Three out-two in and four out-one in are among the most popular sets for motion offenses, and these are the sets covered in this chapter.

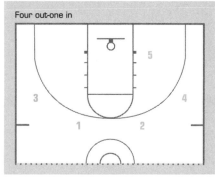

Four out-one in

When installing the motion offense, some coaches like to keep their rules to a minimum, allowing their players to make plays on the fly. Other coaches like to add many rules to keep their offense more structured and disciplined. No matter what category you fall under, here are a few rules that should be followed when running a motion offense.

RULES FOR PERIMETER PLAYERS

1. **Cut to open space.** When a perimeter player makes a cut, he should make sure he is cutting to an open space and not following another player. You rarely want two cutters in the same position at the same time. A perimeter player has many choices: He can make an L-cut or a V-cut (see page 190) to get the ball to the wing without a screen; an inside cut or a basket cut; or a back cut, either a shallow and replace or a paint cut (on pages 190–191).

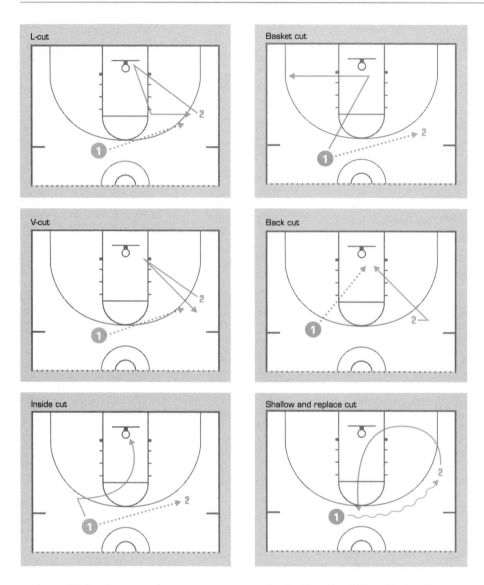

By having your players use a variety of cuts, they should be able to eliminate consecutive cuts and keep good spacing on the floor.

2. **After catching the ball, square up strong to the basket and hold the ball for a two count (hold the ball in a triple-threat position for two seconds).** By doing this, perimeter players will not only have better control of the ball, they will also be able to better read the defense and the cuts and screens of their teammates.

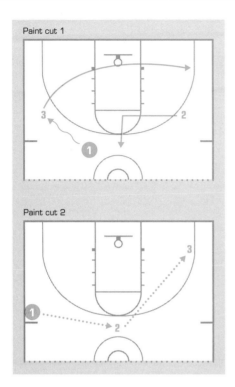

Paint cut 1

Paint cut 2

Down screen

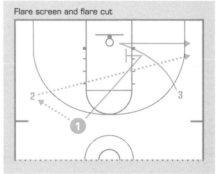

Flare screen and flare cut

3. **Look down to screen.** Successful screens are made when good angles are produced. Better angles are produced by using down screens within your offense. Down screens also increase the amount of possible cuts off the screen. When using a down screen, the player being screened can read the defense and react. If the defense is overplaying the screen, the cutter may flare out (do a flare cut) and away from the defensive player for a jump shot. If the defensive player is following the cutter, the cutter can curl off the screen. If the defensive player overplays the cutter, the cutter may back cut, also referred to as a backdoor cut, (on page 192).

4. **Try to keep fifteen- to eighteen-foot spacing.** Spreading out the offense leads to spreading out the defense, which makes it easier for the offense to attack using dribble penetration or cutting to the basket. Good spacing also makes it difficult for the defense to use good help-side defense. One way to ensure this spacing (see page 192 for four-guard and three-guard spacing) is to assign spots. In four out-one in motion, there should be four spots filled around the perimeter, while in three out-two in motion there should be three spots filled around the perimeter. When a player makes a cut, he should always be looking to fill one of these spots,

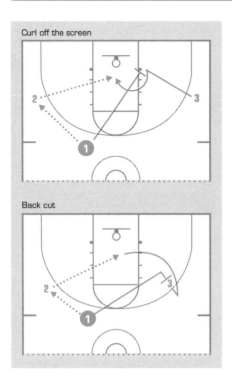

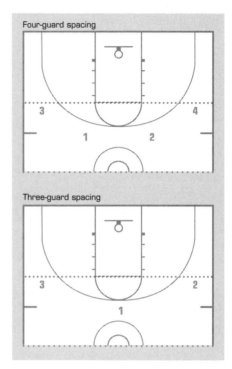

or cut to the basket and then fill an open spot. Perimeter players should also work on staying high above the motion line, or staying "high and wide." This helps to keep the defense spaced out and opens up lanes for dribble penetration. It also gives the post players more room to work.

5. **Reduce the use of the dribble.** The only time a perimeter player should dribble is to move the ball against full-court pressure, take the ball to the basket, or improve a passing angle.

6. **If not cutting, screen.** After a perimeter player passes the ball, he should make a cut to the basket, screen, or receive a screen. Good screens lead to wide-open shots. When players are constantly moving and constantly screening, they are hard to guard. Constant, unpredictable movement causes the defense to get out of position, which leads to easy baskets. Perimeter players may use down screens, cross screens, or back screens (on page 193). (See pages 98–99 for more on screens.)

7. **Look to cut to the high post when it is open.** Cutting to the high post (see page 197) opens up a drive to the basket, a high-low feed, a quick reversal, or an open 3-point shot. Good things usually happen when the ball gets into the high post.

RULES FOR POST PLAYERS

Depending on your team's size, you may want your offense to have two post players, one post player, or none. If you choose to use the post position, here are some rules you might want to employ:

1. **The center should always be in the post.** In most cases, you do not want your center handling the ball on the perimeter. The only time the center comes out of the post is to back screen.

2. **The high post should be on the ball-side.** You want your players to flash to the high post from the weak-side to the ball-side. By having the high post on the ball-side, you ensure safe passes and also open up more options.

3. **The low post should be opposite the ball.** By having the low post work for position on the weak-side, that post player will be in position to receive a pass after a ball reversal or a high-low feed from the high post. If the ball is reversed, and the low post is now on ball-side, that post player should work for position for a two count. If the ball is not fed into the post, that post player should look to seal the opposite side or screen away and fill the weak-side block. The post player should constantly be working to set his man up to seal and score.

4. **When the high post opens up, move to it.** Depending on your talent level at the post position, a post player can drive to the basket, hit a jump shot, feed the post, reverse the ball, or hit an open perimeter player for a 3-point basket, all from the high post.

Down screen

Cross screen

Back screen

5. **The low post should look to set back screens for perimeter players.** Post players should look to set back screens for perimeter players when they pass from the sideline to the top of the key.

MOTION OPTIONS FOR POST PLAYERS

Three out-two in motion screen away and roll high: This option begins with the ball at the top of the key. The ball is then passed to one sideline. The post player on that side automatically screens away for the opposite post player. The opposite post player uses the screen and comes across the lane looking for a feed from the perimeter player. The post player who set the screen now rolls from the screen to the high post also looking for the ball. If the ball is passed to the low post, the high post crashes and looks for a dump pass or rebound from a shot. If the ball is passed to the high post, the low post will seal and look for a high-low feed. The player with the ball in the high post should look to feed the low post, shoot, or penetrate.

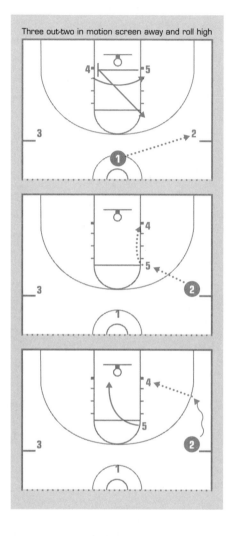

Three out-two in motion screen away and roll high

Two down: In this set, have your post players start on the perimeter and your guards start in the post. The post players set down screens for the guards, and the point guard chooses which side to pass to. The ball-side post player seals his man for a post feed, while the weak-side post player flashes to the high post. (See page 195.)

Four low stack: This is an easy way to open up into your motion offense by having your point guard at the top of the key with the ball while the other four players stack in the low post. In this set you can get the same look as the two down (four low stack two down)

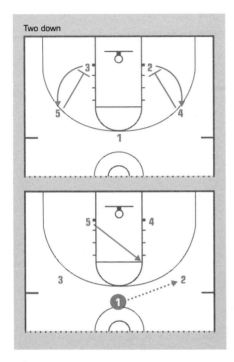

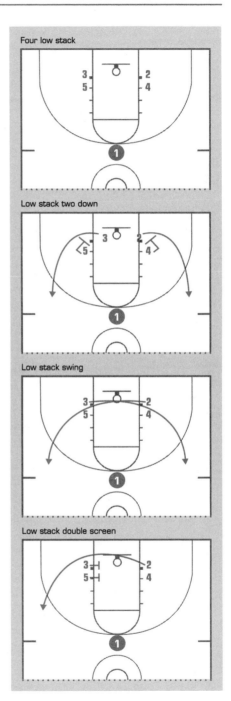

by having your post players screen for your guards. You could also look to swing your guards to get into your motion (low stack swing). This is still the same basic set except you are getting early movement out of your guards, which could help disrupt the defense.

Low stack double screen: Here, have your guard and your post player on one side to set a double screen for a guard coming off the opposite side.

MOTION SETS

Some coaches like to run set plays to get into their motion offense. By doing this, they add a little more structure to their motion, and can get a specific look that they may want to take advantage of. Look at the diagrams for Advanced motion set 1 and 2 for two options. (See pages 206–211 for more set plays that are not part of a motion offense.)

MOTION OFFENSE VS. ZONE DEFENSE

One of the benefits of running a motion offense is that it is very flexible. Your players are reading the defense to see what options they have. This makes the motion offense work well against zone defenses, as well as man-to-man defense. However, when playing against a zone defense, you may want to make a few small changes or tweaks to your motion offense.

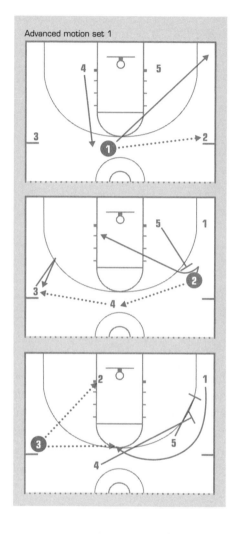

Advanced motion set 1

1. The first change would be having your post players start in the short corners (page 197). This spreads out the zone, which will open up the high post (page 197), as well as create driving lanes for your guards. Once your point guard passes to a side, the opposite post player should flash to the high post. The guard on the wing may now pass the ball to either the short corner or the high post, or reverse it to the guard on the top of the perimeter.

2. If the ball goes to the short corner, the high post should crash to the basket, looking for a feed from the player in the short corner, while the guards should find an open spot on the perimeter in case the ball needs to be passed back out. The post player in the short corner has the option to get to the basket, hit the high-post player crashing to the basket, shoot the mid-range jump shot, or pass the ball

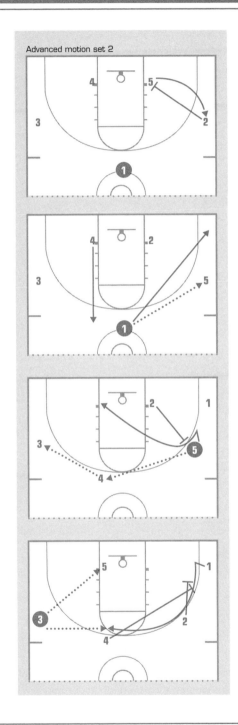

Advanced motion set 2

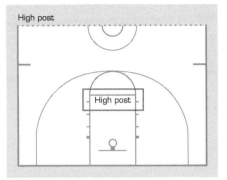

High post

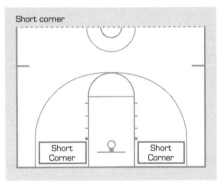

Short corner

back out to a guard spotting up on the perimeter.

3. If the ball is passed into the high post, that player should square up to the basket and look for the drive to the basket, the open jump shot, the player in the short corner, or a ball reversal. Once again, when the ball is passed into the post, the perimeter players should be looking to find new open spots to get a pass from the high post.

4. When running your zone motion offense (see page 198), try and reverse the ball frequently and quickly. By reversing the ball, the defense has to

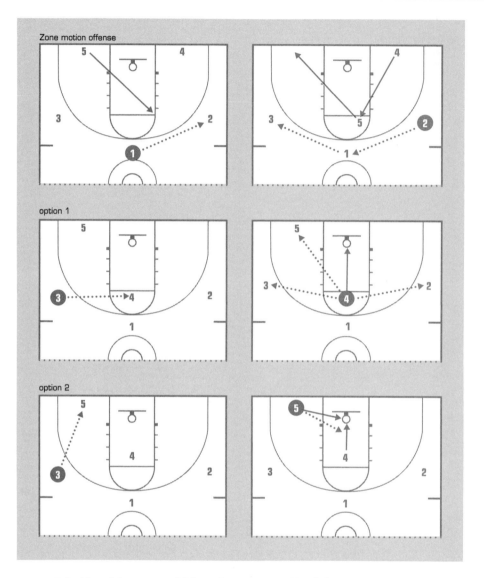

switch sides of the court quickly and occupy one side of the court. The quick reversal can lead to open shots and open lanes to penetrate to the basket.

5. Get the ball into the post. When the ball gets inside the post, the zone will usually collapse and leave guards open for shots on the perimeter.

6. Make sure you attack the gaps. Guards should attack the gaps by dribbling into them, and post players should cut into them when they are open.

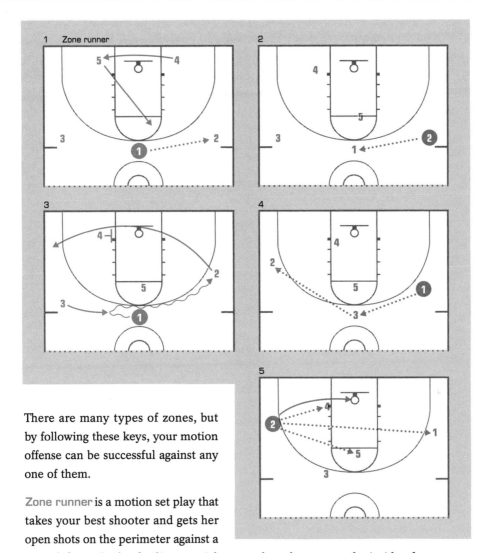

There are many types of zones, but by following these keys, your motion offense can be successful against any one of them.

Zone runner is a motion set play that takes your best shooter and gets her open shots on the perimeter against a zone defense. It also facilitates quick reversals and opens up the inside of any zone.

By running a motion offense, you are developing an offense that has constant movement and keeps all five defenders occupied, making your team harder to defend. Spreading out the floor makes it difficult for defensive teams to help out teammates and recover. Defenses cannot take your team out of your offense and disrupt your plays because your players are reading how they react to their movement. However, motion offense is hard to teach, and hard to perfect. When taught correctly, motion offense is very effective because every player is in a position to score. As a coach, it is your job to make sure your players not only understand the fundamentals of passing, cutting, and screening, but also that each player knows his role within the offense and chooses his shots wisely. When all of this is done correctly, the motion offense can be a very successful and fun offense to run.

THE FLEX OFFENSE

The flex is a very popular patterned offense based on passing, screening, and ball reversals. The flex also consists of many options and counter-options that make it difficult to guard.

BASIC FLEX OFFENSE

1. The base alignment of the flex is a four-low set with a point guard at the top of the key. The point guard (1-man) will decide which way to start the offense by dribbling to one side. When the point guard dribbles to one side of the court, the opposite post (4-man) will flash above the opposite elbow.

2. Once the 1-man has passed the ball to the 4-man, the strong-side post player (5-man) will set the "flex screen" for the strong-side guard (3-man). This cut off the flex screen is also known as the "flex cut," and a majority of scoring opportunities come off of this flex cut. If the 3-man is open, the 4-man should pass the ball to him as he comes off the flex screen for an inside shot. If the 3-man does not receive the pass, he should fill the opposite block position.

3. After the 5-man sets the flex-screen for the 3-man, the 1-man sets a down screen for the 5-man and widens out to the wing. The 5-man comes off the screen from the 1-man and cuts to the elbow. If the 5-man

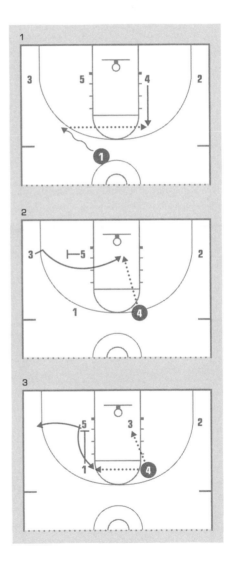

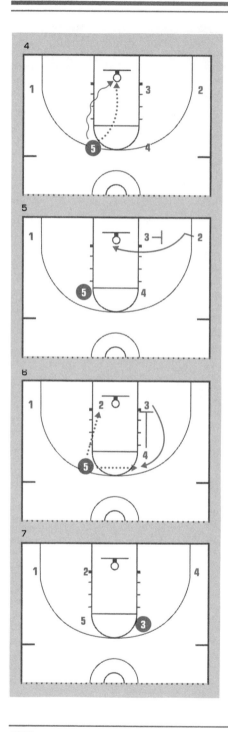

is open on the elbow, he receives a pass from the 4-man. The 5-man is now in a position to shoot a jump shot from the elbow or drive to the basket to make a lay-up. The pattern in the diagram is the foundation of the flex offense. At this point in the pattern, the 4-man has the choice to pass to either the 3-man coming off the flex screen or the 5-man cutting off the down-screen from the 1-man. Most of the scoring opportunities in the flex come off the flex cut or from shots from the high post. The multiple screens used within the offense cause confusion and mismatches within the defense, which, in turn, lead to scoring opportunities.

4. If the 4-man passes to the 5-man, he can shoot or drive to the basket.

5. If the shot or drive is not available when the 5-man receives the ball, the flex is repeated from the other side. The 3-man will set the flex screen on the block for the 2-man.

6. If the 2-man is not open on the flex cut, he fills the opposite post spot. If the 2-man does not receive the pass off of the flex-cut, the 4-man screens for the 3-man, who should catch the ball above the elbow, looking for the open shot, dribble penetration, or the next flex cut.

7. Once your players have gone this far through the pattern, their formation should look like diagram seven. No-

tice that diagram seven looks like the set in diagram two because there are players in identical spots. The pattern can be repeated over and over again if a scoring opportunity does not present itself.

FLEX OPTIONS

The flex can be a very productive offense; however, it is a patterned offense and can become predictable if your players run it like robots. Some simple variations can be installed to make the flex less predictable.

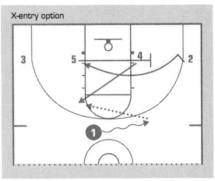

X-entry option: One of the simplest variations is the X-entry. In the X-entry, when the 1-man chooses a side to initiate the offense, the ball-side post (the 4-man) flashes to the opposite elbow, while the 5-man replaces the 4-man and sets the flex screen for the 2-man. After the X-entry is complete, the players are set in their regular flex positions and can continue to run the flex pattern. You would most likely want to run this X-entry when the defense is beginning to deny your entry into the high post.

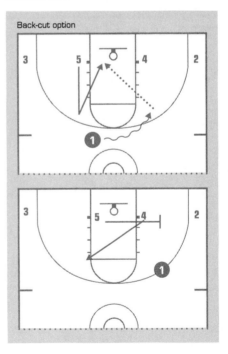

Back-cut option: Another entry option is the back cut. When the point guard (1-man) dribbles to one side to initiate the offense, the opposite post (5-man) flashes to the high post as usual. However, instead of catching the ball at the elbow, the 5-man executes a back cut and looks for the pass from the 1-man for a lay-up. If the 1-man does not make the pass, the 5-man should replace the 4-man, who executes the X-entry. This option can be used when the defense is overplaying the entry pass, as well as when the defense is overplaying.

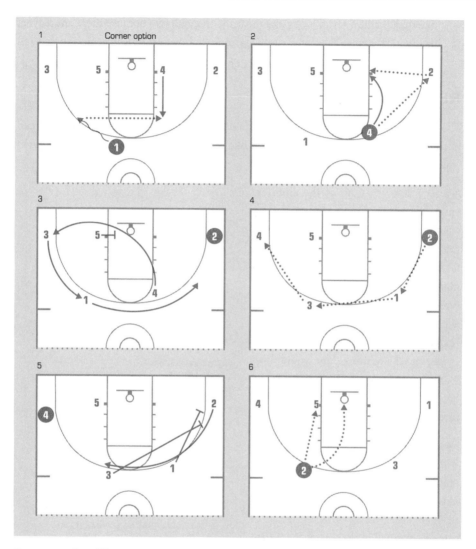

Corner option: The corner option is a very successful variation within the flex offense. When the 4-man receives the entry pass from the 1-man, instead of looking for the flex cut, he will pass the ball to the 2-man in the corner and make a basket cut. The 2-man looks to hit the 4-man cutting to the basket for an easy lay-up. If the back cut is not open, the 1-man fills the 4-man's position, while the 3-man fills the 1-man's old position. While the guards (1-man and 3-man) are sliding toward the ball, the 5-man sets a flare screen for the 4-man. While the 4-man is cutting off of the 5-man's screen, the guards (1-man and 3-man) quickly reverse the ball, looking to hit the 4-man on the wing for an open 3-point shot. After the ball is reversed to the 4-man, the 1-man and 3-man set a double screen for the 2-man, who should get an open look for a shot, basket penetration, or a post feed.

There are many other options your team can use while running the flex. It is important to teach your players to recognize how the defense is playing. If the defense is overplaying and denying passes, your players should look for back cuts. If the defense is switching screens, your players should look for screeners rolling to the ball after screening and look to utilize any mismatches that may occur from the defense switching screens.

OFFENSIVE SET PLAYS

In some cases, running a motion offense does not work effectively for your team. There may be particular situations where you need to run set plays. Beginners, especially, may not be comfortable with a motion offense because it requires a lot of acting and reacting to the defense and other players on your team. So if you have a team of beginning players, you may want to have some set plays you can use.

Other times you may want to use set plays are when you need to score quickly. You can use a set play to get your best shooter open so she has a good look at the basket. You can also use set plays to try and create mismatches on the court. If you notice your opponent switches on all screens, you can run a set play that has a guard screening for a post player. If the defense switches, you then have mismatches, which can create scoring opportunities. For example, your quick guard may be able to drive around a slower post defender. Or your tall post player will be able to shoot over the head of a short guard.

One other situation where you may want to use set plays is if you notice the opponent is great at full-court presses, but that they struggle in the half-court offense. Using set plays can take advantage of their weaknesses and confuse them, especially if you have several different plays you can use.

When using a set play, the point guard typically calls out the name of the play as he dribbles up the court. Or the coach may call out the play from the sideline. Another option is to have some kind of hand signal (like a raised fist) that the point guard can use to indicate the play. If you use hand signals, all four of the other offensive players must be looking at the point guard so that everyone knows what play is being run.

The following pages contain some basic set plays that can be use agains man-to-man and zone defenses.

SET PLAYS VS. MAN-TO-MAN DEFENSE

Thunderhawk: This is an ideal play for intermediate players.

1. Players start in a 1-4 high set with the 4-man and 5-man on opposite elbows and the 2-man and 3-man outside the 3-point arc at the free-throw line extended.
2. The 1-man passes the ball to the best post player (the 5-man here), who steps out to get the ball.
3. Once the 5-man receives the ball, the 3-man runs to the block.

4. The 4-man sets a flare screen for the 1-man, who stays outside the 3-point line. After setting the screen, the 4-man steps out and receives a pass from the 5-man.

5. After the 4-man receives the pass, he immediately passes the ball to the 1-man.

6. The 3-man then sets a diagonal screen for the 5-man, who is looking to get a pass from the 1-man to score (option 1).

7. A second option can be for the 3-man to set the diagonal screen for the 5-man and then receive a down screen from the 4-man. The 3-man comes off the screen looking for a jump shot.

Hammer: This is a great play for beginner teams if you have a standout ball handler who has the confidence and ability to use dribble penetration. (See page 208.)

1. As the 1-man dribbles the ball up the court, the 4-man and 5-man set up on the same block.

2. The 1-man looks for an opportunity for dribble penetration toward the vacated block. He drives, looking to score.

3. As the 1-man drives to the basket, one of the post players (the 4-man here) pops up to the high post.

4. If no one picks up the 1-man, he shoots a lay-up. If other defenders step in to help on defense, the

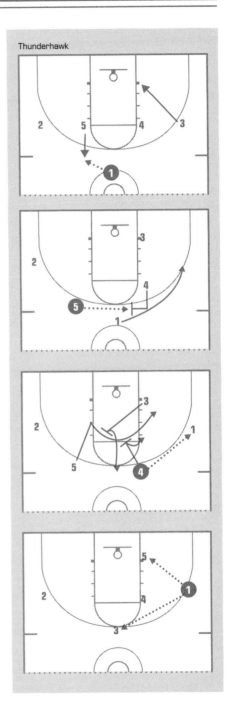

Thunderhawk

1-man looks to pass the ball to his now-open teammates (to a guard on the wing, the low post, or the high post).

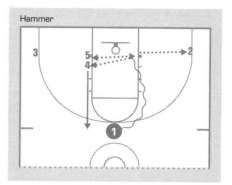

Tiger: This is another great beginner-level play for a team with a superior ball handler.

1. The 2-man is on one wing near the corner, and the 3-man is in the same position on the opposite side of the court. The 4-man and 5-man set up on the same block.

2. The 1-man brings the ball up the court to the top of the key and then dribbles in the direction opposite of where the two post players are lined up.

3. The post players set a double screen for the guard on their side of the court (the 3-man here). The 3-man comes off the top-side of the screen and runs toward the basket.

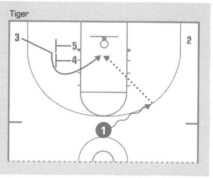

4. The 1-man looks for a quick pass to the 3-man, who should be open for a lay-up.

5. If the 3-man's defender knows the screen is coming and gets through it to the lane, the 3-man can change his cut and instead of going to the basket, he can flare back to the corner where he started. He gets the pass from the 1-man and takes a jump shot.

Box: Use this set play with teams of at least intermediate level.

1. Players line up in a box with the post players at the elbows and the guards at the blocks. The best post player (the 5-man here) and best passer (the 3-man here) should line up on the same side of the court. The point guard brings the ball up the court.

2. The 5-man sets a down screen for the 3-man. The 3-man pops out to the wing and receives a pass from the 1-man.

3. The 4-man sets a flare screen for the 1-man, who runs to the wing. The 2-man runs a curl cut over the top of the 5-man.

4. The 3-man takes one or two dribbles to the baseline to get a better passing angle to the 5-man. The 5-man steps around his defender and posts up.

BASKETBALL DRILLS, PLAYS, AND STRATEGIES

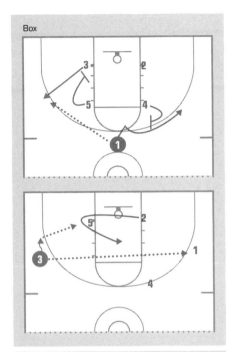

Box

5. The 3-man makes a bounce pass on the baseline to the 5-man, who should have a lay-up opportunity.

6. If the post player is not open, the 3-man can look for a skip pass to the 1-man as he comes off the flare screen.

Lob: This is an advanced play because each player must remember more than one job.

1. Players line up in a box with the post players at the elbows and the guards at the blocks. The best post player (the 5-man here) and best passer (the 3-man here) should line up on the same side of the court. The point guard brings the ball up the court.

2. The 5-man sets a down screen for the 3-man. The 3-man pops out to the wing and receives a pass from the 1-man.

3. At the same time the 5-man sets a screen, the 4-man sets a down screen for the 2-man, who pops out to the wing.

4. The 4-man then screens his own defender (help-side) as the 5-man cuts across the baseline and runs off the 4-man's screen.

5. The 5-man receives a lob from the 3-man. The pass is aimed at the back bottom corner of the backboard. The 5-man then shoots a lay-up.

6. Meanwhile, the 2-man sets a flare screen for the 1-man. Both the 2-man or 1-man are other options for the play if the lob doesn't work.

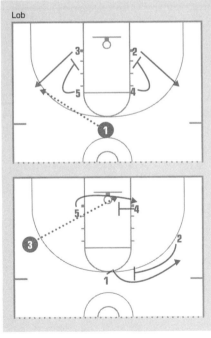

Lob

SET PLAYS VS. ZONE DEFENSE

Flare: This is a beginner-level play to use against a 2-3 zone defense.

1. Players set up in a box around the 3-point arc. The 4-man and 5-man set up at the low block extended, and the 2-man and 3-man set up at the free-throw line extended. The 1-man brings the ball up the court.

2. The 1-man passes to the 3-man, while the 2-man and 4-man set flare screens on the zone players on their side of the court.

3. The 1-man runs to the wing to the spot the 2-man just vacated.

4. The 3-man makes a skip pass to the 1-man, who should be open for a jump shot.

5. If the 1-man is not open, the 2-man can pop up to the top of the key to receive a pass and reverse the ball.

Zone stack: This is an intermediate-level play to use against a 2-3 zone defense.

1. The 1-man brings the ball up the court on one side (left side here).

2. The 4-man and 5-man stack on the low block opposite of the ball. The best shooter (the 2-man here) lines up on the ball-side block. The 3-man comes up the court with the 1-man, parallel to him but on the other side of the court, presenting a two-guard front.

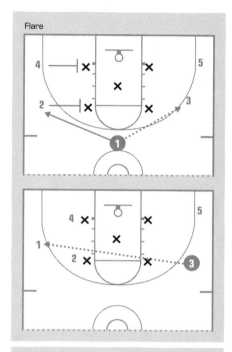

Flare

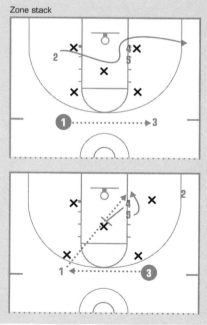

Zone stack

3. The 4-man and 5-man set a double screen for the 2-man, who runs off the bottom of the screen to the wing.

4. Simultaneously, the 1-man passes to the 3-man.

5. The 4-man screens the middle defender in the zone and the 5-man cuts to the basket.

6. Simultaneously, the 3-man reverses the ball back to the 1-man.

7. The 1-man makes a lob pass to the 5-man, who should be open for a lay-up.

Corner: This is an advanced-level play to use against a 2-3 zone defense.

1. Players set up around the 3-point arc. The 4-man and 5-man set up at the low block extended, and the 2-man and 3-man are at the free-throw line extended. The 1-man brings the ball up the court.

2. The 1-man passes to the 2-man and follows his pass.

3. The 2-man passes to the 4-man and then cuts to the basket looking for a pass and easy lay-up (option 1).

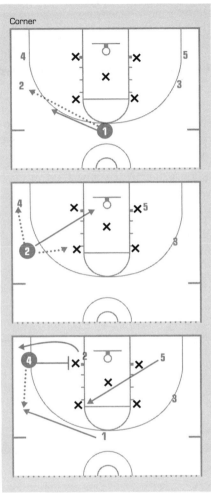

4. The 4-man passes back to the 1-man and then screens for the 2-man, who pops out to the corner, looking for a pass and an open jump shot (option 2). The 4-man then posts up and looks for a pass (option 3).

5. The 5-man flashes to the high post, looking for the pass and an open jump shot (option 4).

10

Defenses

Coaching philosophy varies among coaches at every level; the philosophy of how to win basketball games can be argued forever. Yes, the object is to score more points than your opponent; however, what is the difference between scoring more points and holding your opponent to fewer points than what you have accumulated? You win the game either by scoring more points or holding your opponent to fewer points. This chapter is all about defense and holding the other team to as few points as possible, including discussion on the types of defense to play in the half court. (For full-court defenses, or presses, see chapter eleven.)

The first type is old-fashioned, man-to-man defense, which emphasizes pressuring the basketball. Man-to-man defense is exactly what it says it is, each player matches up with one offensive player whom he is responsible for guarding. Man-to-man defense can have three different schemes for players off the basketball: gap, deny, and switch. The gap defense has a player sitting in the penetrating gap, allowing the pass to be made to his offensive counterpart. The focus is to pressure the basketball because the on-ball defender has help in either direction since the other defenders are playing the gap. The second type of man-to-man defense is denial. This type of defense is an aggressive style of play where the offense is not allowed to make any pass easily. The defenders who are guarding an offensive player one pass away are denying that pass very aggressively. The third strategy is the switch man-to-man defense. This requires the defense to communicate because they must switch every exchange or screen. Coaches might vary any of these strategies, which will be discussed in further detail in this chapter.

Also discussed in this chapter is zone defense, including the 2-3 zone and the 1-3-1 zone. There are different varieties

COACHING KEYS

- Communication is key between coaches and players, but it is even more important between players and players. All five players must be on the same page.
- It is imperative that players work hard on defense; the harder players play, the less they foul.
- All five players on the floor must know where the ball is at all times.
- The personnel on your team will affect the type of defense you will spend the most time practicing.

KEY TERMS

Deny: The defensive philosophy that tries to take away all passing lanes to make one pass between two offensive players very difficult.

Gap: The defensive philosophy that allows the passes from one offensive player to another but tries to take away dribble penetration.

Help-side: See pages 128 and 216.

Show and recover: When a defender that is guarding the screener temporarily guards the ball handler for a split second the screened defender time to recover.

Switch: The defensive philosophy that defensive players shift from one offensive player to another during any screen or exchange.

Three-quarter front: When guarding a post player, the defensive post player has his entire arm and part of his body in the passing lane, blocking the entry of the ball to the post.

of playing 2-3 zone, but the main focus is to keep the basketball out of the lane area. Defensively, the offense should be able to get open looks from the perimeter if the defense is helping out in the lane. The 1-3-1 zone and its variations are also addressed. When a coach has players that do not match up well enough with the personnel on the other team (according to size or speed or strength) to use a man-to-man defense, the zone defense could be a viable option.

The next defenses that are discussed are the box-and-one and triangle-and-two defenses. These defenses are best used when one team is outmanned by the other, and the offensive team has one or two exceptional players that you know your team cannot guard man-to-man. With that being said, the better team might have a few players that the defense would not have to guard as closely as the two best offensive players. The box-and-one defense can be aligned with the traditional two-by-two box, or it can be aligned as a diamond set up one-by-two-by-one. The triangle-and-two set-up is traditionally a one-by-two set-up. In both of the these defenses, the defenders who are not part of the box or the triangle guard the "best" players on offense in a man-to-man-style defense. These junk defenses can be successful if the offensive team begins to stand around and think too much.

The last type of defense to be covered in this chapter is the flip defense. The flip defense is known as the defense that switches from man to zone or zone to man. It is important to be able to flip defenses within the same possession so the offensive team is not sure what defense you are playing and, therefore, has trouble getting into an offensive rhythm. Another variation of the flip could be that after made baskets, the team is in man-to-man defense, and after misses the team is in zone defense, or vice versa.

MAN-TO-MAN DEFENSE

Basketball traditionalists think defense should only to be played man-to-man, with each defender responsible for guarding one offensive player. The man-to-man defense has three different variations: deny, gap, and switch. The major difference between deny and gap is that in deny man-to-man defense, the team defense is denying each passing lane that is one pass away, while the gap defense allows the pass but takes away the dribble penetration to the gap. In the switch man-to-man defense, the defense switches from one offensive player to the next on each screen or exchange.

MATCH-UPS

When guarding man-to-man, it is important for each defensive player to match up with an offensive player that is similar in size and plays a similar position. Each team is different and it is up to the coaching staff to decide how best to match up with the opposing team. For example, your best defensive guard should match up with the opposing team's best perimeter player, while your best post defender should guard their best post player. A general rule might be to always have your guards match up with their guards, forwards with their forwards, and post players with their post players. However, there are exceptions to that rule because a team that you play might have a point guard who cannot shoot. Therefore, the best match for your team might be to match up him up with a post player because then your post player does not have to guard him outside the paint area. As a coach, there is nothing wrong with being creative and thinking outside the box. You know your personnel and what they can and cannot do better than anyone else.

ON-THE-BALL DEFENSE

Defensive ball pressure really sets the tone of what type of defense your team can play. An aggressive, deny man-to-man defense has players pressuring the ball all over the floor, in an attempt to frustrate the opposing team's primary ball handlers. It is important for any defensive player who is guarding the basketball to consistently be in a defensive stance, which includes bending the knees, keeping the butt down, having active hands, and maintaining a certain amount of mental toughness that says "this offensive player will not dribble penetrate the basketball past me."

POST DEFENSE

Within either gap or deny man-to-man defense, there lies a philosophy on how to guard the post. The post is defined in this section as the block area on either side of the floor. The midpost is the area halfway between the post and the elbow area. There are basically two different ways to play the post area, since the post player is either fronted by the defender or the defender plays behind. Fronting the post is a more aggressive way of playing low-post defense. If fronting the post, it is very important then to get excellent ball pressure and great help-side defense, which could also be known as lob help. When fronting the post, the goal for the defense is to eliminate any opportunity for the offense to pass the ball into the post. It is necessary to front the post area, but once the offensive post player moves to the midpost or off the block area, the defense must then work to three-quarter front the post. The problem with this, though, is the offense then has too much space between the defense and basket to throw a lob pass for a lay-up. Once the post player begins to try to move back to the post area, the defender reacts to this and begins to work to front the post.

Post defense with defensive post players who are bigger or taller can adjust their method of playing. They can afford to play behind the offensive player because it would be difficult for the offensive players to score over their bigger bodies and their outstretched arms. Playing behind does not simply mean allowing an offensive player to catch the ball in the post area or closer to the basket. The goal of this type of post defense is to allow for catches but to make the offensive post players get their post catches off the low block, preferably two or three feet off the block. Playing behind the post does not require as much lob help or ball pressure as fronting of the post does. Bigger and stronger post players find this type of defense to be more effective than fronting the post because every offensive post player has to score over the post defenders.

HELP-SIDE DEFENSE

Man-to-man defense relies heavily on good help-side defense. Help-side defense consists of the positioning of the defenders who are guarding the offensive players that are two passes or a skip pass away from the basketball. Usually the help-side defense is the difference between successful and average basketball teams. On-the-ball defense is simple: Players put as much pressure on the basketball as possible but stay in front of the ball. One-pass away (see page 151) defense emphasizes denying any pass that is only

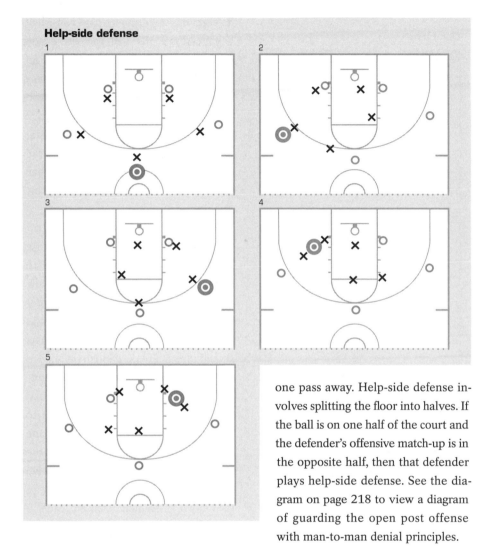

Help-side defense

one pass away. Help-side defense involves splitting the floor into halves. If the ball is on one half of the court and the defender's offensive match-up is in the opposite half, then that defender plays help-side defense. See the diagram on page 218 to view a diagram of guarding the open post offense with man-to-man denial principles.

DENY MAN-TO-MAN DEFENSE

Deny man-to-man defense (page 218) emphasizes ball pressure and extending the defense to take the offense out of their rhythm and timing. Any offensive player one pass away from the basketball should be denied in order to create situations where the defense can get turnovers (stealing the pass) that immediately set up easy baskets on a fast break. One aspect of deny man-to-man defense that needs emphasis is on-the-ball

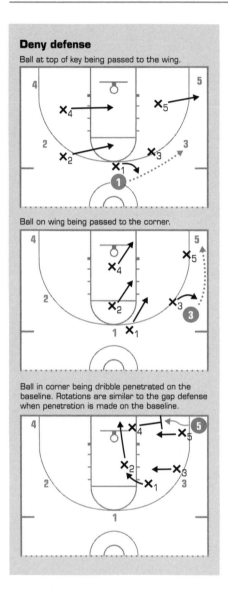

Deny defense

Ball at top of key being passed to the wing.

Ball on wing being passed to the corner.

Ball in corner being dribble penetrated on the baseline. Rotations are similar to the gap defense when penetration is made on the baseline.

defense. It is important to have consistent ball pressure so that with each possession, the point guard has to work hard to get the ball up the floor. Too much ball pressure and gambling may allow a good dribbler to fake out the defender and drive around him, creating 5-on-4 opportunities where the defense is outnumbered. The ideal situation is having as much ball pressure as you can without allowing any dribble penetration.

Guarding one pass away is the difference between gap and deny defense. There are a few variations on how to deny passes to the offensive player one pass away from the ball. The defender can place just his arm or hand in the passing lane to help deny the pass, but he should also maintain enough balance to move with the offensive player if he cuts backdoor for a lay-up. Another method for denial can be for the defender to place his entire body in the passing lane. If he is going to do this, he must trust the help-side defense. Help-side defensive players are the most important part of the deny man-to-man defense because if the offense begins to make backdoor cuts, the defenders playing help-side defense should be in position to stop those cuts.

Players can also use a combination of both hand and body to block the passing lane. When doing this, it is important that players only deny penetrating passes, which means passes will be denied only if the target is an offensive player close to the basket who is a threat to score from that position. This defense combines the pressure from denial but, as a coach, you do not have to worry about giving up many backdoor cuts and lay-ups for easy scoring opportunities.

BASKETBALL DRILLS, PLAYS, AND STRATEGIES

Deny man-to-man defense presents many problems for the offense because the defense is trying to push the offense out of scoring range when they make their first entry pass.

GAP MAN-TO-MAN DEFENSE

Gap man-to-man defense is more conservative than deny man-to-man defense. The main difference in the two defenses revolves around how to guard the one pass away. The gap defense allows the pass but then puts pressure on the ball on the catch. The reason to allow this pass without any denial is that the team's defensive goal is to take away the possibility of dribble penetration from the offense. By allowing the one-pass away catch, defenders are free to hang out closer to the lane until their player catches the ball. The gap defense places an emphasis on defensive positioning and understanding the concept of keeping the ball out of the lane area off the dribble.

On-ball pressure can be more intense in gap defense than denial defense because each on-ball defender has help on each side of him. Intensive on-ball pressure creates havoc without having to gamble and go for steals, and it can even create opportunities for

Gap defense

Ball at top of key. X_2 and X_3 play the dribble penetration gap instead of denying the pass from the 1-man to the 3-man or the 1-man to the 2-man.

Ball on wing, passed to the corner. Notice each defensive player is moving to a different spot.

Ball in corner dribble penetration on the baseline. Notice the rotations from all five players.

backdoor cuts. Playing on-ball defense at any point on the floor will always have two defenders in position to help stop the ball from getting into the lane area close to the basket.

If the offense has a few good outside shooters, even though defenders allow the passes to reach them, it is important for the defense to quickly apply ball pressure once they catch the pass so they cannot just catch and shoot. When guarding certain players who are not outside threats, the individual defenders can help out even more on the dribble penetration from the ball.

Help-side defense would seem to not have much importance in gap defense because the one-pass away defenders are already in help. But the help-side defenders are *always* important because they are the last line of defense against the basket. See the diagram on page 219 to notice how the gap defense would guard against the open post offense. Notice the differences between deny and gap defenses in the diagrams on pages 218 and 219.

Gap defense could frustrate a team that wants to create easy scoring opportunities off the dribble. It could also be an alternative to guarding a great offensive team that can both create off the dribble and shoot off the pass. As a coach, you want to take one out of the equation so gap defense can take away dribble penetration. Gap defense does take disciplined players and a stubborn coach who can stick with the game plan.

SWITCH MAN-TO-MAN DEFENSE

Switch man-to-man defense puts an emphasis on communication among individual defenders to play great team defense. This defense involves players always switching on screens and exchanges. That is, instead of defensive players staying with their offensive match-up on a screen, they switch who they are guarding with another teammate involved in the play. You can play variations of this switch man-to-man defense. First of all, the defense can switch all five players, no matter if a guard is screening a post player or vice versa. This way, there is no confusion because all five players know to switch *all* screens and exchanges. Or guards can only switch with guards and post players with post players. Depending on personnel, you can combine the first and second options with a third option where players who play positions one through four switch, but the 5-man stays with his assignment no matter what. The 5-man could be a big post player or a player who has a lot of strength but not quickness, and this match-up could be the only one that is conducive to the team being successful.

In the switch man-to-man defense, it is up to your preference to play more of a denial or gap defense, switching either to keep the pressure up on denying the one pass away or to keep help for dribble penetration. Switching can keep the help-side defenders in position so they are ready to help off the dribble or pass.

In late-game situations, switch man-to-man defense can provide the opportunity to relinquish any show-and-recover situations, when teams screen and look to score off

Switch defense

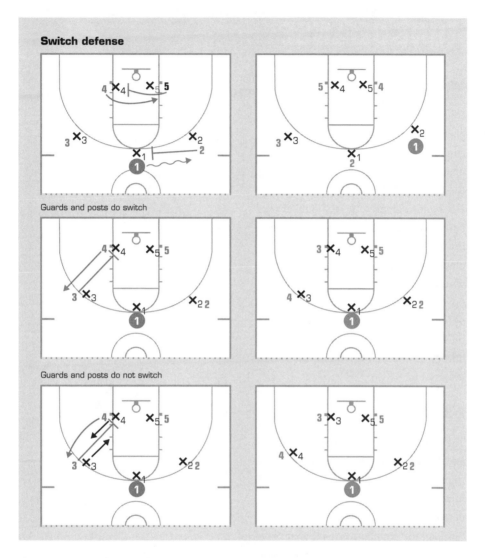

Guards and posts do switch

Guards and posts do not switch

those screens. (Show-and-recover situations involve the defender helping out too much on an offensive player coming off a screen, allowing the screener to be open for a scoring opportunity.) Switching usually forces offensive teams to make a second read or use their second or third option on an offensive set play. If you decide to use the switch man-to-man defense, it is very important to use practice time to go over certain situations and allow players the opportunity to communicate with their teammates. Mistakes in late-game situations because one player switched while another did not can result in lost games.

ZONE DEFENSE

The zone defense is an alternative to the man-to-man defense. Instead of each defensive player being responsible for guarding one offensive player, each defender guards a specific zone on the court and any offensive player who enters that area. When playing zone defense, it is still important to use man-to-man principles when guarding the basketball. Within either the 2-3 or 1-3-1 zone defenses, there should always be a defender responsible for guarding the basketball. Many young basketball players think they can stand and watch when playing zone defense. That is far from the truth. In order for a zone defense to be effective, players must be willing to play just as hard or even harder on the defensive end than they are used to.

2-3 ZONE DEFENSE

The basic 2-3 zone defense takes away an offensive post presence that a coach thinks his team cannot effectively guard in a man-to-man defense. The 2-3 zone defense can be summed up by one word: "inside-out." Emphasize to all your players that they must take away the inside game from their opponents. That means they might be giving up something, usually outside jumpers.

The 2-3 zone alignment is usually set up with the two guards or two smallest players up top. They might start

2-3 zone defense

Pass from top of key to wing.

3 comes out until 1 can bump him down. Once this happens, 3 goes back down to short corner and 5 and 4 both rotate back.

Skip pass from O₂ to O₃. 4 has the ball until 2 can bump him down.

BASKETBALL DRILLS, PLAYS, AND STRATEGIES

around the elbow area but can extend to the 3-point line or beyond. The bottom three players are usually the three tallest players who can rebound the best. The 2-3 alignment allows for good defensive rebounding position because you have your three tallest, biggest players near the basket.

The 2-3 zone defense takes away the post presence but it gives up something: An offensive team can get open shots at either the wing if the defense allows or at the elbow. But if you have two really great shooters on the wing, you do not want to give them open looks. Therefore, your top two guards are going to favor the wing area, and if they do that, it will open up the elbow area, which is usually where the two guards are positioned. Many times, the elbow area is where the offense wants to get the ball, but as the defense, would you rather give an elbow jump shot to an offensive player who does not want to take that shot or an open 3-pointer to a great shooter? That answer is simple: the nonoffensive threat shooting an elbow jumper. Always keep the offensive personnel in mind for opposing teams. If you know they have two players who are low-percentage 3-point shooters, there is no need to have the defense sprint out to guard them when they catch a pass beyond the 3-point line.

The 2-3 zone can be varied any way you feel comfortable; the middle player, which usually is your 5-man or your biggest player, can extend out to the free-throw line or stay right underneath the basket. This will probably depend on what you want to give to the offense. With high-school teams and some junior-high teams, scouting might play an important role into your 2-3 philosophy because you can get an idea of what type of offense the opponents will run against your 2-3 zone. This allows for certain adjustments and variations for specific teams.

1-3-1 ZONE DEFENSE

The 1-3-1 zone defense (see page 224) can create great opportunities for the defense to trap players with the ball in the corners against either the half-court line or baseline. This defense can also be played strictly within the 3-point line, which provides an alternative defense to the 2-3 zone. It can also be a combination of both a trapping 1-3-1 half-court trap or a regular 1-3-1 zone defense that is played at the 3-point line and in. The 1-3-1 zone defense forces an opponent to spend extra time preparing because most teams practice against a man-to-man or 2-3 zone defense.

The positions of players in the 1-3-1 can vary. The player at the top of the key is a great spot for a long-armed wing player or a point guard who can really pester the opposing team's point guard. It is important that whoever you place in these spots

1-3-1 zone defense

Weakside wing has to drop to protect against the diagonal skip pass.

Ball in corner. 3 steps out to take the ball. 4 drops to the middle of the lane. 2 drops into the passing lane from O_4 to O_3. 1 tries to hide behind O_3 to steal

Skip pass from corner to opposite wing. All 5 players must sprint and get there as quickly as possible.

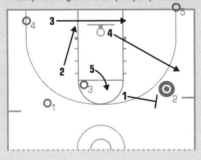

forces the ball to one side, usually the left because majority of the players are right-handed, which forces them to use their weak hand. The offense will try to reverse the basketball from one side to the other, so if you have a defender who can make this reversal very difficult, the top spot should go to that defender.

The second row of defenders has three spots. The middle spot should probably go to your biggest player since he must cover the two elbows and two low blocks. The two wing spots can be covered by guards or forwards. If possible, it would be great for these player to be good rebounders; however, they just have to be active and able to read the shoulder of the passer.

The most important rotation in the 1-3-1 zone is the wing opposite the ball rotating down to the opposite block. If the ball is above the top of the key on one side where the wing has to guard, the opposite wing has to rotate down to the opposite block to take away that diagonal passing lane.

The last line of defense in a 1-3-1 zone is the bottom player, who roams the baseline. Some coaches think they should place their 1- or 2-guard at the bottom because he has to go from sideline to sideline. But the best option would be a long-armed wing player who can go from sideline to sideline and can also trap the ball in the corner and force turnovers. The bottom player needs to be able to rebound since he is going from corner to corner, but if a shot is taken from one side of the floor, the rebound is more than likely going to come off to the opposite side, so he may get fewer rebounds than you might think.

BASKETBALL DRILLS, PLAYS, AND STRATEGIES

The 1-3-1 zone forces the offense to pass the ball to the corners because it takes away the shots from the wings. All five players in the 1-3-1 zone have to work extremely hard for it to be an effective defense.

The extension of the 1-3-1 half-court defense into a **1-3-1 half-court trap** is dependent on the personnel you have to work with. The best places to trap are the four corners, the four corners being the sideline and half-court line once the offense comes across the half court and the other two corners formed by the baseline and the sideline.

The 1-3-1 half-court trap presents an alternative to a man-to-man defense for the losing team that needs a change of pace to put pressure on the offense and get back into the game. The traps near the half-court line use the top player and one of the wings, depending on what side of the floor the ball is on. The traps between the sideline and baseline include the wing player on the ball-side of the court and the bottom player who is running the baseline. It is very important, no matter where the trap is, that the other three players on defense realize that those two players are trapping the ball and it is their job to anticipate where the ball will be thrown out of the trap. In an ideal game, the pass is stolen every time out of the trap, but in reality, it depends on how effective the trap is. The better the trap, the more aggressive the three other

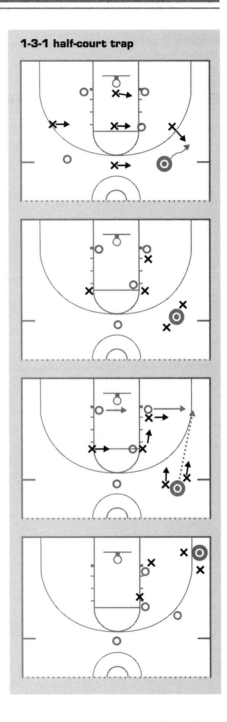

1-3-1 half-court trap

players can be in anticipating where the next pass will go while reading the offensive player's shoulders. Those shoulders will usually give away where he's looking to pass out of the trap. A half-court 1-3-1 zone trap needs all five players willing to give their total effort because, if not, those passes out of the traps will lead to lay-ups since the remaining defenders are outnumbered by the offense.

The 1-3-1 zone defense has a unique set-up compared to a man-to-man defense or 2-3 zone defense. The offense must adjust how they attack this type of defense and it usually forces them to use the corners, which then allows the defense to trap.

JUNK DEFENSES

These so-called junk defenses are more commonly known as the box-and-one defense and triangle-and-two defense. Junk defense is the term associated with these types of defenses because they are not traditional ways to stop the offense. However, it does not take away the effectiveness of either one if played correctly with the right personnel. The box-and-one defense focuses on the best player from your opponent. Your best defensive player's only responsibility is to stay with that offensive player wherever he goes on the court. The triangle-and-two defense is a nice alternative if the opposing team has more than one outstanding offensive player. These two defenses are affected by how skilled and talented the other three or four offensive players are. These defensive schemes provide an opportunity for the defense to really make the offense think about how to successfully attack the basket.

BOX-AND-ONE DEFENSE

The box-and-one defense is focused on taking away the opponent's best player and forcing the other four players on the floor to beat you. The responsibility of your best defensive player is very easy: all he is worried about is denying the best player the basketball. The all-out denial frustrates the offensive player to the point where he might become disinterested in what is going on in the game because he is accustomed to touching the ball many times throughout the game. When the offensive player does catch the ball, the other four players on defense must help on the ball. Remember, the object is to make the other four players beat you. On the other hand, you do not want the other defender to over help and thereby allow one of the four offensive players to shoot a lay-up. The

Box-and-one defense

Box-and-one vs. open post. Man-to-man vs. O_1. O_1 passes and cuts through and 1 stays with him. 2, 3, 4, and 5 stay in their box.

Box-and-one vs. down screen or baseline. O_4 screens 2 and tries to screen 1 to get O_1 an open shot. 1 gets through the screen the best he can. 5 might have to show and recover if needed.

box-and-one defense can also be referred to as "inside-out" because you want the other four players shooting outside jump shots instead of wide open lay-ups. This type of defense requires the five players to communicate and know where each teammate is located on the floor.

The other four players in this defense can be aligned two different ways. The traditional box-and-one defense is a two-by-two set-up and has two players at the elbows and two players at the blocks. The two players up top are usually the guards and the smaller players. The two players on the blocks are usually the bigger, taller players who are also the best rebounders. The box-and-one defense should force the other four offensive players to beat you from the outside by hitting jump shots instead of

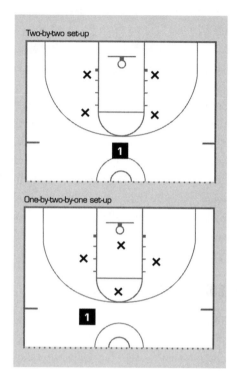

lay-ups or shots from the lane. Once a shot is taken, it is important that all five players go the glass and rebound to finish each possession.

The other type of alignment the box-and-one can have is the one-by-two-by-one diamond box. One player is at the top of the key or in the middle of the free-throw line. The next two players are located around the midpost area halfway between the elbow and the low block. The last player is positioned in the middle of the lane between the low blocks. This could also provide another adjustment you could make within the game to change up the pace or to confuse the offense. Just a simple adjustment to what the offense is used to looking at could give the offense something else to think about and throw them out of rhythm.

The box-and-one defense is a combination of both man-to-man and zone defensive principles. It could be a game plan to take away the opponent's best player and force the other four players to beat your team. It is hoped that the four players are not accustomed to that role and it takes a while for them to adjust to their new role. The box-and-one defense could also be a change in the flow for just a few possessions in the game.

TRIANGLE-AND-TWO DEFENSE

The triangle-and-two defense is best used against a team with two outstanding offensive players. Two defenders play the two most outstanding offensive players. The hope of this defense is to force the other three players to beat your team. The defenders playing the dominant offensive players man-to-man have difficult responsibilities. The defenders must deny the basketball to those players as much as possible all over the court, which is easier said than done.

While the two defenders play their respective deny man-to-man defense, the other three players line up in the triangle alignment. This alignment consists of one defender, probably your smallest but quickest player, going from elbow to elbow while the other two defenders start out on the low blocks. Those two defenders have to be

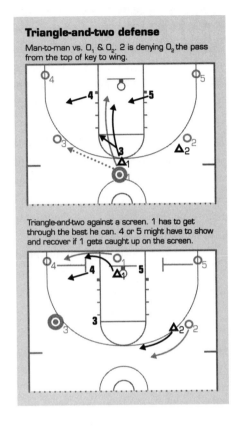

Triangle-and-two defense

Man-to-man vs. O₁ & O₂. 2 is denying O₂ the pass from the top of key to wing.

Triangle-and-two against a screen. 1 has to get through the best he can. 4 or 5 might have to show and recover if 1 gets caught up on the screen.

the best two rebounders left because they play closest to the basket. This is another "inside-out" type of defense because taking away the best offensive scoring options forces the other players to make plays they are not accustomed to, which is making outside shots or scoring over the top the defenders' outstretched arms. The three defenders lined up in the triangle need to guard the basketball when it is in their area like they are playing man-to-man defense. Also, if one of the great offensive players does catch a pass, the other defenders must help against dribble penetration and force the player with the ball to give it up. A variation on this defense could be for one of the three triangle defenders to help the man-to-man defenders immediately trap the basketball when one of the two best offensive players receives a pass. In this case, it is imperative that the other two players in the triangle anticipate where the pass out of the trap will go. It is necessary that all five players understand each of their roles and responsibilities in the triangle-and-two defense.

FLIP DEFENSES

Playing a flip defense means that your team switches defenses within the same offensive possession, usually switching between man-to-man defense and a zone defense. This is an excellent option for college and NBA teams because of the shot clock. It confuses offenses and wastes precious seconds as the offense is forced to adjust to a new defense. But even at levels without a shot clock, flip defense could still be implemented to guard out-of-bounds plays from underneath the offense's own basket. It could be effective against a team of bigger, stronger athletes who might stand around in their zone offense. So, show your zone defense, then after the first, second, or third pass, switch to a man-to-man defense to catch the offense off guard and leave them running their zone offense against man-to-man defense.

The flip defense needs all five players to communicate among each other, but it also requires great communication from the coaching staff to the players. This type of defense requires sufficient practice time to go over many situations.

As mentioned, an ideal situation to use a flip defense is when guarding an out-of-bounds play. The flip defense for this situation is to start in a zone as the ball is inbounded, then switch to man-to-man once the ball is in play. Playing the offensive set for an out-of-bounds situation with a zone defense is a conservative way to guard against possible scoring opportunities, but once the pass is made, the defense can match up with the closest offensive player and guard them man-to-man. Within your defense, each defender must be able to guard any player on the floor, and all five players must communicate in case the match-ups are not conducive.

In the flip defense, all five players work together to guard the ball, not just their assigned zone or man. Each player must communicate and understand his responsibility when switching defenses within the same offensive possession to ensure that no offensive player is left alone or is forgotten.

Presses

The effectiveness of a press is based on the theory that all five defenders on the court are playing as hard as possible. The purpose of pressing a team is to increase the tempo of the game. Pressing teams are usually athletic and quick; however, a team does not have to be athletic to press. For example, a team with several long-armed players may be able to trap in the half-court setting. There are several reasons a team may want to press. The obvious reasons are to create turnovers and to wear down the opposing team. In order to press for an entire game, a team must be in great condition.

An important part of an effective press is trapping. Trapping requires one defensive player to be able to guard at least two offensive players. Also, an effective trap gives the offense a sense of claustrophobia because the ball is restricted to a small, confined area. An effective trap is often done as a surprise, possibly after a free throw or a time-out because a team can get better organized out of a dead-ball situation.

There should only be two defensive players trapping the basketball at all times. The players should not reach for the basketball, but should mirror the movement of the ball ("trace" the movement with their hands). By mirroring or tracing the basketball, a defender will not get called for a foul. If the offensive player tries to split the trap by dipping his shoulder, the two defenders should fall to the ground as though fouled by a charge.

Any defensive player not guarding or trapping the ball should anticipate a pass being made. It is critical that a defensive player is not "hugging" his opponent by standing so close to him that a pass out of a trap will result in an easy

COACHING KEYS

- Defenders should be prepared to guard multiple players on a single possession. As a coach, you must be comfortable with this situation because there may be mismatches in personnel.
- Players not guarding the ball should be several feet away from the player they are guarding, rather than "hugging" him. Anticipation of passes is vital.
- Players should not reach for the ball when setting a trap because this usually results in fouling the offensive player.
- Effort by all five players is the only way a press will work.

KEY TERMS

Centerfielder: The player on the court who is designated to cover an area on the court rather than a specific person (see gold press on page 247).

Hugging: Guarding a player who does not have the basketball too closely, which decreases the defender's chances of stealing a pass.

On the line / up the line: The position of a defensive player on the court that is between the ball and the player he is guarding. For example, if the ball has not passed half court, the defender should be between the ball and the player he is guarding, which will allow him to recover or even steal the pass if it is attempted.

Read: To anticipate stealing a pass by deceptively positioning oneself in the press.

scoring opportunity. A way that a player can anticipate a pass is by looking at the shoulders of the player with the ball—their position will usually determine where the ball will be passed.

Teams should try to trap the ball in the corners of the court. The best place to trap is just past half court because of the over-and-back rule, which prohibits the offense from crossing to the back court with the ball once they have passed half court with it. So, trapping just past half court is like trapping with four defenders (two defenders, the sideline, and the half-court line).

There are many types of presses discussed in this chapter, from half court, to man-to-man, to zone. The reoccurring principle is that, in most instances, the trap must come from the backside of the offensive player. By having the defender come from the backside, the offensive player does not see the trap coming and cannot adjust. Many of the presses discussed in this chapter involve trapping offensive players who are dribbling. Trapping dribblers limits what the offense can do. If a team follows a pass and traps the ball, the offensive player can dribble around the press. If a dribbler is trapped, this will limit his ability to break the trap because he will not be able to begin dribbling again. His only option is to pick up the ball and pass it.

Keep in mind that as a pressing team, your team will not steal every pass or get a turnover each time down the court. Also, they may give up some lay-ups. The nature of pressing is to gamble and take chances. Many times, the effects of a press will start appearing late in a game, when the other team has been worn down by your continual pressure.

BASKETBALL DRILLS, PLAYS, AND STRATEGIES

INSTRUCTIONS

1. The defensive team matches up in a full-court, man-to-man press.
2. The most athletic player (X_4 in the diagram) guards the player taking the ball out of bounds, making the entry pass very difficult.
3. Players X_1 and X_2, guarding the front-line offensive players, are on the side of their offensive opponent (in or near the lane, forcing the offense to the sideline), aware not to give up the baseball pass.
4. Players X_3 and X_5, guarding the offensive players near half court, are a few steps in front of the players they are guarding. Make sure they are not "hugging" their opponents because it will be more difficult to steal the ball if a long pass is attempted.
5. Player X_4 forces the inbounder to make the entry pass near the corner of the baseline and sideline.
6. Player X_4 follows the pass and traps the ball with player X_1.

TIPS

Use this press if your team is in superior condition and is quicker than the opponent, but undersized. This is a great press to use to speed up the tempo of the game.

7. Once the trap has occurred, the remaining three defenders split the four offensive players.
8. The only pass available to the player being trapped is the long baseball pass, but even this pass is difficult to make if the trap is solid.
9. If the ball is reversed out of the trap, player X_2, guarding the middle, waits a split second before covering the player who received the reversal, allowing the rotation of the other defensive players to occur.
10. Player X_4 remains guarding the same player, but player X_1 replaces player X_2 in the middle of the press.
11. As the ball is dribbled, the closest player behind the basketball anticipates trapping the dribbler. (Note: It is important that the trap comes from behind so the dribbler is not able to see it coming. Ideally, the second trap happens just after the ball is dribbled across half court.)
12. The defense again rotates and splits responsibility to guard the remaining offensive players, anticipating or reading passes.

Continued on next page

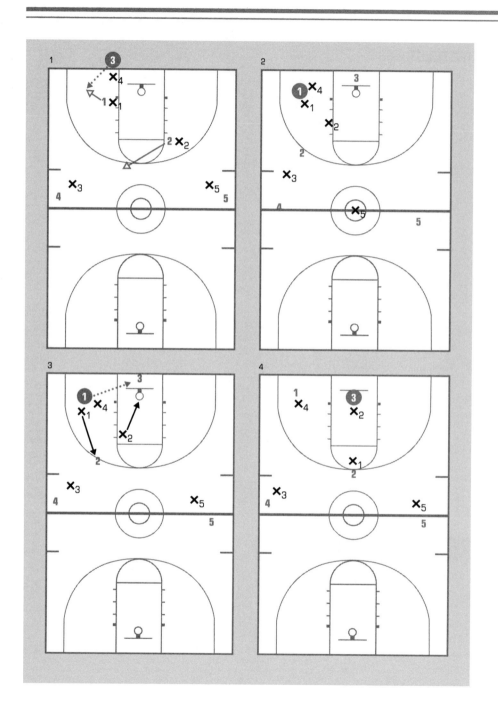

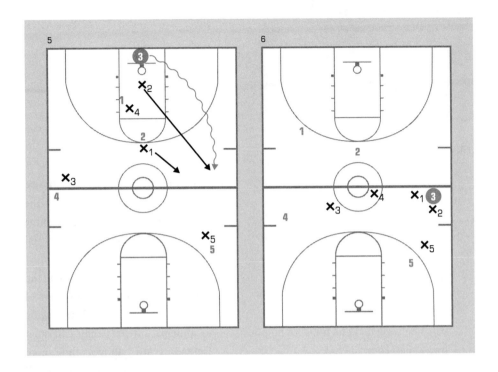

51 PRESS

Difficulty Level: Intermediate

Ideal Game Situation: On the spur of the moment and at unexpected times, such as after a time-out or made free throw

INSTRUCTIONS

1. The defense plays man-to-man at least three-fourths of the court. They do not look to trap until past half court.
2. The defensive player guarding the ball forces the ball to be dribbled to the sideline.
3. As soon as the ball approaches half court, the defensive player on the ball-side wing makes a move to help trap at half court.

TIPS

Guard three-fourths of the court so the defenders can push the ball near the sideline to make for a more effective trap.

4. Once the trap has occurred, the remaining three defenders split the four offensive players, meaning each defensive player gets between two offensive players.
5. The players who are not trapping the ball see which way the shoulders of the player with the ball are facing to anticipate a pass they can steal. Defenders are "above" their man, meaning they are closer to the ball than the player they are guarding is.

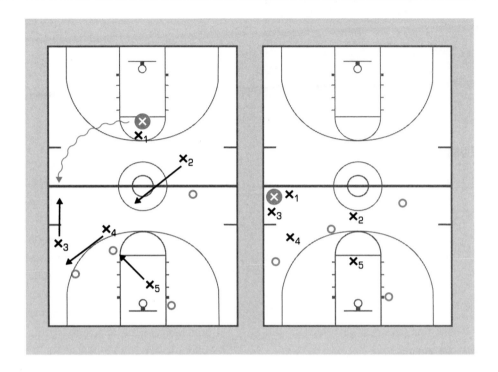

52 PRESS

Difficulty Level: Intermediate

Ideal Game Situation: On the spur of the moment, such as after a time-out or a made free throw

INSTRUCTIONS

1. The defensive team plays at least half-court man-to-man defense.

2. Once the ball is passed to the wing in the front court, the player guarding the ball follows the pass and traps the ball on the corner with the defender guarding the player who receives the pass. In other words, the first pass past half court should be trapped.

3. Once the ball is trapped, the three remaining defenders are each between two offensive players. The only pass open is the crosscourt skip pass.

4. If the ball is passed out of the trap, the defense communicates and rotates accordingly.

5. Traps are thrown to the baseline, on the wings, and in the corner. Passes away from the basket are not to be trapped. It is recommended that only one trap occurs per possession (preferably on the first pass to the outlet player).

TIPS

1. Traps should occur on passes toward the basket (e.g., a wing to a corner pass equals a trap, but a corner to wing pass is away from the basket so there is no trap).

2. Only use this trap a few times during the game.

BASKETBALL DRILLS, PLAYS, AND STRATEGIES

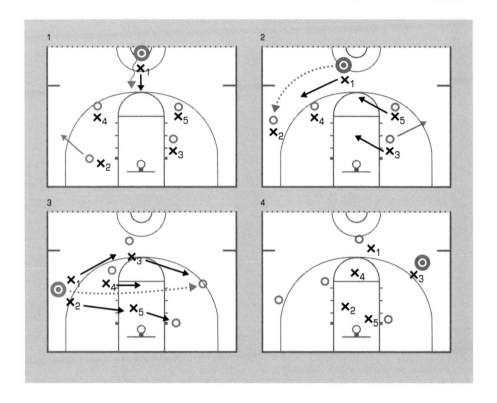

DIAMOND PRESS

Difficulty Level: Intermediate

Ideal Game Situation: After made baskets; if you have several athletic players

INSTRUCTIONS

1. Two guards (players X_1 and X_2) line up, one on each elbow. Two wings line up: player X_3 five feet in front of the free-throw line and player X_4 behind the free-throw line. The post player (player X_5) lines up at half court.

2. A trap does not occur until the ball has passed the free-throw line in the back court. The defense is not denying the inbound pass.

3. Once the ball has passed the free-throw line, player X_2 on the elbow and the player X_3 in front of the free throw line, trap the ball.

4. While the trap is occurring, player X_1, on the opposite elbow, splits two offensive players.

5. Player X_4, behind the free throw line, and player X_5, at midcourt, may cheat and give up the deep pass. The players are anticipating a pass other than a long pass (this is part of the gamble with this press).

6. If the ball is reversed, the players rotate accordingly with player X_1 in the middle moving to the opposite wing, and player X_3 in the trap sprinting to the middle (illustration three).

7. This press is not meant to have multiple traps.

TIPS

A team can trap in all corners of the court, but It is recommended that only one trap occurs for beginners.

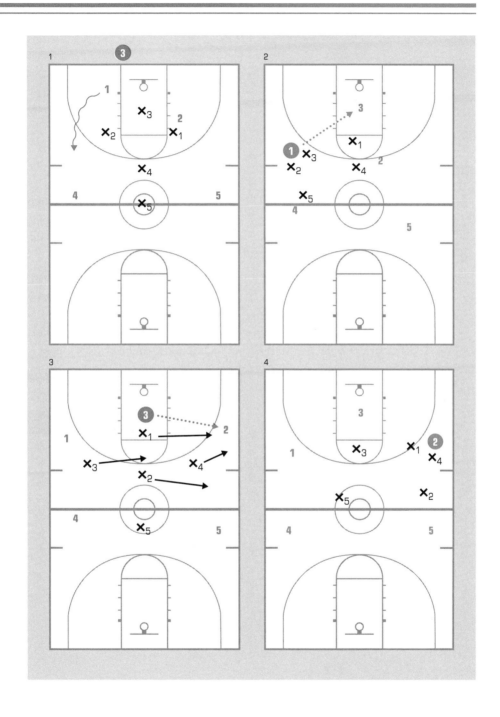

1-3-1 PRESS

Difficulty Level: Intermediate

Ideal Game Situation: After made baskets; if your team has several athletic or tall players with long arms

INSTRUCTIONS

1. An athletic, long-armed player (player X_3) plays three steps above the top of the key.

2. The center (player X_5) stands on the free-throw line with the point guard (player X_1) on the left wing and the shooting guard (player X_2), on the right side. (It is better to put the taller guard on the right side since this is where most offenses are run.)

3. The power forward (player X_4) is under the basket.

4. After the first pass past half court, players X_3 and player X_2 trap. Player X_5 anticipates and tries to steal the reversal pass. The opposite guard (player X_1) anticipates the high post pass and the player under the basket (player X_4) anticipates the corner pass.

5. Most of the time, this is a one-trap-per-possession press, but trapping more than once is an option if the opportunity arises.

6. If the ball is reversed, the closest guard (player X_1) and the closest forward (player X_5) trap, while the opposite guard (player X_2) covers the basket, and player X_3, who is at the top of the key, guards the reversal pass.

TIPS

Use this press if you have a long-armed player who is athletic and quick enough to play the top of the 1-3-1 trap.

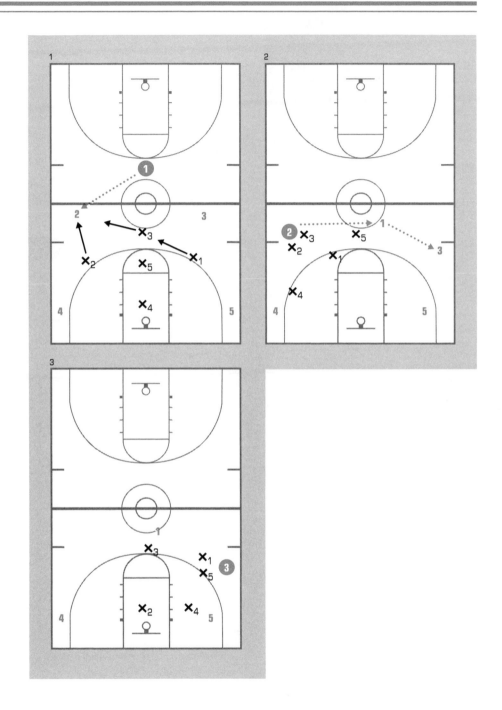

WHITE PRESS

Difficulty Level: Advanced

Ideal Game Situation:
After made baskets against teams that have a good, quick point guard.

INSTRUCTIONS

1. Player X_4, who guards the ball out of bounds, is the most athletic on the team. He has his back facing the ball and helps player X_1, who guards the point guard. This will force someone other than the point guard to catch the ball.

2. Once the ball has been entered to the opposite guard, the defender forces the ball up the sideline.

3. The closest player from the blind-side (player X_4), other than the point guard (the player guarding the point guard should never leave to trap the basketball), anticipates and traps the ball going up the sideline.

4. The remaining players that are not trapping get between each of the remaining offensive players.

5. If the ball is reversed, the defense rotates to the same players they were guarding at the start of the press.

6. The press continues to follow the same principles from this point forward until a steal or until the ball crosses half court.

TIPS

This is a good press to use when trying to stop the other team's point guard or to slow the game up a bit.

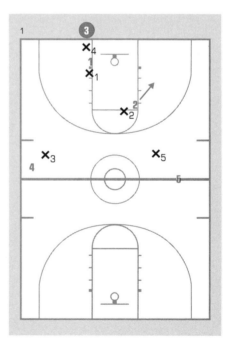

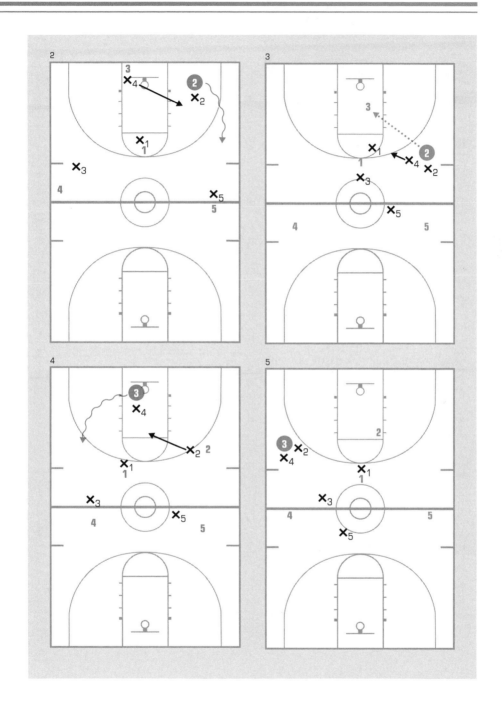

BLACK PRESS

Difficulty Level: Beginner

Ideal Game Situation: After made baskets

INSTRUCTIONS

1. This press has two guards at the elbow and top of the key, with two wing players about seven feet behind them and a post player in the backrow on the other side of half court.

2. The object of this press is to force the dribbler up the sideline.

3. Once the dribbler has reached the sideline, the ball-side guard and the ball-side wing (players X_2 and X_4) trap the ball just past half court. By waiting until after the dribbler crosses half court, the defenders take away his option of throwing behind him because he would be called for an over-and-back violation.

4. The remaining three players are all in between the remaining offensive players (illustration 2).

TIPS

This press is used to slow a team down more than it is used to create turnovers.

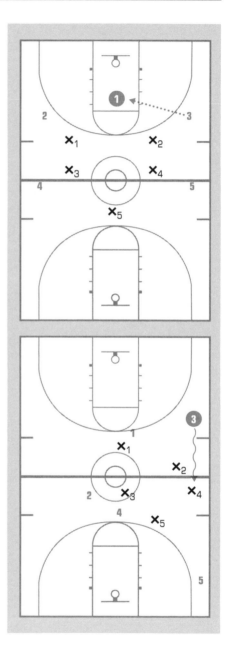

GOLD PRESS

Difficulty Level: Advanced

Ideal Game Situation: On a dead ball or after a made free throw; when trying to make entry passes very difficult for the opposing team; when trying to get a five-second call; if your team's post players are not very skilled

INSTRUCTIONS

1. Players X_1 and X_2 are positioned in the front of the press and faceguard (face the offensive players, not the inbounder) and deny the ball from being entered to their players.

2. The centerfielder (player X_3) helps players X_1 and X_2 and is responsible for any passes made over their heads.

3. The backrow players (players X_4 and X_5) play above their players, meaning they play between them and the ball, anticipating stealing a pass.

TIPS

Use this press when you need to create an immediate turnover. It is difficult to get set up after a made basket.

4. If the defense is unable to get a five-second count, and the ball is entered to the wing, the defensive players match up accordingly, with the center defender (player X_3) guarding the inbounder.

5. Once the ball is dribbled, the closest player from the blindside (player X_3) traps the ball, and the remaining three defenders split between the four remaining offensive players.

6. If the ball is passed out of the trap, the rotation can vary.

Continued on next page

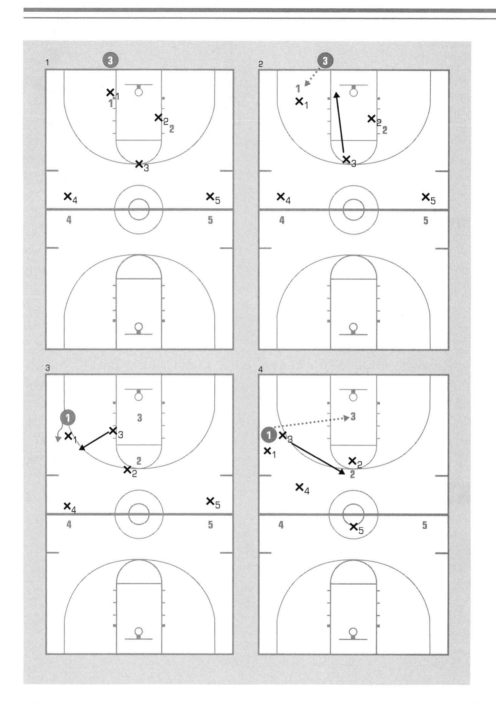

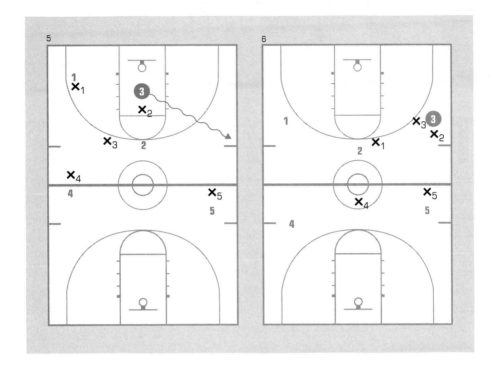

Press Breaks

The word "press" is short for "pressure," meaning to speed up or make uncomfortable. A misunderstanding when trying to break a press is that a team must have good ball handlers on the court. In reality, what a team needs are good decision makers that will use their dribbles wisely or make the easy pass. Breaking a press isn't as much about Xs and Os as it is about getting the ball to correct spots on the court and having the proper spacing necessary to break a press. Ultimately, the defense should be at a disadvantage by pressing because the offense is getting good shots at the offensive end of the court. A defensive team may take chances by double-teaming a player. So, if proper passes are made, the offensive team should have an advantage, such as a 2-on-1, when trying to score. Doing simple things like pass fakes can go a long way in helping the offensive team break the press.

As discussed in this chapter, there are many different ways to break a press, but ultimately, the same principles apply no matter what press break is being used. There are two important things to remember when breaking a press:

- The offense must have good spacing so that one defensive player cannot guard two offensive players.
- The ball should ultimately be passed to the center of the court and stay out of "hot spots." Hot spot areas of the press would be any corners of the court.

It is important that the offensive players realize they have ten seconds to advance the ball beyond half court. Also, an offensive player being closely guarded has a

KEY TERMS

On a string: Two players around half court that work in tandem—one flashes to the middle of the court and the other flashes to the ball-side sideline. As the ball is reversed, the players do the same thing on the other side of the court.

Release valve: The player who is behind the ball in a press break.

Seam: An imaginary line down the middle of the court from hoop to hoop.

minimum of twelve seconds if the ball is past half court: four seconds to hold the ball, four seconds to dribble, and four more seconds to hold the ball again before the referee will call a five-second count. Not only should players remember how much time they have, but they should also count in their heads and have a sixth sense about knowing the time situation.

In a press break, the offensive player receiving a pass should not wait for the ball to arrive, but instead should aggressively go after the pass. It is critical that the offensive players never turn their backs to the ball and begin running down the court, or they will not be able to see if a trap is occurring behind them. In order to avoid this problem, the offensive players should run down the court with their backs on the same side as the sideline—this will enable them to see things both in front of and behind them.

The best way to break a press is to

have a good passer take the ball out of bounds. Usually this would be the small forward, since this player will have some size. Often, the defense will have a tall, athletic defender guarding the inbound pass to make it difficult to enter the pass. After inbounding the ball, the player should sprint to the top of the key, looking at the ball the entire time. Ultimately, this is the spot where the basketball needs to be passed to.

The guard who receives the ball should not catch it in the corner, because then the offense could immediately get trapped. The player at center court will flash to the top of the key as the ball is reversed. The player who flashes should be the post player on the same side of the court at which the ball was entered. The other post at the top of the key should run to the basket in the front court. This means the small forward at the top of the key and one player at half court would rotate at the top of the key position looking to receive the ball. Once the ball is passed to the center of the court, the press will be able to be broken, since the player cannot be trapped in the center of the court. Another helpful hint to remember is if it is a man-to-man press, the offensive team can clear to the opposite end of the court and have the offense dribble up the court against only one defender.

Difficulty Level: Beginner

Ideal Game Situation: After a made basket or dead ball, against man-to-man or zone defense

INSTRUCTIONS

1. The 3-man inbounds the ball. The 1-man and 2-man line up single file facing the ball. (Lining up behind each other makes for better screening angles and sealing after screening.) The 4-man and 5-man are at half court.

2. The 1-man screens for the 2-man if it is a man-to-man press.

3. The 3-man enters the ball to the 2-man, but not in the corner. The ball should be entered about twelve feet from both the sideline and the baseline.

4. After entering the ball, the 3-man steps in bounds on the seam, about a step behind the 2-man, who has the ball.

5. The 1-man sprints to the top of the key. The 5-man sprints toward the opposite basket.

6. At this point, the 1-man and the 4-man are "on a string," working in tandem. If the ball is reversed to the 3-man, the 4-man flashes to the top of the key and the 1-man sprints to the ball-side sideline. Also, the 2-man, after reversing the ball, returns to the seam. The 5-man moves so he is always on the offside block.

7. The ball is eventually passed to the center of the court. If the ball is not reversed to the 3-man, it can be passed directly to the 4-man when he is at the top of the key.

8. After passing the ball to the 4-man in the center of the court, the guard (the 3-man) who is closest to the player with the ball (the 4-man) stays in place as a release valve, and the player on the wing (the 1-man) and the opposite guard (the 2-man) sprint down each sideline. This will make the press break appear as a 1-3-1, with one guard as a safety, the ball in the middle with a player on each side of it, and the post player on the block at the other end.

Continued on next page

TIPS

1. Positions 1, 2, and 3 are interchangeable, as are positions 4 and 5.

2. If the ball cannot be reversed, the player with the ball looks to the sideline, the middle of the court, or the deep outlet (in order of those progressions).

3. When breaking a press using the 21 press break, it is vital that the player who is the release valve stays a step behind the ball in the middle of the court to give the offense better spacing.

4. If possible, the offensive team should clear out everyone who doesn't have the ball to see if the defenders will follow the offensive players down the court, so they will not be able to trap.

5. If a post player catches the ball in this press break, she should not dribble more than one or two times, realizing defenders may be behind her.

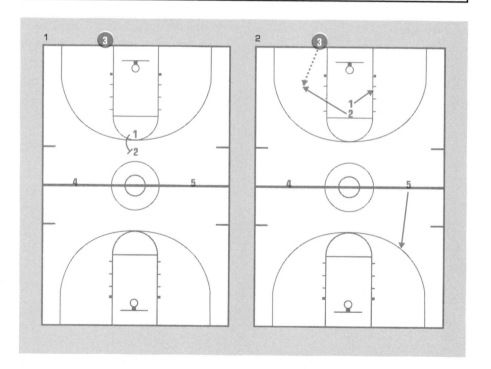

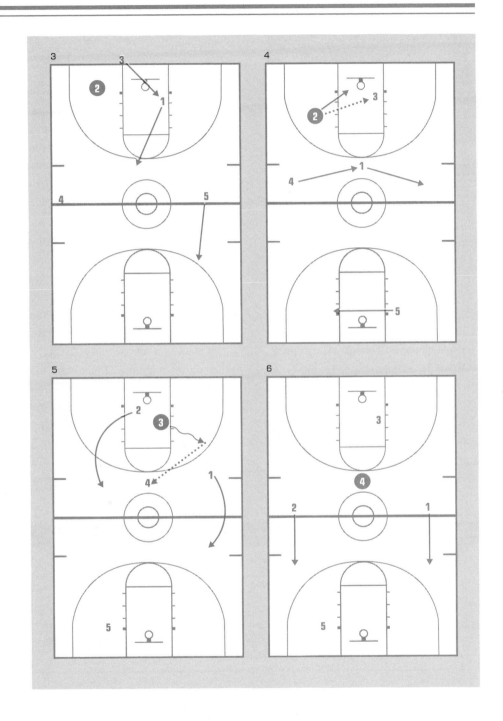

21 THROUGH

Difficulty Level: Beginner

Ideal Game Situation: After a made basket or dead ball, against a man-to-man or zone defense

INSTRUCTIONS

1. The 3-man inbounds the ball. The 1-man and 2-man line up single file facing the ball. (Lining up behind each other makes for better screening angles and sealing after screening.) The 4-man and 5-man are at half court.

2. The 1-man screens for the 2-man if playing against a man-to-man press.

3. The 3-man enters the ball to the 2-man, but not in the corner. The ball should be entered about twelve feet from both the sideline and the baseline.

4. After entering the ball, the 3-man sprints to the top of the key and faces back toward the basketball. The 1-man sprints to the seam about a step behind the basketball, and the 5-man sprints toward the opposite basket.

5. At this point, the 3-man and the 4-man are "on a string." If the ball is reversed to the 1-man, the 4-man flashes to the top of the key and the 3-man sprints to the ball-side sideline. Also, after reversing the ball, the 2-man returns to the seam, one step behind the ball.

6. The ball is eventually passed to the center of the court.

7. After passing the ball to the 4-man in the center of the court, the guard (the 1-man) who is closest to the player with the ball (the 4-man) stays in place as a release valve. The player on the wing (the 2-man) and the opposite guard (the 3-man) sprint down each sideline. This makes the press break appear as a 1-3-1, with one guard as a safety, the ball in the middle with a player on each side of it, and the post player on the block at the other end.

TIPS

1. Positions 1, 2, and 3 are interchangeable, as are positions 4 and 5.

2. This is a variation of the 21 press break; however, the same points or tips should be stressed.

3. Players must communicate to the player with the ball when a defender is behind her. When dribbling past a defender in the press, the offensive player crosses over to protect the defender from tipping the ball from behind.

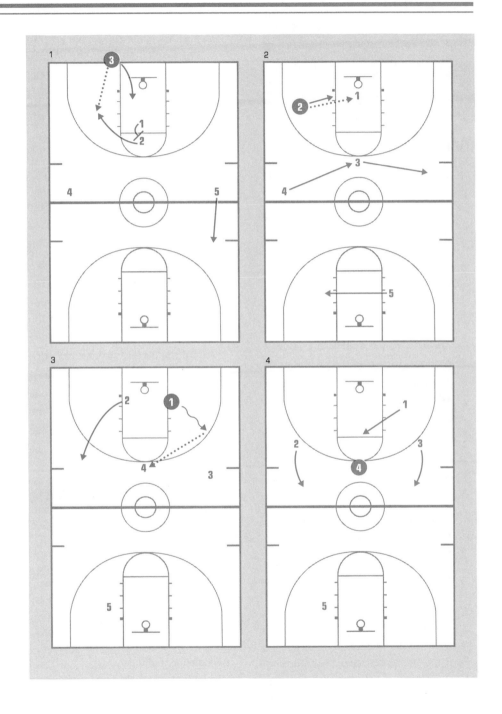

1-4 PRESS BREAK

Difficulty Level: Intermediate

Ideal Game Situation: After a made basket or dead ball, against a man-to-man defense

INSTRUCTIONS

1. The 3-man takes the ball out of bounds. The 1-man and the 2-man line up on opposite elbows. The 4-man and 5-man line up at the free-throw line extended on opposite sides.

2. The 5-man pretends that he wants the ball, but instead, he screens the 1-man on the opposite elbow then sprints toward the opposite basket. (Note: Surprising as it may sound, this baseball pass over the top of the press is open many times, especially if you have an athletic 5-man who can run and catch the ball under control. Worst-case scenario, the team switches and your guard is bringing the ball up the court against the other team's 5-man.)

3. The 4-man screens for the 2-man on the opposite elbow, and then goes to the top of the key.

4. After the 3-man inbounds the ball to the 1-man, the 4-man goes to the ball-side sideline and the 2-man replaces the 4-man at the top of the key. The 3-man steps inbounds one step behind the ball on the seam.

5. If the ball is reversed to the 3-man, the 4-man and the 2-man are "on a string," meaning the 2-man goes to the ball-side sideline and the 4-man replaces the 1-man at the top of the key. Also, the 1-man replaces the 3-man on the seam about a step behind the ball.

6. After the ball is entered, the press break is similar to the 21 press break (see page 253).

7. The ball is eventually passed to the center of the court.

8. After passing the ball to the center of the court, the guard (the 3-man) who is closest to the player with the ball (the 4-man) stays in place as a release valve. The player on the wing (the 1-man) and the opposite guard (the 2-man) sprint down each sideline. This will make the press break appear as a 1-3-1, with one guard as a safety, the ball in the middle with a player on each side of it, and the post player on the block at the other end.

TIPS

1. Positions 1, 2, and 3 are interchangeable, as are positions 4 and 5.

2. This is a good press break to use out of a time-out because it is a different look with all four players at the foul line. Most presses do not have everyone this close to the ball. It should only be used a few times a game to catch the defenders off guard.

BASKETBALL DRILLS, PLAYS, AND STRATEGIES

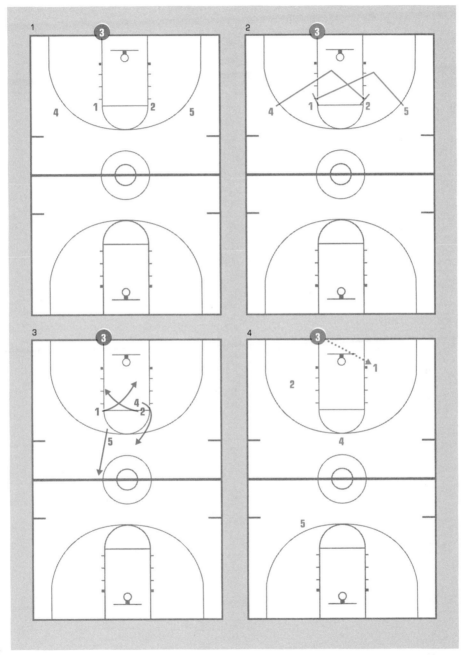

Continued on next page

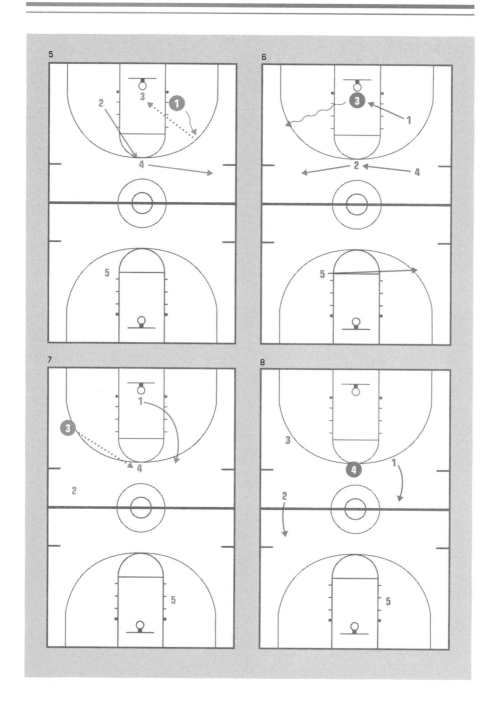

INSTRUCTIONS

1. The 1-man stands in the middle of half court, while the 2-man stands between the top of the key and half court. The 4-man stands on the ball-side at half court near the sideline. The 5-man stands opposite the ball-side at half court near the sideline. The 3-man takes the ball out of bounds.

2. The 2-man sprints toward the ball and, after getting to the free-throw line, should break either left or right. (In illustration two, he breaks right.)

3. The ball is not entered to the 2-man. After not receiving the ball, the 2-man runs up the sideline opposite the ball. The 1-man follows the 2-man, but breaks the opposite way.

TIPS

This press break is effective when an offensive team is having difficulty getting the ball inbounds. It makes it tougher to deny the inbounds pass because the offensive team has more space, allowing them to get more momentum and make more cuts.

T PRESS BREAK

Difficulty Level: Advanced

Ideal Game Situation: After a made basket or dead ball against a man-to-man or a zone defense

4. The 4-man follows the 1-man, but stops at the top of the key.

5. The 3-man enters the ball to the 1-man, then steps in bounds on the seam, a step behind the ball.

6. After the ball has been entered, the 4-man flashes to the ball-side sideline, and the 5-man replaces the 4-man at the top of the key.

7. Once the ball is thrown to the center (illustration six), the 4-man and the 3-man sprint down each sideline, and the 1-man remains back as the release valve.

Continued on next page

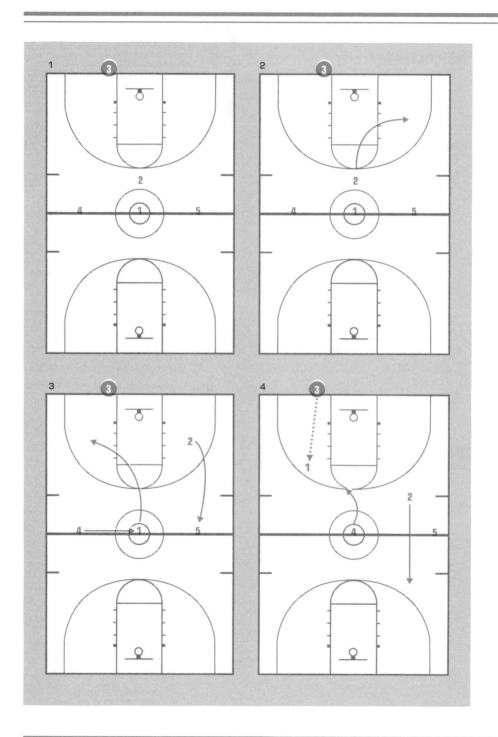

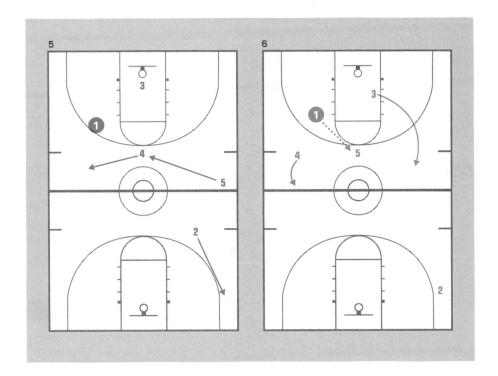

THROW BACK

Difficulty Level: Advanced

Ideal Game Situation: After a made basket, at the end of the game when leading, against a man-to-man defense that is not guarding the ball when out of bounds

INSTRUCTIONS

1. Have a good free-throw shooter take the ball out of bounds (the 3-man in the diagram).

2. The 1-man lines up at the free-throw line, while the 2-man lines up on the block opposite where the ball is being taken out.

3. The 2-man screens for the 1-man, who runs out of bounds about fifteen feet away from and parallel to the inbounder.

4. The 3-man passes the ball to the 1-man and steps in bounds.

5. From this point, the 3-man will not be covered and a press break can be run accordingly.

TIPS

This is a great press break to use late in the game when your team is winning by a point or two and no defenders are guarding the inbounder.

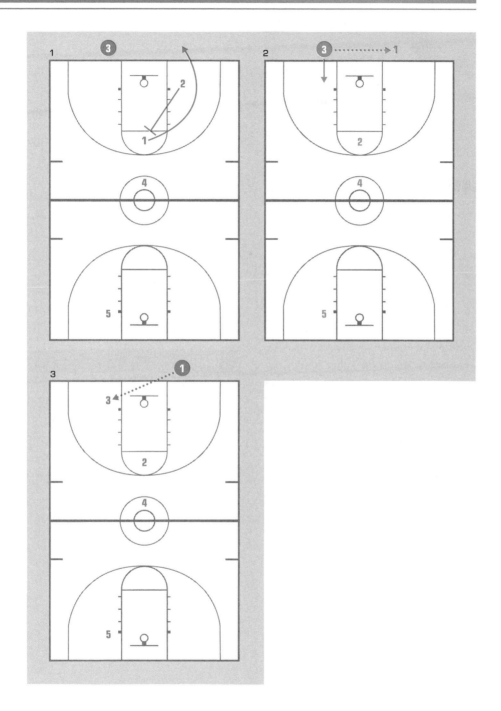

HOME RUN

Difficulty Level: Advanced

Ideal Game Situation: When losing at the end of the game, if there are less than three seconds left at the end of a quarter, against a man-to-man or zone defense

INSTRUCTIONS

1. The best passer (the 3-man in the diagram) takes the ball out of bounds. The other players take position at half court or at the other end of the court. The 1-man lines up at the top of the key at the other end of the court. The 2-man and 5-man line up at the opposite corner of the inbounder on the other end of the court. The 4-man lines up at half court near the opposite sideline of the ball.

2. The 5-man sets a back screen for the 1-man at the top of the key, and the 1-man curls around to the ball-side corner. After setting the back screen, the 5-man looks for the pass.

3. The 4-man fakes coming up for the ball and breaks down the sideline.

4. The 3-man passes to the 5-man, at which point the 2-man sets a back screen for the 4-man running down the sideline.

5. If the defense doesn't switch, the 4-man is open for a lay-up.

6. If the defense switches, the 2-man opens up and looks for the 3-point shot.

TIPS

This is a press break that is great if a team needs a basket near the end of the quarter or the end of the game.

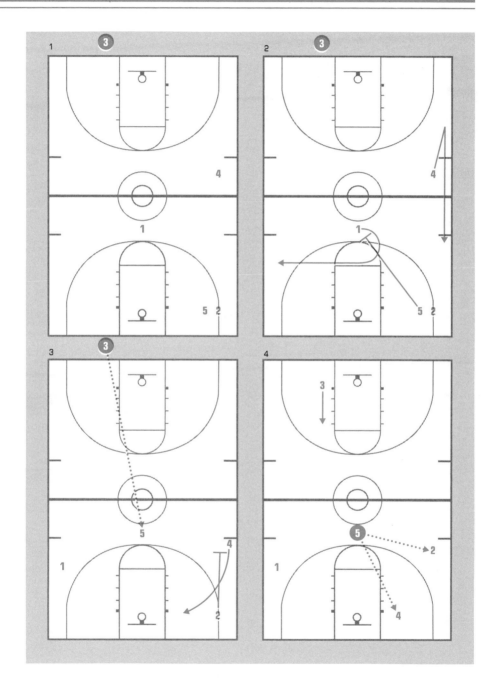

12 PRESS BREAK

Difficulty Level: Intermediate

Ideal Game Situation: After a dead ball at half court against a half-court man-to-man or zone trap

INSTRUCTIONS

1. The ball needs to be inbounded to the point guard (1-man). Usually, this is not a problem because this is used on half court traps only.

2. The point guard has the ball in the center of the court, just before the half-court line, with both wings in the back court. The post players are at opposite sides of the court, at the top of the key extended.

3. The point guard picks a side and dribbles toward it. Whatever side he dribbles toward, that wing circles to the middle of the court and the guard on the opposite side replaces the point guard in the middle as a release valve.

4. If the ball is reversed, the point guard stays in the same spot, and the guard in the middle moves to the opposite wing.

5. The object is either to get the ball to the middle of the court, or beat the defense down the sideline with a quick, hard dribble.

TIPS

Half-court traps are most effective with a taller, long-armed team. In order to successfully run the 12 press break, the offensive team must keep the ball out of the corners. Also, the offense should try to throw the ball diagonally over the press.

BASKETBALL DRILLS, PLAYS, AND STRATEGIES

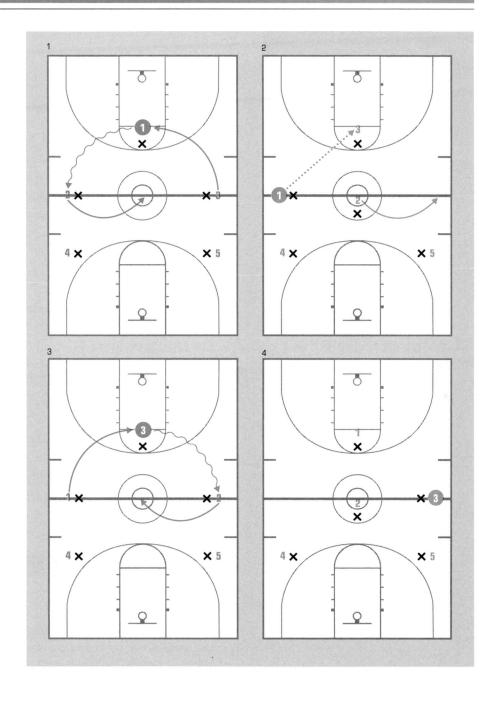

13 PRESS BREAK

Difficulty Level: Intermediate

Ideal Game Situation: After a made basket or dead ball, against a man-to-man defense; if you have athletic forwards

INSTRUCTIONS

1. The 3-man takes the ball out of bounds. The 4-man stands at the top of the key, facing the ball. The 1-man and 2-man are at half court, one on each side about a foot from the sidelines. The 5-man is on the ball-side block at the opposite end of the court.

2. The 1-man and 2-man run their defensive men at an angle off of the 4-man at the top of the key. (Advanced teams can have the 1-man and 2-man cross.)

3. The ball is entered to either the 1-man or the 2-man. Upon entering the ball to the 1-man, this break is similar to the 21 press break (see page 253).

4. After entering the ball to the 1-man, the 3-man moves to the seam, about a step behind the basketball. The 2-man sprints to the top of the key and faces back toward the ball. The 4-man sprints to the sideline on the side where the ball was entered.

5. At this point, the 2-man and the 4-man are "on a string." If the ball is reversed to the 3-man, the 4-man flashes to the top of the key and the 2-man sprints to the ball-side sideline. Also, the 1-man, after reversing the ball, returns to the seam, one step behind the ball.

6. The ball is eventually passed to the center of the court.

7. After passing the ball to the 4-man in the center of the court (illustration five), the guard (the 3-man) who is closest to the player with the ball (the 4-man) stays in place as a release valve. The player on the wing (the 1-man) and the opposite guard (the 2-man) sprint down each sideline. This will make the press break appear as a 1-3-1, with one guard as a safety, the ball in the middle with a player on each side of it, and the post player on the block at the other end.

TIPS

1. Positions 1, 2, and 3 are interchangeable, as are positions 4 and 5.

2. Use an athletic 4-man or 5-man in this press break to force teams to press by bringing up the post players (who may be slower).

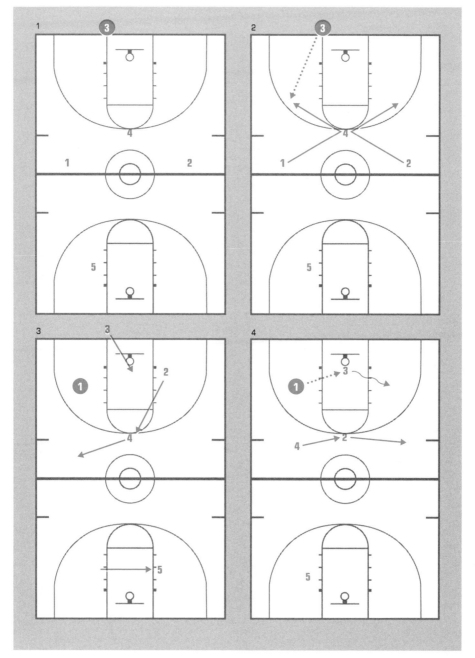

Continued on next page

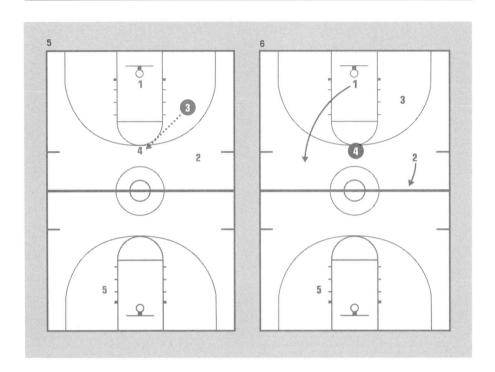

Inbound, Tip-Off, and Last-Second Plays

The key to being a great basketball team rests on execution on both the offensive and defensive ends of the floor. In this chapter, you will find a mixture of underneath and sideline inbound plays (or out-of-bounds plays) and last-second, full-court plays that, if executed properly, can be the difference between a loss and a win. Also included are two tip-off plays to help teams get a quick score on the first play of the game.

As a coach, it can be easy to neglect these parts of the game because your main focus is on offensive and defensive execution, which it should be. But, always leave time in your practice plan to go over out-of-bounds plays.

Watch games that come down to the wire where one team loses by one or two points. There is a great chance that in a close game, the team that executes their out-of-bounds plays and scores on these possessions walks away with a win.

COACHING KEYS

- Look at out-of-bounds opportunities as a chance to put points on the board. An aggressive mentality should be your only mentality.
- Emphasize the importance of setting up quickly for out-of-bounds plays. If your team can get set up before the defense is set, you have an increased chance of scoring.
- Choose your inbounder based not on size or position, but on the abilities to execute the play. First, your inbounder needs to communicate to everyone on the court what play is being run. Confusion leads to missed opportunities and turnovers. Second, you need a player who sees the play before it happens and is ready to deliver a pass when his teammate comes open. Third, the player needs to be able to make passes to open players in positions where they can put the ball in the basket.

Stress to your players the importance of winning the out-of-bounds "war." Your goal is to hold your opponents scoreless on their out-of-bounds plays, while scoring as much as possible on the offensive end.

The following is a list of rules to remember when inbounding the basketball:

1. A smart, skilled passer who works well under pressure takes the basketball out of bounds.

KEY TERMS

1-4 low set: A formation where all four players (excluding the inbounder) are spread horizontally across the floor, near the baseline.

Box set: A formation where two players are set up on opposite blocks and two players are set up on opposing elbows. This formation has the appearance of a box.

Five-second rule: The inbounder has five seconds to pass the ball to a teammate or the possession results in a turnover.

Inbounder: The player passing the ball to a teammate from out of bounds.

Rolling back to the basketball: A player quickly coming back to the basketball after he sets a screen for a teammate.

Stack: A formation where players are lined up vertically. Players can be lined up tightly or they can have space between them.

2. The player inbounding the ball makes sure he is aware of the backboard, and gives himself room to enter the ball. (He should not have his toes crowding the baseline.)

3. The inbounder must communicate what the play is with his teammates before he takes the ball from the official.

4. Once the official hands the inbounder the ball, he has five seconds to enter the ball, or it will be given to the other team. The inbounder uses ball fakes to shift the defense before passing.

5. The inbounder counts to himself, and roughly knows how much time he has to enter the basketball.

6. Players must not leave the inbounder out to dry. If the five-second call is close to being made, the other players have to get open (not stand and watch).

7. When a player enters the ball on the sideline, he must know where half court is. There is no more frustrating turnover in basketball than when an inbounder throws the ball to his teammate who catches the ball in the front court and his momentum takes him into the back court for an over-and-back violation.

8. When taking the ball out for a last-second, full-court play, the inbounder must be aware of anything that may be hanging from the ceiling. If the ball hits an obstruction while in flight, the opponents would receive the basketball underneath their hoop.

If you follow these basic guidelines and have a team that executes well, your team should win the out-of-bounds "war." And several of the inbounds plays in this chapter may help you win the game by setting your team up for successful last-second shot attempts.

Tip-off plays aren't always necessary and may be difficult for beginner teams. However, they can be effective and help give your team momentum right from the start of the game. If you have a tall player who can jump well and you're fairly confident that you can win most tips, using tip-off plays may be another extra edge you can have over your opponent.

SIDELINE ENTRY

Difficulty Level: Beginner

Ideal Game Situation: Inbounding from the sideline to set up a half-court offense

INSTRUCTIONS

1. The 3-man takes the ball out of bounds. The 1-man is in the middle of the court at ball level. The 5-man is at ball level, close to the inbounder. The 4-man is on the ball-side block, and the 2-man is on the opposite block.

2. The 3-man smacks the ball to signify the start of play.

3. The 5-man turns and sets a screen for the 1-man, who runs to the back court. After screening for the 1-man, the 5-man flashes back to the ball. The 2-man runs off of a screen from the 4-man to the ball-side corner.

4. The 3-man enters the ball to the 1-man.

5. If the 1-man is not open, the inbounder can enter the ball to the 5-man, who is flashing back to the ball.

6. If neither option is open, the 2-man, who flashed to the corner, must come back to the ball to help for an entry.

TIPS

When entering the ball near half court, inbounders must make sure their teammate is not just inside the half-court line, but moving toward the back court when the ball is passed in. This can create an over-and-back situation. It is okay, however, to pass the ball into him when he is in the back court.

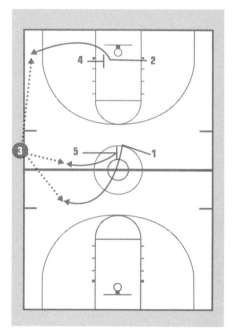

INSTRUCTIONS

1. Players set up in a 1-4 low set. The 2-man starts on the ball-side block while the 4-man starts on the opposite block. The 5-man starts in the ball-side corner, with the 3-man in the opposite corner.
2. The 1-man takes the ball out of bounds and smacks it to signify the start of the play.

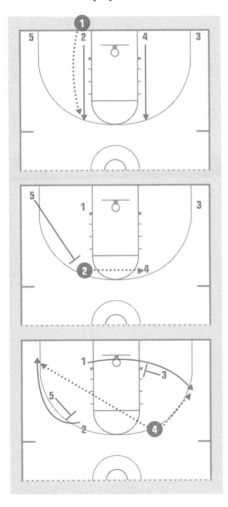

Difficulty Level: Intermediate

Ideal Game Situation: Scoring when the ball is being taken out under your basket

3. Simultaneously, the 2-man and the 4-man pop up to the 3-point arc.
4. The inbounder lobs the ball to the 2-man, who catches the ball near the 3-point line. After lobbing the ball, the inbounder steps into the block, replacing the 2-man.
5. The 2-man passes the ball across the lane to the 4-man.
6. Simultaneously, the 5-man sets a flare screen for the 2-man, who comes off the screen looking for a 3-point shot. The 3-man sets a down screen for the 1-man, who comes off on the opposite side of the floor also looking for a scoring opportunity (as a second option).

TIPS

1. You want your best shooter to receive the initial inbounds pass and then receive the flare screen from the 5-man.

2. When setting the flare screen, if the 5-man's defender helps on the 2-man, the 5-man should immediately flash to the basket looking to receive a pass for a lay-up.

STACK

Difficulty Level: Beginner

Ideal Game Situation: Scoring when the ball is being taken out under your basket

INSTRUCTIONS

1. Players line up in a tight stack outside the lane on ball-side with the 5-man is closest to the ball (halfway up the lane), followed by the 3-man, 4-man, and 2-man.

3. The 1-man takes the ball out of bounds and smacks it to signify the start of the play.

4. Simultaneously, the 5-man, 3-man, and 4-man rush across the lane opposite the ball.

5. The 2-man flashes right to the ball. The 1-man passes it to him for the lay-up or jumper.

6. If the 2-man is not open when he flashes, the other players must scramble back to the ball for an entry.

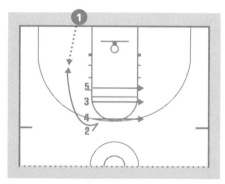

TIPS

This is a very simple, but very effective at the beginner levels. If the 2-man's defender plays on the inside of the stack, at the smack of the ball when the 4-man rushes across the lane, he is setting an inadvertent screen on the 2-man's defender. The 2-man quickly flashes to the ball and he is open.

CROSS

Difficulty Level: Beginner

Ideal Game Situation: Entering the basketball underneath your basket

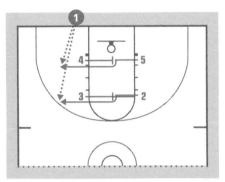

TIPS

If the inbounder has trouble getting the basketball inbounds, players must help by making themselves available for an entry, and must not stand around and watch.

INSTRUCTIONS

1. The players set up in a box formation. The 4-man starts on the ball-side block, while the 5-man starts on the opposite block. The 3-man starts on the ball-side elbow, while the 2-man starts on the opposite elbow.
2. The 1-man takes the ball out of bounds and smacks it to signify the start of the play.
3. Simultaneously, the 4-man sets a cross screen for the 5-man. The 3-man sets a cross screen for the 2-man.
4. The first option is to hit the 5-man, as she comes off the cross screen from the 4-man.
5. The second option is to hit the 2-man as she comes off the cross screen from the 3-man.

SIDELINE STACK

Difficulty Level: Beginner

Ideal Game Situation:
Getting the ball inbounds from the sideline

INSTRUCTIONS

1. Players line up in a straight line at ball level in the following order: 5, 4, 3, 1. (The 5-man is closest to the sideline.) The 2-man takes the ball out of bounds.

2. The 2-man smacks the ball to signify the start of the play.

3. The 4-man loops around the outside of the 1-man and 3-man toward the basket, hoping his defender chases him around the stack.

4. Simultaneously, the 3-man breaks hard directly to the basket. The 5-man loops around the outside and sets a screen for the 1-man, who breaks into the back court to receive the entry pass.

5. After the 5-man screens, he rolls back to the ball for an entry pass if the 1-man is not open.

TIPS

This play is designed to get the ball in and set up your half-court offense. Rarely will you score off of this play. What makes this play effective is that you have the 5-man screening for the 1-man, making it difficult for the defenders to switch.

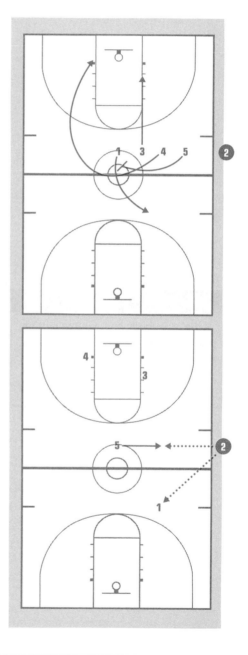

INSTRUCTIONS

1. Players set up in a 1-4 low set. The 5-man starts on the ball-side block, while the 2-man starts on the opposite block. The 4-man starts in the ball-side corner, while the 3-man starts in the opposite corner. (The 3-man has his hands and feet ready for a catch-and-shoot opportunity if his defender

Difficulty Level: Intermediate

Ideal Game Situation: Scoring when the ball is being taken out under your basket

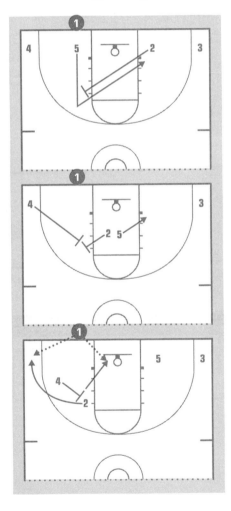

isn't paying attention or he must get open deep if no player is open.)

2. The 1-man takes the ball out of bounds and smacks it to signify the start of the play.

3. The 5-man pops up to the elbow and the 1-man fakes a lob pass to him.

4. The 2-man sets a diagonal back screen for the 5-man, who then cuts to the opposite block.

5. The 2-man then receives a screen from the 4-man (outside the lane and below the free-throw line extended) looking for a shot or scoring opportunity. After the 4-man sets the screen, he flashes to the basket if his defender helps. If not, he releases deep for the over-the-top safety pass.

TIPS

1. Your best shooter should be in the 2-man position in this play.

2. The 2-man must set a solid screen to get the play started. The better screen the 2-man sets, the more likely he will be open when he comes off the screen set by the 4-man.

SIDELINE BOX

Difficulty Level: Intermediate

Ideal Game Situation: Inbounding the ball from the sideline on your end of the court, looking to score

INSTRUCTIONS

1. Players line up in a box formation. The 4-man and 5-man start on opposite elbows. The 3-man starts on the block closest to the sideline, while the 1-man starts on the opposite block.

2. The 2-man takes the ball out of bounds and smacks it to signify the start of the play.

3. The 3-man screens for the 1-man, who goes to the ball-side corner (the screen should take place near the middle of the lane).

4. The 4-man and 5-man come together, shoulder to shoulder, to set a double screen for the 3-man (the double screen should take place around the free-throw line).

5. If the 3-man sees that his man has been screened, he can come off the screen looking for a 3-point shot. If he is not wide open, he can pop to half court to receive an entry pass.

6. After setting the double screen, the 5-man rolls back toward the ball to look for an inbound pass if the 3-man wasn't open.

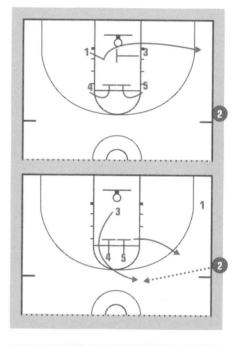

TIPS

Put your best shooter on the ball-side block as you want that player coming off the double screen.

INSTRUCTIONS

1. The 1-man sets up at ball level near the middle of the court. The 2-man sets up on the ball-side block, with the 5-man on the opposite block. The 4-man sets up near the top of the 3-point arc.

2. The 3-man smacks the ball to signify the start of the play.

3. The 2-man screens in the middle of the lane for the 5-man, who now looks to post up on the ball-side block.

4. The 4-man sets a down screen for the 2-man, who can come off the screen looking for a shot, or come to the ball looking for an entry pass.

5. If no players are open, the 1-man makes the necessary cuts to get open for an entry pass.

TIPS

1. When the 5-man comes to the ball-side block, if his man fronts him, the inbounder can look to lob the ball over the top because there is no backside defensive help.

2. Put your best shooter or scorer in the position occupied by the 2-man in this play.

Difficulty Level: Intermediate

Ideal Game Situation: Inbounding the ball from the sideline on your end of the court, looking to score

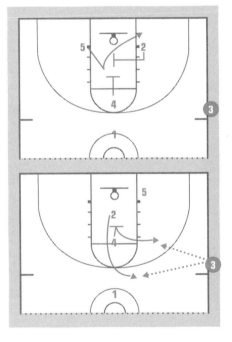

Difficulty Level: Intermediate

Ideal Game Situation: Scoring when the ball is being taken out under your basket

INSTRUCTIONS

1. Players set up in a box formation. Player 5 starts on the ball-side block with player 4 setting up on the ball-side elbow. Player 2 starts on the opposite block, and player 3 is at the opposite elbow.

2. Player 1 takes the ball out of bounds and smacks it to signify the start of the play.

3. Simultaneously, player 5 pops to the ball-side corner while player 2 sets a diagonal back screen for player 4. Player 3 releases deep to act as a safety lob pass.

4. Player 4 cuts off the screen to the opposite block, looking for the ball. After player 2 sets the screen, he rolls back to the ball.

5. If neither player 2 nor player 4 are open, the inbounder looks to pass over the top of the defense to player 3, who is in the safety position.

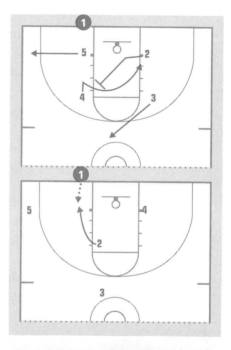

TIPS

1. The person who usually scores the most in this play is player 2, who sets the screen and rolls back. The better the screen, the more open the 2-man will be when he rolls back.

2. This play is effective because there is a guard screening on a forward, which makes it difficult for the defense to switch.

3. The players in this play are interchangeable, so you can mix up the positions.

INSTRUCTIONS

1. Players 2, 3, 4, and 5 line up in a tight stack outside the lane opposite the ball. Player 2 is above the free-throw line with player 5 on the block.

2. Player 1 takes the ball out and smacks it to signify the start of the play.

3. All four players break hard across the lane. However, player 2 only takes two to three quick steps in the lane and cuts back hard to the opposite block, looking for the ball.

4. If that option is not open, player 5 settles on the ball-side block. Player 4 releases deep for the over-the-top safety pass, and player 3 cuts to the ball-side wing.

TIPS

1. This is a good play to run if there are only a few seconds left in the quarter or the game.

2. In order to score off this play, player 2 must do a good job selling his cut across the lane in order to convince his defender, then cut quickly back to the opposite block looking for the open lay-up.

STACK OPPOSITE

Difficulty Level: Intermediate

Ideal Game Situation: Scoring when the ball is being taken out under your basket

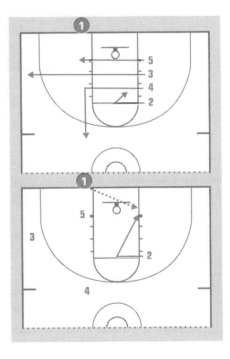

PICK THE PICKER

Difficulty Level: Intermediate

Ideal Game Situation: Scoring when the ball is being taken out under your basket

INSTRUCTIONS

1. Players set up in a box formation. The 5-man starts on the ball-side block, and the 4-man starts on the opposite block. The 3-man starts on the ball-side elbow, and the 2-man is on the opposite elbow.

2. The 1-man takes the ball out of bounds and smacks it to signify the start of the play.

3. Simultaneously, the 5-man sets a back screen for the 3-man, who flares to the ball-side corner. The 4-man looks to set a diagonal back screen for the 5-man. The 2-man releases deep to act as the over-the-top safety pass.

4. The 5-man cuts to the opposite block off of the 4-man's screen. Once the 4-man sets the screen, he rolls back to the basket looking for the ball.

5. If those options are not open, the inbounder looks to the over-the-top safety pass to the 2-man.

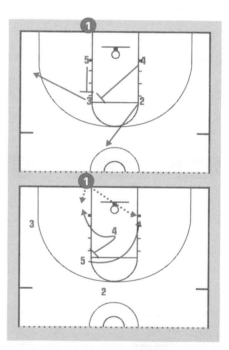

TIPS

The person who will usually score the most in this play is the 4-man, who sets the screen and rolls back. The better the screen, the more open the 4-man will be when he rolls back.

INSTRUCTIONS

1. Players set up in a 1-4 low set. The 5-man starts on the ball-side block, while the 4-man starts on the opposite block. The 3-man starts in the ball-side corner (occupying his defender but can be used as an entry if no other players are open), while the 2-man starts in the opposite corner.

2. The 1-man takes the ball out of bounds and smacks it to signify the start of the play.

3. The 5-man pops up to the elbow and the 1-man fakes the lob pass.

4. As the 5-man pops up to the elbow, the 4-man sets a diagonal back screen for him.

5. The 5-man then cuts off the screen to the opposite block. After setting the screen, the 4-man rolls back to the basket to look for the inbound pass on the ball-side block.

6. If neither option is there, the inbounder throws the over-the-top safety pass to the 2-man, who has released deep.

TIPS

The person who will usually score the most in this play is the 4-man, who sets the screen and rolls back. The better the screen, the more open the 4-man will be when he rolls back.

1-4 HIGH

Difficulty Level: Intermediate

Ideal Game Situation: Scoring when the ball is being taken out under your basket

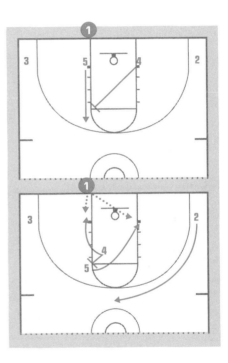

41

Ideal Game Situation: Scoring when the ball is being taken out under your basket

INSTRUCTIONS

1. Players set up in a 1-4 low set. The 5-man starts on the ball-side block with the 4-man on the opposite block. The 3-man starts in the ball-side corner with the 2-man in the opposite corner.

2. The 1-man takes the ball out of bounds and smacks it to signify the start of the play.

3. The 5-man and the 4-man flash to the top of the key.

4. The 1-man lobs the ball to the 5-man, who catches the ball near the 3-point line. After lobbing the ball, the 1-man steps in to the block replacing the 5-man.

5. The 5-man passes the ball across the lane to the 4-man, who has also popped up around the 3-point line.

6. The 1-man then sets a flex screen for the 3-man, who cuts across the lane looking for the ball.

7. The 5-man down screens for the 1-man, who pops to the elbow looking for a shot. The 5-man posts up after setting the screen.

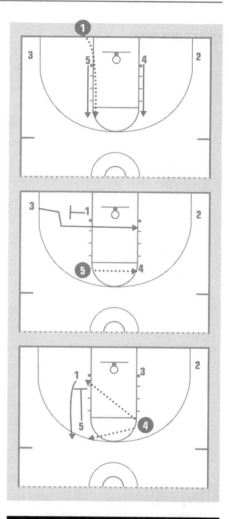

TIPS

1. Make sure the inbounder knows that the initial lob pass is crucial to starting the play. If the pass is not thrown far enough out, it can congest the play.

2. The 5-man, who receives the first pass, must hold off his defender until the ball has been lobbed, otherwise, he risks the chance of a stolen pass.

INSTRUCTIONS

1. Players set up in a box formation. The 5-man starts on the ball-side block with the 4-man setting up on the ball-side elbow. The 2-man starts on the opposite block with the 3-man at the opposite elbow.

2. The 1-man takes the ball out of bounds and smacks it to signify the start of the play.

3. The 2-man sets a back screen for the 3-man, who cuts to the opposite block looking for the ball. The 5-man slides up the lane to set a shoulder-to-shoulder double screen with the 4-man.

4. After setting the back screen, the 2-man runs off the double screen set by the 4-man and 5-man, and looks for a shot or scoring opportunity.

5. The 5-man then flashes hard to the basket while the 4-man releases deep for an over-the-top safety pass.

TIPS

1. You want your best shooter or scorer to occupy the 2-man position in this play.

2. When the 4-man and 5-man are setting a double screen for the shooter, if either of their defenders jump out to help on the 2-man, the player left unguarded should immediately flash hard to the basket for a lay-up.

DOUBLE

Difficulty Level: Intermediate

Ideal Game Situation: Scoring when the ball is being taken out under your basket

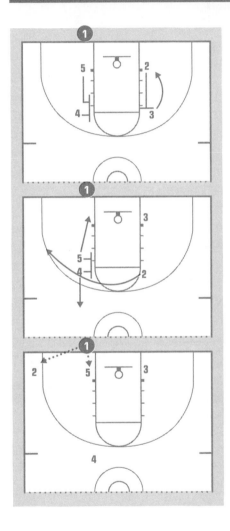

RED

Difficulty Level: Advanced

Ideal Game Situation: Going the length of the floor to score a basket with fewer than three seconds left on the clock

INSTRUCTIONS

1. Your best thrower (player 2) takes the ball out of bounds underneath your opponent's hoop. (Make sure he knows to avoid the backboard, as well as anything else hanging from the ceiling when inbounding the ball.)

2. Place your point guard (player 1) on the elbow opposite the ball. Your best shooter (player 3) is placed at half court, inside the circle. Place your one of your forwards (player 4) at half court, ball-side, near the sideline. Place your best athlete or tallest player (player 5) at the opposite end of the floor on the free-throw line.

3. The inbounder smacks the ball to signify the start of play. Player 3 takes one step deep, then comes back and receives a screen from player 4 at half court. Player 1 does not move because he is trying to occupy a defender. Player 5, on the opposite end of the floor, prepares for a potential pass.

4. The inbounder's first look is to hit player 3 on the move as he is coming off the screen.

5. The second option is to hit the screener (player 4), who comes back to the ball after screening for player 3.

6. The third option is to throw it deep to player 5 on the opposite free-throw line.

7. After catching the ball, a player only can take one or two dribbles and then must shoot the ball.

TIPS

With three seconds on the clock, a player has a maximum of two dribbles and then must shoot the ball.

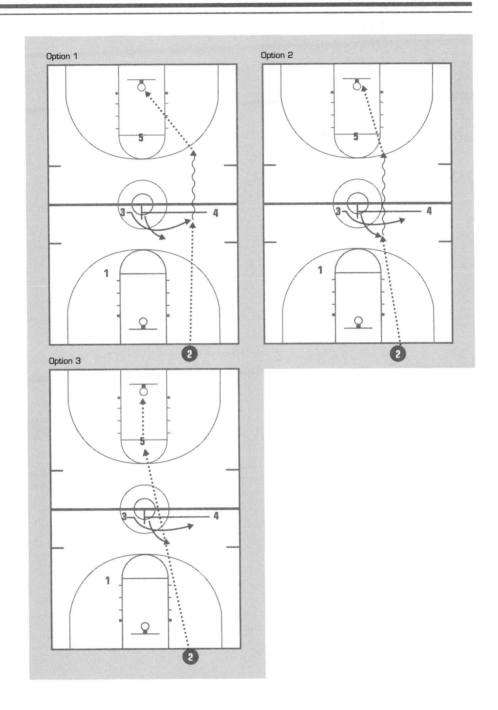

Option 1

Option 2

Option 3

LION TIP-OFF

Difficulty Level: Intermediate

Ideal Game Situation: When your center is the taller player or better jumper and is likely to get the tip-off

INSTRUCTIONS

1. The tallest and quickest jumper (player 5) lines up for the tip-off. If he is right-handed, the best passer (player 1) lines up to the left, just outside the circle over the half-court line (line up on the right if player 5 is left-handed). The next-best athlete (player 3) lines up opposite of player 1, but two steps farther down court. One player (player 2) lines up directly behind player 5, and the last player (player 4) lines up in the midde of the free-throw line down court.

2. Player 5 tips the ball to player 1, who immediately dribbles toward the basket.

3. As soon as the ball is tipped (and is still in the air), player 3 breaks toward the basket. Player 4 runs and sets a back screen for him near the top of the 3-point arc.

4. Player 2 acts as a safety to prevent the other team from scoring if they happen to win the tip-off.

5. Player 1 looks to lob the ball to player 3 as he comes off the screen for a lay-up.

TIPS

1. This should be done quickly to catch the opponent off guard by scoring at the start of the game.

2. If player 3 is not open after the back screen is set for him, the pass should not be forced. Player 1 should make the decision to set up the offense.

3. Make sure none of the players line up directly behind the referee, so that the jumper is able to tip the ball directly to any of them.

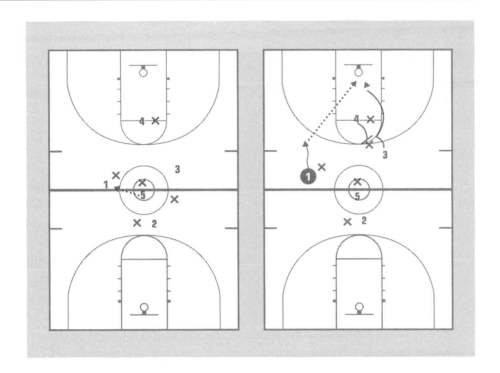

RAM TIP-OFF

Difficulty Level: Advanced

Ideal Game Situation: When your center is the taller player or better jumper and is likely to get the tip-off

INSTRUCTIONS

1. The tallest, quickest jumper (player 5) lines up for the tip-off. If the player is right-handed, the best passer (player 1) lines up just outside the circle on the left (on the right if player 5 is left-handed). One player lines up opposite of the best passer (player 3). One player lines up outside the circle directly behind the jumper (player 2) and the last player (player 4) lines up directly in front of the jumper just outside the circle.

2. Player 5 tips the ball to player 1, who immediately dribbles toward the basket.

3. After player 5 tips the ball, player 4 sets a back screen on player 5's defender. Player 5 then spins toward the basket.

4. Player 2 acts as a safety to prevent the other team from scoring if they happen to win the tip-off.

5. Player 1 looks to lob the ball to player 5, who should be open for a lay-up. Or, if he is open, player 1 can drive to the basket and score.

TIPS

1. This should be done quickly to catch the opponent off guard by scoring at the start of the game.

2. If player 5 is not open after the back screen is set for him, the pass should not be forced. Player 1 should make the decision to set up the offense.

3. Make sure none of the players line up directly behind the referee so that the jumper is able to tip the ball directly to any of them.

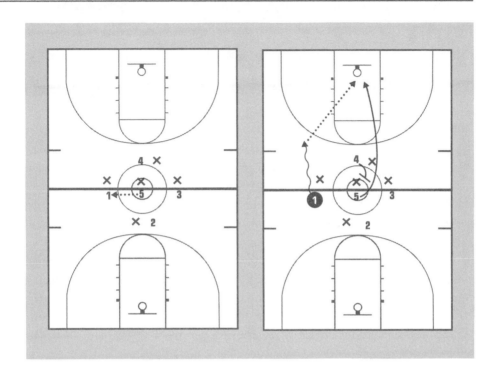

APPENDIX:
Choosing Game Strategies

Personnel is the key factor in determining what offensive and defensive strategies will be used to ensure success during the game. Knowing each individual player's strengths and weaknesses is crucial because this will ensure that the best lineup is on the court at all times. If players know their roles, substitutions will flow easier and no player will become selfish (this is known as team chemistry). Personnel is also the biggest factor in determining what style of basketball a team will be successful at playing. For example, a team that has strong guard play or a deep bench should play an up-tempo game and press on defense. On the other hand, a team that is inside-oriented with taller, slower players should stick to the half-court game and perhaps even play zone defense.

In preparing for a game, knowing your personnel is only half of the game. Knowing and understanding the opponent's personnel is the other half. Learning about your opponent is accomplished by scouting. Scouting is more prevalent on the collegiate and high-school levels, but this is an excellent way to gain an edge on the competition. Going to opponents' games, watching tapes of their play, and looking for player statistics are great ways to scout. Technology has changed the tools available to basketball coaches. For example, most high-school player and team statistics are on the Internet, and sometimes even games are streamed on the Internet. Scouting will help teams prepare a strategy that can be practiced in the days leading up to the game. Most teams do not change the names of their plays, so listening for calls on offensive sets is a great way to have defenders steal passes.

Basketball is a game of statistics. A good team will play based on percentages accomplished through scouting. For example, if an opposing player has only made five out of thirty 3-point attempts, then the defender should not guard this offensive player very closely around the 3-point arc. Or, if the opponent plays at a slow pace and only allows 40 points a game, your team needs to really take care of the ball and get good shots because the number of possessions may be limited. When giving the pre-game speech, remind players of the strengths and weaknesses of each individual on the opposing team.

HELPFUL HINTS: PREPARING FOR GAMES AND IN-GAME ADJUSTMENTS

- Shake the referees' hands and find out their names. Treating the referees with respect is vital because often times a team will have the same referee for several games throughout a season. Knowing the referees' names will ensure a good working relationship.

- Be sure that you and your players are acquainted with your surroundings, especially if you have never played on the court before. Many times a court will have several lines, such as volleyball lines, which can be confusing when shooting a 3-point shot.

- Never have just one name for a play. Opponents can pick this up and anticipate the play coming. A suggestion would be using nicknames. For example, if the play is called "North Carolina," use "Tar Heel" as the play name as well.

- Always know which direction the possession arrow is pointing. Example: If there is a loose ball and a pile up, it is not a wise decision to use a time-out if your team would receive the ball from the possession arrow. This is especially important late in the game, when time-outs are limited and each possession can mean winning or losing.

- Know how many team fouls your team has. This is especially important in the first half. In order for the opposing team to shoot a one-and-one bonus, your team must have seven fouls. If there are only thirty seconds left in the half and your team only has three team fouls, then your team can be aggressive because another foul would not put your opponent in the bonus.

- Communicate how many time-outs are left to you players, especially if you have none, so they do not attempt to call one. Also, if your team is losing by 4 points and makes a shot with fewer than five seconds remaining in the game, have a player on your team swat the ball so the referee has to blow the whistle to stop the clock. This is known as a team's "delay of game," which is the only way to still have a chance at winning if the clock continues to run on made baskets.

- Substitute wisely. If your team has a great offensive player in foul trouble, it may be a good idea to use the "offense, defense" substitution method. This is used in the fourth quarter to substitute a good offensive player out so that she does not pick up another foul, possibly fouling out. However, any time there is a dead ball and the team will be on offense, substitute the good offensive player back into the game.

- Late in the game, always be aware of free-throw shooters. If winning, keep your best free-throw shooters on the court. If losing, know what player to foul on the opposing team (the worst free-throw shooter).
- Holding for the last shot of the quarter or the game is a key factor to success. If there is thirty seconds remaining, it may be a good idea to hold for the last shot. This will ensure that your team will maintain momentum, and it will not be seized by the opponent.
- If there is no doubt that your team will win the game, never shoot a shot at the buzzer or continue to press full court. This is a sign of running up the score and poor sportsmanship. Not to mention, this fuels the opponent for the next time you will meet.

SUBSTITUTION STRATEGY

Every coach has his own substitution strategies. These strategies vary from year to year or even game to game. When you look down your bench, you hope to have many options to turn to. A successful team is one that has bench, players that can step in and, if not raise the level of play, at least keep it at the same level as the starters. Many coaches feel that one of the most important players on the team is the sixth man, that first player to come off the bench and take the place of a starter. This sixth man can often bring a much needed spark to your team when one of your starting players needs a break.

Obviously, you want your best five players on the floor at a time. However, in some situations you may want certain personnel on the floor. For example, if you are up by only a few points at the end of a game, the other team will want to foul to stop the clock, so you definitely want your best free-throw shooters in the game.

You also need to watch your players to see if they are running out of gas. Sometimes assistants are asked to watch players to see if they show signs of fatigue, or coaches may have their players tug at their jerseys when they are tired and need a break. Well-conditioned players may need only a few minutes to catch their breath and jump back in the game.

Fouls can often have a tremendous effect on your substitution strategy. If a player has three fouls in the first or second quarter, you may decide to take that player out of the game so she doesn't foul out and is available toward the end of the game.

If you have the benefit of five very athletic players on your bench, you may use the "scrambled egg" method of substitution. Take five of your most athletic, defensive-minded bench players and put them in the game when the team needs a spark. Whether the starters aren't playing well or if you want to speed things up toward the end of a quarter or a half, substitute all five of these scrambled-egg players in. These players' job is to just play tough defense and try to get easy lay-ups through their defense. Coaches who use this method usually have these players trapping all over the floor and look to pick up the pace of the game to make the other team uncomfortable.

Ultimately, your substitution method is determined by the players you have. As a coach, you need to get to know your players and decide what kind of substitution patterns will be best for your team. Your strategies need to be flexible from year to year depending on your personnel, or game to game depending on match-ups with your opponents or game situations.

GAME-DAY WARM-UP ROUTINE

Your players must be focused on the game they are about to play. Many games can be won or lost due to the level of your players' focus. By building a consistent game-day routine, you may help your players keep their focus throughout the game. Here are some tips that you may find helpful to building a game-day routine:

1. If your game is on a school day, have the players wear something that will help them stay focused on the game later that day. Whether you choose a shirt and tie or a team jacket or t-shirt, the players have a consistent reminder that it is a game day.

2. If there is no school on a game day, you may want to have a shoot-around early in the day, i.e., a time when the team can get together and loosen up by taking some shots and doing some very easy drills. This way, you can make sure that they get out of bed and break a little sweat before the game. If players lay around and sleep all day, they can be sluggish during the game. Make sure your players get plenty of shots in. You may also want to go over scouting reports for the game. The shoot-around can help your team focus on what they will be running and what their opponent will be running during the game.

3. Players should drink plenty of water—not just on game day, but on the days leading up to it as well. It is important that your players stay hydrated throughout the season. Dehydration can lead to cramping and other health problems.

4. On game day, players should eat healthy throughout the day and then eat a healthy meal three to four hours before the game. This meal should be high in carbohydrates and low in fat and protein. Fats and proteins can stay in the players' bodies and weigh them down. Carbohydrates (pasta, rice, bread, vegetables, and fruits) will help provide energy for the players throughout the game.

5. Arrive at the venue at a consistent time. Will your team arrive at the gym an hour before the game? Thirty minutes? You know your team better than anyone else; decide how much time your players will need to get ready for the game.

6. Have a consistent warm-up routine. Your team will have twenty minutes to warm up on the floor. By having a routine, you can quickly get your players ready and keep them focused on the game rather than on the warm-up.

Every coach has a different warm-up routine. You need to build and develop yours before your first game. Before the warm-up clock starts running, make sure players are dressed and have stretched. Once the clock starts, they should be ready to go. Here is a sample of a twenty-minute warm-up routine:

20:00–15:00	Two lines of lay-ups from half court
15:00–10:00	Two lines of shooting from under the basket, then moving to other spots
10:00–5:00	shell drill, concentrating on defense (see page 140)
5:00–1:30	Free shooting and zigzag. Half of the team shoots shots they will take in the game. Starters and players who get significant playing time should be getting the most shots, while other players rebound for them. The other half of the team should do zigzag drills near half court to give more room for shooting and allow them to work on dribbling and defense. Switch from shooters to dribblers halfway through this time.
1:30–0:00	Players hit the bench. This is your time to talk to the team. Quickly go over the scouting report and remind them who they will be guarding.

There are many different and more complex warm-up routines. Some coaches prefer to run back into the locker room during warm-ups to quickly review the scouting report or just to pump up their team. Other coaches stay out on the floor and coach their team during warm-ups, while others let their captains run warm-ups. It is your team; you know them better than anyone else, so decide what you want to do. Once you've decided on a warm-up routine, stick to it so that it becomes second nature to your players, and then they can focus on the game instead of warming up.

BASKETBALL DRILLS, PLAYS, AND STRATEGIES

INDEX